Projections of Demand for Care among the Elderly in Poland

Polish Studies in Economics

Edited by Ryszard Kokoszczyński

Volume 14

Wojciech Łątkowski

Projections of Demand for Care among the Elderly in Poland

PETER LANG

Berlin - Lausanne - Bruxelles - Chennai - New York - Oxford

Bibliographic Information published by the Deutsche Nationalbibliothek
The Deutsche Nationalbibliothek lists this publication in
the Deutsche Nationalbibliografie; detailed bibliographic
data is available in the internet at http://dnb.d-nb.de.

Library of Congress Cataloging-in-Publication Data
A CIP catalog record for this book has been applied for at the
Library of Congress.

This publication was financially supported by the grant of the
National Science Centre, Poland [2016/23/N/HS4/03827].

ISSN 2191-8848
ISBN 978-3-631-89410-1 (Print)
E-ISBN 978-3-631-91630-8 (E-PDF)
E-ISBN 978-3-631-91631-5 (E-PUB)
DOI 10.3726/b21678

© 2024 Peter Lang Group AG, Lausanne
Published by Peter Lang GmbH, Berlin, Deutschland

info@peterlang.com - www.peterlang.com

This publication has been peer reviewed.

Acknowledgements

Research presented in this book was carried out within a project 'Projections of demand for care among the elderly in Poland including health status and family situation' supported by the grant of the National Science Centre, Poland [2016/23/N/HS4/03827].

This monograph is based on data from Eurostat, European Union Statistics on Income and Living Conditions (EU-SILC), years 2005–2015. The responsibility for all conclusions drawn from the data lies entirely with the author.

This paper uses data from SHARE Waves 6 and 7 (DOIs: 10.6103/SHARE.w6.710, 10.6103/SHARE.w7.711).

The SHARE data collection has been funded by the European Commission through FP5 (QLK6-CT-2001-00360), FP6 (SHARE-I3: RII-CT-2006-062193, COMPARE: CIT5-CT-2005-028857, SHARELIFE: CIT4-CT-2006-028812), FP7 (SHARE-PREP: GA N°211909, SHARE-LEAP: GA N°227822, SHARE M4: GA N°261982, DASISH: GA N°283646) and Horizon 2020 (SHARE-DEV3: GA N°676536, SHARE-COHESION: GA N°870628, SERISS: GA N°654221, SSHOC: GA N°823782) and by DG Employment, Social Affairs & Inclusion. Additional funding from the German Ministry of Education and Research, the Max Planck Society for the Advancement of Science, the U.S. National Institute on Aging (U01_AG09740-13S2, P01_AG005842, P01_AG08291, P30_AG12815, R21_AG025169, Y1-AG-4553-01, IAG_BSR06-11, OGHA_04-064, HHSN271201300071C) and from various national funding sources is gratefully acknowledged (see www.share-project.org).

Contents

Introduction

The most distinctive feature of demographic developments, debated increasingly since the 1960s, are changes in the age composition of populations. They are manifested by the increasing number of older people and their share in the total population and labelled as population ageing. This process, approached from the perspectives of different disciplines (demography, economics, sociology, psychology, political sciences, social policy, life sciences, etc.), constitutes the leading topic of research and policy debates. While the 20th century has been marked as the period of the population growth, the 21st century will be dominated by the global population ageing. Consequently, the population ageing process and its diversity across regions and countries are under focus along with multifaceted consequences at both the macro and micro levels (Kotowska, 2019a).

One of the effects of population ageing is the increasing demand for care among older people – a subject of a scientific debate and public policy concerns. Researchers conclude that requesting a care need by older persons is above all related with their health status (e.g. Czekanowski & Bień, 2006; Doblhammer et al., 2008). Health together with income are also the most important factors determining the use of institutional forms of support (Gaymu et al., 2006), while household composition is a predictor of receiving informal support (Gaugler et al., 2007; Wingard et al., 1987). Meeting care need of dependent older people is becoming more urgent as the pace of population ageing in many developed countries, including Poland, is accelerating. The essential ingredients of population ageing, that is, the increasing number of older people and their proportion in the total population, can be considered as a challenge for care arrangements globally. In most countries worldwide, the supply of formal care services for older people is generally underdeveloped; coverage of not-for-profit organisations is limited, while private markets usually cannot offer sufficient and affordable provision of help (WHO, 2011). That makes older people with functional limitations strongly rely on practical support from others, mainly from their family network members (both close members like spouses, children, siblings, but also more distant relatives), friends and neighbours. However, changes in family-related behaviours, both demographic (associated with timing, frequency and sequence of family events) and organisational (connected with labour market involvement of men and women and patterns of housework division between them) call into question the traditional intergenerational care exchanges and their sufficiency to meet the augmented care needs in the future.

Recognition of the future demand for care and its estimation is, therefore, a key priority for social policy considerations.

Estimation of the future demand for care among older people in terms of the number of persons in need should be based on developments in the older population. However, the official population projections are traditionally available only by age and sex. Discussions how to satisfy the future care demand from older people should be based on population projections that go beyond the traditional breakdown. Ideally, they should account for indicators of care needs (e.g. dependency/health status) and care supply (e.g. kinship and social networks) to understand how caring responsibilities could be shared between family members and professional carers. In practice, such projections are rarely prepared with data unavailability being the main limitation. Currently, there are limited examples of studies that would account for both dimensions simultaneously (Eggink et al., 2016; e.g. Gaymu et al., 2008; Geerts et al., 2012; Kingston et al., 2018).

In Poland, the substantial increase in the absolute number of older people and their share in the total population in the coming decades is prominent which makes the country an interesting case study. In recent years Poland's population has been decreasing – both the natural and the real increase have been negative for 7 and 8 years in a row, respectively. The population as of 31 December 2019 was 38,382.6 thousand people which was less by 28.6 thousand than year before and 147.3 thousand than in 2010. At the same time the population of Poland is ageing – the number of people aged 65 and more was 6,947.0 thousand and was higher by 214.7 thousand than in 2018 and 1,756.6 thousand than in 2010 (GUS, 2020a). Along with the growth in the number of older people there is an accelerating increase in the proportion of older adults. It reached 12.4 % and 13.5 % in 2000 and 2010, respectively, and was already equal to 18.1 % in 2019. Among people aged 65 and above the most numerous (35.4 %) were the youngest older people (aged 65–69 years), while the least numerous (11.7 %) were the oldest persons aged 85 and more years (GUS, 2020a). However, the coming years are projected to bring more balance between the proportions of the subpopulations of the youngest and the oldest of older persons leading to the 'double ageing' – an increase in the proportion of the oldest-old among the population aged 65 and above. While the more numerous cohorts will become older and their health will naturally deteriorate due to senescence, an inflated demand for care services among future older people can be expected.[1] In the years 2018–2060, the number of people aged 65 and over will grow by 4.5 million

---

[1] It has to be noted that the core of this book was written before the outburst of the Covid-19 pandemic caused by the SARS-CoV-2 virus and, therefore, the world

with a simultaneous reduction of people in working age (15–64 years) by 7.9 million (Eurostat, 2019). It determines not only the change in the relation between the number of producers and consumers in the economy but also the shift between the number of potential caregivers and care recipients: the old-age support ratio, defined as the number of the population aged 15 to 64 per member of the population aged 65+, is projected to go down from 4.0 to 1.6 persons between 2018 and 2060. The analyses dealing with the current resources of care point out that the institutional care supply is already fulfilling just a very small fraction of older peoples' care needs (ca. 1 % of the population in Poland according to the 2011 population census). Care needs of older people are met mainly by informal caregivers who, first and foremost, are the family network's members. However, the supply of informal care is predicted to diminish mainly due to changes in the family structures. The ideational changes driving family formation patterns add uncertainty about the intergenerational care exchanges. Moreover, access to informal care is also affected by the changes in older people's living arrangements.

The aim of this monograph is to estimate future demand for care among people aged 65 years and over in Poland by preparing appropriate population projections. The demand for care is defined as the number of older people in need of care due to their health status. Predicting the number of older people in need of care rather than percentages is legitimate as the stock of middle-aged adults is already known, while percentages depend to a considerable extent on the future numbers of children yet to be born. For that purpose the following partial theses are formulated:

1. Despite the potential health improvement by age, an increase in the demand for care among older people is expected. This is due to the intensity of the population ageing process in Poland, which is leading to a fast increase in the number of older people who are living longer than ever. Therefore, estimation of this demand requires linking changes in the population age structure with changes in the health status. Consequently, the changes in the individual health of older persons should be incorporated into the projection model.
2. The changes in the family model and living arrangements of older adults result in both shrinking (informal) family care resources and the increasing demand for formal care. In particular, the growing number of people living

---

described appears as if it had never happened. Epilogue appended at the end of the monograph attempts to address the significant impact of Covid-19 on health and care needs of older people and how it could be possibly incorporated into projections.

in single households is augmenting the demand for formal care among older persons. Therefore, to estimate the macro-level effects of these developments for care demand, the projection model should take into account changes in living arrangements of older adults observed at the micro-level.

To prepare population projections that would assess the number of people in care need, I propose the analytical approach which integrates microsimulation of health and living arrangements changes with macro-level projections of the population by age and sex. The proposed approach is driven by the following main thesis:

To estimate the future demand for care among older people changes in the age composition of the population should be linked with changes in the individual health status. In addition, developments of living arrangements of older people need to be accounted for. The projection tool with microsimulation modelling of individual-level behaviours incorporated in the population projections at the national level provides better predictions of the future care demand.

There are relatively few studies in the Polish literature dealing with the future demand for care among older people with activity limitations (Abramowska-Kmon, 2011; Bonneux & van der Gaag, 2012; Szukalski, 2004; Szweda-Lewandowska, 2016). This book attempts to contribute to the field by performing a study that combines changes of the population age structure with changes in the health status and the living arrangements status in a dynamic setting using microsimulation methods. The research makes use of a dynamic multistate projection model that takes into account both characteristics at micro-level – the health status and the family situation (living arrangements) of older persons. It allows estimation of the effect of change in the health status by age over demand for care according to morbidity hypotheses used to formulate projection scenarios. Including into the projection the information about older persons' living arrangements allows assessment of the influence of diminishing informal care resources on the demand for formal care.

Life abhors a vacuum and is difficult to predict, which applies both to the subject as well as the writing period of this book. This monograph is a product of my doctoral dissertation which advanced between 2017 and the beginning of 2020, and, inevitably, had not foreseen two major events that have happened later. Both are critical in the context of care demand and care supply. The first was the outburst of Covid-19 pandemic in 2020 that changed the global landscape in terms of health, but also had its consequences on care provision. The second was the Russian invasion of Ukraine on 24 February 2022, which considerably changed the demographic and labour market situation in Poland, and affected the potential domestic supply of caregivers due to unprecedented forced migration flows from Ukraine. I decided not to revise the main body of the book as it should not affect the perception of the analytical part. However, during the final stage of the book's compliation, I included my remarks on the above-mentioned events in the epilogue, to keep it up-to-date and inquire the reader for their significance. I hope this structuring will be met with understanding.

The goal of the monograph is achieved through the following basic research tasks:

1. to explore the health and the family situation of older people in Poland and their changes over time based on the available empirical data;
2. to estimate the parameters reflecting the older peoples' dynamics of health and living arrangements for the population projection model;
3. to formulate a population projection model which accounts for the health status and the living arrangements of older people and aims to project the future demand for care among the older people in Poland.

The structure of the book reflects the subsequent research tasks. It consists of four chapters that are preceded by the introduction and surmounted by the conclusions section and epilogue. In the first chapter, I provide an overview of demographic change in developed countries and its consequences for care among older people. Its goal is to set the stage for the empirical part of the study. In the beginning, I describe historical and projected trends of population ageing and highlight its diversity from the geographical – global and regional – perspective. I also present different methods of measurement of the advancement of population ageing and provide a brief overview of its selected main consequences. Then, I move on to the description of interrelations between the family model and care provision. At first, I look into family changes in developed countries, that is, how behaviours related to family formation, development and dissolution as well as gender roles within families have evolved in the context of the intergenerational exchanges of care. The more detailed description of family networks' changes in Poland since 1989 follows. In the last part of this chapter I focus on care arrangements for older people. I start with introducing the concept of care to outline different care regimes in Europe and characterise predictors of care provision towards older people. Then, I scrutinise care provision for older people in Poland. Lastly, I review existing pieces of literature about projections of demand for care among older people in European countries and Poland in particular.

The second chapter is devoted to the family and health situation of older people in Poland and basically covers the first research task. In the first subsection the detailed information on living arrangements of older persons is provided. It starts with trends in living arrangements of older persons in a comparative perspective and continues with the summary of the determinants of living arrangements formed of older people. Then, the presentation of living arrangements of older adults in Poland follows by specifying the older population by marital status and their household composition mainly with the use of the available official statistics from registers and censuses. The picture is completed with insights into living arrangements of older people in Poland based on own tabulations of survey data. The second subsection of this chapter mirrors the structure of the first one but describes health status of older people. It starts with clarification about the concept and measurement of health and disability to proceed with description of trends in health and healthy life expectancy among older people. Special attention is paid to the selected theoretical concepts and some empirical findings on the future of morbidity. Next, available survey data on health of older people in Poland is summarised. The chapter closes with a review of the relationship between living arrangements and health.

The aim of the third chapter is to model the dynamics of health and living arrangements of older people in Poland using individual-level longitudinal data. It opens the empirical part of monograph and fulfils the second research task. It begins with the outline of the population projections' modelling scheme that is realised throughout the last two chapters of the book. Then, in the theoretical subsection I distinguish between the incidence and prevalence measures in population description and consider multistate models as a tool for modelling social processes. In the empirical part, I first discuss datasets considered and used for the analysis. Next, I examine the relationship of health and living arrangements with age, sex and education in separate models and then formulate a joint model of health and living arrangements transitions with sex as covariate. This part indirectly leads to answers on additional research questions, such as: what is the relationship of health and living arrangements status with age at older ages, or what is the influence of sex and education on the risk of change in health or living arrangements status among older people, or what is the relationship, if any, between the health status and family situation of older adults. The chapter closes with the discussion of the estimation results.

The final chapter culminates the previous parts of the research. It fulfils the ultimate goal of the thesis formulated as the preparation of projections of future demand for care among people aged 65 years and over in Poland. The chapter starts with discussing microsimulation for population projections. Then, all the steps of preparation of the population projection model are highlighted. They include overview of the simulation projection model along with discussion of the Eurostat population projections and assumptions about the initial population structure and mortality. The final section of the chapter presents the results of the simulation projection model and compares them with the additionally performed sensitivity tests.

In conclusion, I summarise and debate the results obtained from the empirical parts of the study with reference to the formulated aim of the study, the theses and the associated research tasks. I also discuss the strengths and limitations of my research approach. Finally, I attempt to formulate some reflections about further research in the field and policy implications. At the very end, the reader will find epilogue that is a comment on the recent demographic developments that have happened after the core of the book had been finalised. It provides some thoughts on the consequences of the Covid-19 pandemic that has recently left its mark on many aspects of our life and how it could and should be incorporated into our considerations. It also discusses implications of the unprecedented inflow of Ukrainian refugees to Poland – a consequence of unprovoked military aggression of the Russian Federation against Ukraine in February 2022 – on the potential supply of care for older people in Poland.

Chapter 1. Demographic change in developed countries and its consequences for care for older people

In the beginning, I introduce the topic of population ageing with a focus on the components of population dynamics as its main determinants. Then, I juxtapose traditional measures with alternative (prospective) measures of ageing and their use to present the advancement of population ageing in the global and regional perspectives. A brief discussion about consequences of population ageing completes this section. Beside population ageing, which is the main driver of demand for care among older people, I account for changes in the family as they affect provision of elderly care, which is a constitutive component of care arrangements. Family changes are examined in the context of transformations in demographic behaviours and family relations. The main and final section focuses on care arrangements for older people. The conceptualisation of care and care regimes in Europe is followed by a discussion on drivers of care provision. Next, a detailed investigation of care provision for older people in Poland is presented. Finally, a review of existing pieces of literature that focus on the outlook of the older peoples' care needs and care provision in the future concludes the chapter.

1.1 Population ageing in the spotlight

1.1.1 The population reproduction and population ageing

Population ageing is manifested by defined changes in the population age composition. Traditionally, the changes are thought of as an increase in the percentage of the population aged 65 and over. Other threshold of later life is age 60; however, it is more relevant in developing countries characterised by shorter-lived populations.[2] Although the expansion of the numbers of the aged usually

---

2 According to the Law on elderly people dated 11th September 2015 (Ustawa z dnia 11 września 2015 r. o osobach starszych (Dz. U. poz. 1705)) older people in Poland are understood as persons aged 60 and more. As a consequence, many statistics reported for the population of older people in Poland concern this subpopulation. In this monograph I define older people as persons aged 65 and more following the more internationally common standard and, where possible, I present relevant statistics for this age group.

alter the population age structure, a substantial growth in the numbers of older people may reveal in the absence of population ageing defined in percentage terms (Rowland, 2009). It is, therefore, equally important to track changes in the size of older population expressed in absolute terms.

The ageing population structure is inevitable, but also fundamentally positive. It is the consequence of changes in fertility and mortality characteristic of the first demographic transition, that is, dropping death rates followed by a prominent drop in birth rates (e.g. Kirk, 1996). Lee (2011, p. 573) calls population ageing "a necessary by-product of the demographic transition". Declining mortality increases the size of the cohorts that begin to reach advanced ages, while the sustained decline in fertility reduces the size of the successive new cohorts. Consequently, the population structure by age is changing. The changes in the age composition take time as the larger cohorts move up the age pyramid (Rowland, 2009). The pace of the population ageing depends on the delay between the onset of mortality improvement and the start of fertility decline as well as on how rapidly both changes happen. Steep slumps in fertility and the emergence of below-replacement fertility accelerated population ageing in many countries worldwide (Kinsella & Phillips, 2005). International migration flows complement the overall effect of mortality and fertility developments and often cannot be neglected.

Europe has been a pioneer of the demographic transition. As regards its development in the 20th century attributed to relevant stages of the transition, the primacy of fertility decline in population ageing in the period up to 1950 in Europe was taken over by the direct mortality effects in the second part of the century (Murphy, 2017). Murphy notes that these findings are consistent with traditional (monotonic) depiction of trends on population ageing described in the third and fourth phases of the demographic transition, which characterised Europe at that time. However, one needs to be aware that the birth cohort effects in the post-war period in Europe (baby boom) temporarily distorted the stylised pace of ageing (Murphy, 2017). Eventually, the pattern set by Europe has had to become global (Demeny, 2007). Indeed, populations in every country in the world are experiencing the longevity revolution. Moreover, the outlook for a further growth in life expectancy is promising (Janssen & de Beer, 2019; Oeppen & Vaupel, 2002; Vaupel, 2010). The increasing survival rates have been a universal phenomenon for decades now, with the pace of change concordant with the stage of the demographic transition in particular country. Sweden is often put as a forerunner of the revolution. The chance of surviving to age 65 in Sweden has risen from less than 50 % in the 1890s to exceed 90 % today, a standard in countries with the highest life expectancy (UN, 2019c). Reductions in the overall level of mortality are being achieved through improved survival both in young ages and beyond the age of 65, but the impressive growth in the number of octogenarians, nonagenarians and centenarians is caused by improvements in survival among the oldest-old, that is, among persons aged 80 and more (Kannisto et al., 1994; Rau et al., 2008). Poland is no exception. The proportion of adult life spent beyond age 65 increased from 19 % and 16 % for females and males, respectively in the 1960s to 24 % and 20 % today. According to the Eurostat's EUROPOP2018 population projections, this proportion will reach 27 % and 24 % in 2050 for women and men, respectively and 30 % and 28 % in 2100 (Eurostat, 2019).

The second half of the 20th century in Europe and other developed countries was initially characterised by the post-war baby boom depicted in the fertility increase, and later by a rapidly declining fertility leading to near- or below-replacement fertility levels. The near- and below-replacement fertility levels became apparent in countries accounting for the majority of world's population (Kohler et al., 2002). Fertility in the developed countries has been continuously reduced and delayed, and reached in many cases, particularly in Europe, low and lowest-low levels (total fertility rate (TFR) below 1.5 and 1.3, respectively) (Bongaarts, 2002; Frejka & Sobotka, 2008; UN, 2019d).[3] A recent rise in TFR in the late 2000s was attributed to a diminishing pace of the postponement of childbearing (Bongaarts & Sobotka, 2012). However, this fertility upswing was later hampered by worsening economic conditions in the continent (Matysiak et al., 2020). Changes in the age pattern of fertility, especially huge drops in teenage and below age 25 fertility, demonstrate a delay in the timing of childbearing in Europe marked also by a higher mean age of women at first childbirth. It has become a universal and steady trend in the increasing number of European countries, beginning with northern, then western, since the 1980s southern countries, and including central and eastern European countries since the 1990s (Frejka & Sobotka, 2008).

Since the 1990s Poland has been characterised by similar changes in fertility patterns, that is, a substantial decrease in the quantum of reproduction (reaching the minimum TFR of 1.22 in 2003) followed by the postponement of

---

3   The below-replacement fertility is nowadays reported in a total of 93 countries including all Europe, Northern America, Australia and New Zealand, 26 countries of Asia and Northern Africa, and 20 of Latin America and the Caribbean. Moreover, from 1990 to 2019 the total number of countries with very low fertility below 1.5 children per woman increased from 8 to 25, with 13 of them in Europe (UN, 2019c).

childbearing (Kotowska et al., 2008; Tymicki et al., 2018) which were catalysed by the political and economic transformation that began in 1989 (Fihel et al., 2017). The lowest-low fertility levels together with spectacular improvements in survivorship have amplified the increase in the elderly population and its share in the total population. Even though the period TFR in Poland is projected to gradually increase from the current (2019) 1.42 to 1.63 in 2050 and 1.72 in 2100 according to the Eurostat's EUROPOP2018 population projections, the size of the new birth cohorts will drop quickly from around 400 thousand in 2015–2020 to 300 thousand already in 2030 through 2050 and drop further down to 240 thousand in 2100, mainly due to declining numbers of women in the reproductive age and their age composition (Eurostat, 2019).

The impact of migration, the third component of population dynamics, on population ageing has been relatively minor in Europe in the past (Murphy, 2017). Yet, it has become an important factor of the population growth in modern Western Europe[4] for the last couple of decades, especially for countries facing a natural population decline (Coleman, 2008). The effect of international migration on population ageing may be direct via changes in the population size and the age composition, but also indirect through the number of future births given the most of migrants are in the (prime) working and reproductive age. The influence of migration on population may be diverse depending on whether the perspective of the origin or the destination country is used. Migration outflows in the net-emigration countries contribute to population ageing, while the net-receiver countries may experience population rejuvenation[5] (Fihel et al., 2018). Countries with a negative natural population growth are often able to maintain a positive real growth thanks to incoming migrants, however, in the long-term "immigration cannot solve population ageing or provide other than a moderate amelioration even with high inflows" (Coleman, 2008, p. 472). Replacement migration, which refers to immigration needed to offset a population decline and population ageing, has been proven highly unrealistic. In order to maintain potential support ratios in the developed countries with low

---

4   Western Europe is understood as group of countries that historically, up to 1990s, were on the western side of the 'Iron Curtain', i.e., the Mediterranean, Anglo-Saxon, German-speaking, the Benelux and Nordic countries.

5   "Sporadically, in specific circumstances an inflow from abroad can help to fill a generation gap (…). Alternatively, from the perspective of the sending country, a massive and age-selective outflow can upset the quantitative ratios in the age structure, affecting the population's natality and demographic prospects" (Fihel et al., 2018, pp. 1306–1307).

fertility and mortality rates, the immigration flows would need to highly exceed those observed in the past (United Nations, 2001). Offsetting negative economic consequences of population ageing in 27 European countries, including Poland, solely with immigration is implausible[6] (Bijak et al., 2007, 2013). However, promoting education-selective migration together with high integration efforts may cushion the negative effects of ageing (Marois et al., 2020).

Poland has been experiencing a negative net migration rate for decades but the migration outflow intensified after Poland's EU accession in 2004 (Fihel et al., 2018). The volume of temporary migrants grew by 1 million in just 6 years to reach 1.5 million within less than 15 years. The official statistics indicate that the vast majority of those who left Poland in the first years after the accession have stayed abroad until now (GUS, 2019). The analyses for Poland show that despite the massive scale of emigration the direct effect of migration on the population's age composition is much smaller relative to effects of mortality and fertility. However, the overall impact of outflows will intensify in the future due to indirect effect of 'missing' births and the decline in the size of future cohorts (Fihel et al., 2018). Although there has been no permanent return wave of Polish migrants after 1989 (White et al., 2018), the ageing process could be deepened in the future by migrants willing to come back to Poland for retirement.

1.1.2 Diversity in population ageing

To understand population ageing process the difference between ageing at the individual and population level has to be highlighted: "Population ageing differs from the ageing of an individual. People who survive grow older with each year they live. Populations, on the other hand, can grow younger" (Sanderson & Scherbov, 2005, p. 811). In other words, populations may become younger in the context of the changes in its age composition. On the contrary, individuals are subject to a natural biological process of senescence which is irreversible. Here, the focus is on changes in the age composition of populations and their measurement.

The usual way to measure population ageing is to follow changes in the proportion of the people who are perceived as old. There are different perceptions of what the old age is, however, the cut-off point is a fixed chronological age, usually

---

6 "With respect to immigration alone, in order to keep the population structure of Europe relatively young, many more immigrants would theoretically be needed than it is currently assumed in the High variant of the projection, seen as the high bound of the possible future immigration size" (Bijak et al., 2007, pp. 27–28).

age 65 years. Alternatively, population ageing can be measured by tracking changes in the median age of the population.[7] Both the proportion of the old and the median age have advantage of being easily accessible and comparable across countries.

Historical trends of both measures show that the advancement of population ageing around the globe is substantially diverse. The course of the demographic transition is strongly heterogeneous across regions due to its onset and the patterns of changes in mortality and fertility. Figure 1 summarises the past and future trends in the share of population aged 65 and over globally and by continents. According to the United Nations' estimates and projections (UN, 2019d), the share of older population globally amounted to 5 % in 1950 to nearly double in 2020 and to reach 15.9 % in 2050 and 22.6 % in 2100.[8] The dispersion of the measure across continents has been increasing over the observed and projected period due to regional differences in the pace of ageing. The steepest rise in proportion of older people in most continents is projected to take place in the upcoming three decades, in Europe, Asia and Latin America especially. Poland between 2010 and 2060 distinguishes itself as an extreme example. Starting from well below the share reported for Europe, the share of older population in Poland from 2045 is going to surpass it to reach 35 % in 2060 and 34 % in 2100.

The course of the median age of the population over the previous and current centuries is presented in Figure 2. In the 1950s the median age of the population in Europe, North America and Oceania was reaching 30 years, the highest at that time. The populations of Asia, Latin America and Africa were the youngest with the median age close to 20 years. Since back then the median age for Europe has been picking up continuously. The other regions have been experiencing a drop until the 1970s when the trend had reversed. The only exception was the population of Africa, which has started to get older only since the 1990s. Today, the range between the highest and the lowest median age amounts to about 22 years, twice as much as in 1950. Europe and Africa have the oldest and the youngest populations respectively again, and the median age of Africa's population has not surpassed the 1950s level and is the single one below the median age of world's total

---

7   The median age of the population is age (expressed as years) that divides the population in two parts of equal size. The number of persons with ages above the median is the same as the number of persons with ages below the median.

8   The corresponding increments expressed in absolute terms are even more persuasive. The number of people aged 65 and over was nearly 130 million in 1950 and reached almost 728 million in 2020. The global older population in 2020 is projected to double within the next 25 to 30 years (nearly 1.55 billion people aged 65 and over expected in 2050). The projected number in 2100 exceeds 2.4 billion older people.

population. The common feature for future is the further growth in the median age globally. The fastest pace of ageing until the end of the century is expected in Latin America, while the median age for Europe is to stabilise at 48 years. Poland has been historically below the median age for Europe. However, it is projected to exceed it since the 2020–2030 decade and oscillate around 51 years since 2050.

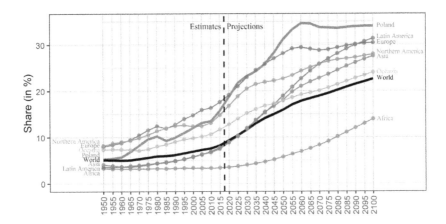

Figure 1. The share of the population aged 65 and over by world's regions and in Poland, 1950–2100.

Source: Own elaboration based on (UN 2019d). Medium fertility variant for projections.

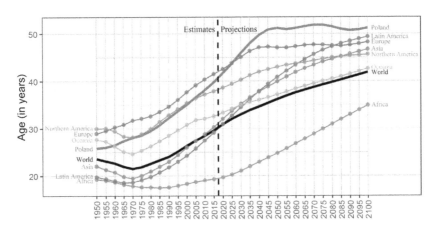

Figure 2. Median age of the population by world's regions and in Poland, 1950–2100.

Source: Own elaboration based on (UN 2019d). Medium fertility variant for projections.

The population ageing process is not uniform in Europe as it is not uniform across the world. Figure 3 shows the age structure of the European population at the regional level with a colour-coding scheme representing relative dominance of functional age groups, that is, youth (0–14 years), working age (15–64) and elderly people (≥65 years), in contrast to the overall European population as a standard. The European population is characterised by clear large-scale and small-scale differences at the regional level that are driven by the interplay between fertility, mortality and migration in different regions (Kashnitsky & Schöley, 2018). In 2015, Poland remains relatively homogeneous within its administrative borders and stands out with a higher share of working-age population and a lower share of aged older than 65 years when compared to age structure of the European population.

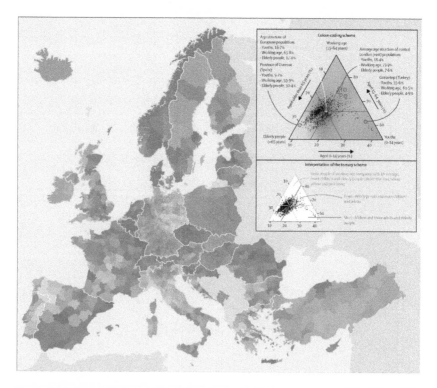

Figure 3. Colour-coded map of population age structures in European Nomenclature of Territorial Units for Statistics 3 regions in 2015.

Source: Kashnitsky and Schöley (2018, p. 210).

The measures that use the relations between the functional age groups, namely demographic dependency ratios and support ratios, are also widely used indicators for monitoring changes in the age composition of populations. They are treated as good indicators of economic pressures imposed by population ageing. One of the most popular measures is the old-age dependency ratio (OADR) defined as the number of persons aged 65 years and above per 100 persons of working age (aged 15 (or 20) to 64 years). In the context of declining fertility and increased longevity, it shows that the relative size of older age groups increases while that of younger age groups declines (UN, 2020). The reverse of OADR, that is, the ratio of the population aged 15–64 to the population aged 65+, is the potential support ratio (PSR) which highlights the potential level of support from the working-age adults towards the population of the old. However, they come under increasing criticism for clinging on to conventional measurement of ageing rather than incorporating increases in longevity and health to adjust forecasts (Sanderson & Scherbov, 2010).

Next to traditional measures of population ageing there are also other measures to analyse this phenomenon. Essentially, the idea is to change the way of thinking about age beyond maturity moving from the number of years that have been lived so far to the number of years yet to be lived (Ryder, 1975). In the vanguard of the development of those measures are Warren Sanderson and Sergei Scherbov who incorporate the concept of a fixed remaining life expectancy and advocate supplementing chronological age with prospective age in population ageing analyses. Sanderson and Scherbov (2005, 2007) introduced the median age of the population standardised for expected remaining years of life called the prospective median age. They argue that using the concept of a fixed remaining life expectancy, but also other characteristics, such as health-based measures, enhance more comprehensive and accurate analysis of population ageing (Scherbov & Sanderson, 2016). The most recent investigation on the ageing trends in high- and middle-income countries over the 2015–2100 period is provided by Sanderson et al. (2018). The authors use the United Nations probabilistic population forecasts to see if the populations of these countries will grow older continuously using both the conventional and prospective measures of ageing. They found that the conventional proportion of the population aged 65 and older and the conventional median age of the population suggest continued advancement in population ageing throughout the century (see left panels in Figures 4 and 5). In the short run, the increases in the conventional measures can be attributed mostly to the past fertility declines and then to the increases in life expectancy at older ages.

In contrast, the corresponding prospective measures (right panels) indicate that ageing will stagnate in the long run due to increases in life expectancy at older ages. The authors conclude that "adjusting to population aging will still be challenging, but there is no point in exaggerating the challenge through mismeasurement" (Sanderson et al., 2018, p. 170). They also suggest using alternative indicators for dependency measurements that incorporate additional aspects such as health care or pension costs. These results are in line with previous considerations by Sanderson and Scherbov (2015, p. 2): "When prospective age is used, increases in measures of population aging are slower when the pace of life expectancy improvements is faster. This is the opposite of the conventional view that faster increases in life expectancy will cause the speed of aging to increase." The more important question remains unanswered of what quality or of what health those extra years of life will be lived. The newly proposed measures of ageing are aiming at grasping multiple dimensions of ageing and account not only for the number of years but also for their quality (Balachandran & James, 2019).

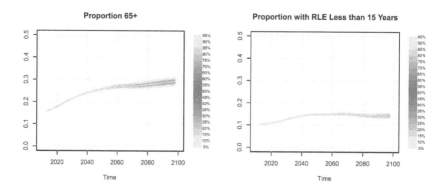

Figure 4. Proportions aged 65+ and proportions with remaining life expectancy (RLE) of 15 years or less. Evolution of probability distributions of the conventional proportion of the population counted as old and its prospective analogue, World Bank high-income countries, 2015–2100.

Note: The thick line in the middle indicates the median of the distribution, and the legend to the right of the chart indicates percentiles.

Source: Sanderson et al. (2018, p. 166).

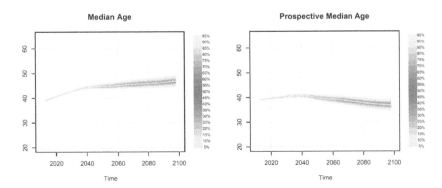

Figure 5. Conventional and prospective median age. Evolution of the probability distributions of the conventional median age and its prospective analogue, World Bank high-income countries, 2015–2100.

Note: The thick line in the middle indicates the median of the distribution, and the legend to the right of the chart indicates percentiles.

Source: Sanderson et al. (2018, p. 168).

The data for Poland provide a similar picture to the overall results obtained for high-income countries. The proportion of people aged 65 years and over is projected to increase from 17 % in 2018 to a maximum of 33 % in 2063 and then stabilise at 32 % up to the end of the century. The prospective proportion of people with remaining life expectancy of 15 years or less is expected to reach a maximum of 20.2 % in 2065 between 2018 (12.0 %) and 2100 (17.2 %). The growth is steeper for the conventional measure than for the prospective one. However, both measures indicate that the changes in the age composition in Poland will be marked with further advances in population ageing in the next four to five decades, followed by its stabilisation until the end of the time period considered (Figure 6).

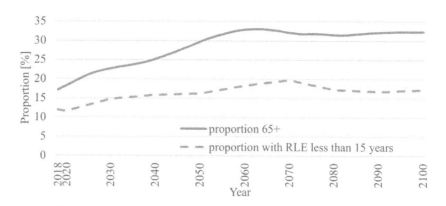

Figure 6. Proportions aged 65+ and proportions with remaining life expectancy (RLE) of 15 years or less, Poland, 2018–2100.

Source: Eurostat online database [proj_18np, proj_18nalexp], baseline projections, own calculations.

The comparison of projections of the conventional and the prospective median ages in Poland allows for quite diverse conclusions (Figure 7). The traditionally computed median age for females and males is expected to grow by 8.6 and 9.1 years respectively over the projection horizon to reach 50 and 47 years in 2100. Clearly, the population of Poland will become older. The picture for the prospective median age[9] adds a new perspective as the median ages are projected to go down in 2100 by 1.9 and 5.3 years for females and males. Until the first half of the century population ageing is projected to progress, but in the second half the process is projected to stagnate. This long-run tendency can be explained by increases in life expectancy at older ages. Therefore, if the years until death are the threshold of old age, then the 'ageing' population will in fact become relatively younger.

---

9   The prospective median ages are computed as the ages in the life table of 2018, in which people have the same remaining life expectancy as at the median age in specific years (see Sanderson, Scherbov and Gerland (2018) Appendix A.1 for details and the mathematical formulation).

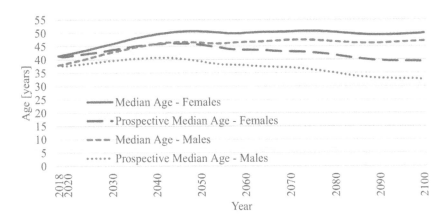

Figure 7. Conventional and prospective median age by sex, Poland, 2018–2100.
Source: Eurostat online database [proj_18np, proj_18nalexp], baseline projections, own calculations.

Demographic dependency ratios do not include any information about the economic activity that is important from the macroeconomic perspective, such as employment or productivity. Therefore, the economic dependency ratio (EDR) defined as a ratio of the number of retired to the number of employed people is also widely used. A comparison between different dependency ratios can be found in Loichinger et al. (2017). The authors use different definitions of dependency that incorporate both changes in the age composition of the populations as well as age-specific profiles of economic activities. They compare the standard demographic dependency ratio with measures that include economic activity characteristics, for example, data on labour market activity, but also data on income and consumption over the life course in line with the National Transfer Accounts (NTA) approach[10] (Lee & Mason, 2011). The level of

---

10 "The economic old-age dependency ratio, or economic OADR, is defined as the effective number of consumers aged 65 years or over divided by the effective number of workers at all ages. (…) One advantage of this measure is that it incorporates age-specific variations in labour income and consumption resulting from differences across countries in labour force participation, unemployment, hours worked, labour productivity and consumption. In other words, the ratio reflects the resource needs (consumption) of older persons relative to the resources produced (labour income) by all workers, irrespective of their age. An increasing economic OADR indicates that the number of effective older consumers per effective worker is increasing. This, in turn, can change the demand for, and the means of, financing the consumption

dependency is concluded to vary significantly between the indicators used. The projected economic dependency may be affected by changes in labour market participation, labour income and consumption patterns (Loichinger et al., 2017). It is a valuable information for adapting public policies and individual strategies to manage population ageing.

The similar comparison for Poland using demographic and NTA dependency ratios is presented in Table 1. The increase in the demographic dependency ratio between 2012 and 2016 was evident (18 % growth, a corresponding increase of 3.9 older persons per 100 people). In the same period the economic dependency for old age, that is, the share of consumption of elderly which is not financed out of their own labour income in relation to total labour income, remained stable. It suggests that the observed increase in the demographic pressure of the older population on the working-age population has not necessarily translated into an increase in the economic pressure of older consumers over the population of producers.

Table 1. NTA dependency ratio and demographic dependency ratio for old age in Poland, 2012 and 2016, per 100 people.

	2012	2016
Demographic old-age dependency ratio (OADR)	21.9	25.8
NTA old-age dependency ratio (NTA DR$_{old}$)	26.6	26.4

Source: Chłoń-Domińczak and Łątkowski (2019).

In summary, population ageing is a global process that is regionally diverse. The advancement of population ageing varies geographically. However, it may also be assessed differently depending on the measures used. The conventional measures, based on a fixed threshold for old age, show more advanced population ageing than the prospective measures, which refer to the old age adapted to increasing longevity. Using measures other than conventional ones provides a new perspective on the future evolution of population ageing. It also refers to new developments extending dependency ratios with advanced economic activity measures that take the age-specific differences in needs and productivity into account as well as information on quality of life. It also calls for reassessment of the challenges stemming from population ageing.

---

of goods and services at older ages, including with pension and health care benefits" (United Nations, 2020, pp. 19–20).

1.1.3 Selected main consequences of population ageing

Population ageing is the subject of keen interest of scientists and policymakers as its consequences widely affect economies and societies. These consequences are applicable to the macro-level perspective but are also relevant for individuals (the micro-level). What demography is certain about is that population ageing leads to slowdown in the population growth. However, the social and economic consequences of ageing are debatable (Bloom et al., 2003; Goldstein, 2009). The aspect that gets the most attention is the relationship between population ageing and economic growth, labour market, consumption, health and care services, and public finance. Sustainability of pensions and social security with respect to the expected inflated number of beneficiaries, employment at older ages, income inequality in later life as well as changes in labour supply – ageing of workforce, future labour productivity and technological progress – are widely discussed. Equally important is the association of population ageing and health (care). Population health and disability in later life, health and social care expenditures, and informal caregiving are the public policy concerns too. Awareness of unequal ageing, which refers to inequality that develops throughout the life course[11] and materialises in old age, is rising and is put to the top of the international policy agenda (OECD, 2017). More and more attention is also given to the demographic and social aspects of population ageing related to families, their composition and kin networks (especially in the context of childlessness), intergenerational transfers and well-being in old age (Uhlenberg, 2009).

The importance of the population age structure for the economy stems from the age-related differences in economic productivity, that is, the economic life cycle, which undergoes changes because of living longer and having fewer children later in life. Children require care and education, they have to consume, but cannot produce which makes them economically dependent.[12] Adulthood comprises mostly of periods of production and savings allowing for financing own consumption needs and accumulating wealth. Thus, the middle-aged are net producers. Finally, older people rely mostly on transfers from younger generations and dissaving, therefore, are mostly classified as net consumers

---

11 Disadvantages in health, education, employment and earnings start early in life, reinforce each other and compound over the life course (OECD, 2017).

12 According to the Minimum Age Convention adopted by the International Labour Organization in 1973 the general minimum age for admission to employment or work shall not be less than the age of completion of compulsory schooling and, in any case, shall not be less than 15 years.

similar to the youngest generations. Changes in the population age structure affect all of the age groups and determine the number of net consumers and net producers which is the most important from the economic point of view (Goldstein, 2009).

The National Transfer Accounts (NTA) approach allows depiction of an interplay of consumption and labour income over the lifecycle, that is, a lifecycle deficit in the NTA terminology.[13] The generational distribution of consumption and labour income in Poland that results in the lifecycle deficit is presented in Figure 8. In 2016 the economically active group that on average produced a surplus from labour income over individual consumption (the negative lifecycle deficit, or LCD surplus) contained between age 27 and 57. The younger (below 27 years of age) and more senior (above age 57) were on average not able to finance their consumption by themselves. Population ageing that results in the growing aggregate consumption and the lifecycle deficit of the senior generations relative to the younger generations adds extra pressure on the current working-age population.

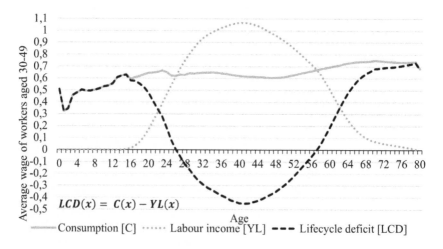

Figure 8. Normalised per capita labour income, consumption and lifecycle deficit age profiles for Poland, 2016.

Source: Own elaboration based on Chłoń-Domińczak and Łątkowski (2019, pp. 11–13).

---

13 The lifecycle deficit is the excess of consumption over labour income, [C(x) – YL(x)], at each age x. The excess of labour income over consumption for prime-age adults is referred to as the lifecycle surplus (Lee & Mason, 2014, p. 56).

Changes in the age structure of populations characterised by the reduction in the share of working-age population with accompanying increase in the cohorts of older people are most likely to result in modest declines in the rate of economic growth (Bloom et al., 2010). Economic projections foresee that demographic changes will put the EU Member States under a strong fiscal pressure (European Commission, 2018; Goldstein & Kluge, 2016). Many concerns are related to the future sustainability of pension provision and the adequate levels of pension benefits. Europe is the only continent with a shrinking working-age population, driven by past and present fertility decline below-replacement accompanied by an increase in the number of retirees due to longevity improvements. This change along with the ageing of the labour force and population in general challenge maintaining the sustainability of pension systems. Additionally, the average length of life after the labour market exit has been increasing over time (OECD, 2019c).

The increasing costs of health care systems and the future productivity of the European economy are also of growing concern. Even though the older population has become healthier over the years, their needs and behaviours vary from younger individuals. They require more health care and most of their income comes from social pensions (Bloom et al., 2010). Sustainability of health care provision is challenging as health care expenditure is unproportionally higher for those aged 65 and over in comparison to those aged under 65. Trends in the prevalence of disability are highly associated with age which implies increased care needs of older people and particularly higher costs of long-term care in the future (Gaymu et al., 2007; Murphy et al., 2006). Thanks to old-age mortality improvements and subsequent increases in survival of spouses and siblings, the pool of the kin to provide care has expanded in the recent years thanks to relatively wide (horizontal) network of siblings among the baby-boom cohorts. However, the long-term decline in fertility will have a stronger effect on care provision from relatives that will be shrinking relatively further in the future leading to more pronounced informal care burden (Agree & Glaser, 2009). It needs to be kept in mind that family networks are in fact potential (rather than factual) care resources which are subjective to change because of demographic change (that affects the size of the network) as well as changes in lifestyles (that influence kinship interrelationships and actual behaviours). Observation of the real transfers of care suggest that the horizontal relationships (between siblings) are becoming weaker. The topic of care needs of older people and provision of care in the future will be scrutinised and discussed in more detail in Section 1.3.

Population ageing contributes also to the increasing economic inequality. The direct effect of change in the age composition on inequality is found minor, but both increasing capital intensity due to slower population growth and increasing period of savings accumulation due to longevity improvements have a substantial effect on growing unequal wealth distribution (Goldstein & Lee, 2014). Last but not least, one needs to draw attention to take care about the well-being of older people which is certainly determined by their personal independence. The welfare needs of older people require special recognition as they deal with age-related vulnerability (Rowland, 2009).

The economic consequences of population ageing can be mitigated by behavioural responses at individual level and by policy reforms carried out by governments (Bloom et al., 2010). For example, population ageing leaves an imprint on both the economy and the labour market. From the human capital perspective, the decline in the relative size of the economically active population requires higher labour productivity and, therefore, encourages human capital investments. It also changes the structure of demand for goods that, in turn, alters employment patterns across sectors of economy and pushes for labour mobility (Börsch-Supan, 2003). Also on positive note, Lee and Mason (2014) argue that low fertility is not a serious economic challenge provided a greater investment in human capital is observed as the loss in employment and taxpayers is offset by enhanced productivity. They also find out that "fertility below replacement and modest population decline favor higher material standards of living" (Lee & Mason, 2014, p. 233).

There are mechanisms that allow adaptation to the upcoming changes. Firstly, individuals may want to extend their working life thanks to increased life expectancy and better health. Increases in labour force participation in the older (pre-retirement) age groups and among women (thanks to average lifespan increases and smaller family sizes) are of high importance to compensate at least partially for a drop in labour supply. Secondly, maintaining high standard of living in retirement may be achieved by increased propensity to save over the working life (Bloom et al., 2010).

Individual decisions that would translate into macroeconomic effects have to be supported by adequate policy adjustments. In order to encourage longer labour market careers a rather obvious solution is to raise a statutory retirement age and offer more flexible old-age pension arrangements. Unwanted, but probable actions are pension cuts and higher tax rates. Another strategy to cope with consequences of population ageing is to improve labour market flexibility by promoting part-time work given the ongoing health improvement at older ages and the fact that jobs require less strength nowadays. It would allow economically active adults to extend working life to earn income but without bearing the full-time job workload (Christensen et al., 2009). Initiatives such as lifelong learning to improve professional skills or preventive screening to maintain health are also encouraging older working population not to exit labour market too early.

Immigration to the EU countries cannot counteract the ongoing population ageing process but can play a complementary role with other measures promoting labour participation and postponement of retirement. It is worth noticing, however, that migration brings in potential social pressures that may be difficult to overcome by domestic citizens (Gil Alonso, 2009).

In countries in which the effect of the first demographic dividend is fading away, that is, the temporary positive effect of population change on economic growth due to increases in the size of the population at the working ages relative to the size of the young and the old, the economic and social situation is bound to change. The consequences of ageing on the economic growth to a large extent depend on the policy environment, especially on flexibility and adequacy of policy responses targeted to address economic challenges (Bloom et al., 2010; Kotowska, 2009). Seizing the opportunity of the development of the silver economy (considered as a part of the general economy relevant to the needs and demands of older adults) should be prioritised as the development of services dedicated to seniors as well as their engagement in socio-economic life is a source of potential growth (Abramowska-Kmon et al., 2020). OECD report on ageing and employment policies (OECD, 2015) found positive changes in this respect in Poland, for example, the increasing employment rate for older workers,[14] but also pointed at areas that could provide more improvement. The recommendations focus on the overall strategy to encourage longer working lives with the following areas of action: (1) better incentives to carry on working (e.g. improving women's labour market conditions, supporting work incentives, preventing early labour market exit); (2) tackling employment barriers on the side of employers (e.g. promoting age management, better dissemination of good practices); and (3) improving the employability of older workers (e.g. relieving older women from responsibilities toward their families, focus on preventive measures in occupational health services, more work-focused training for adults and older workers). The consequences of population ageing seem to be manageable to

---

14 The increase in the employment rate at older ages has been hampered by the decision to decrease the legal retirement age from the scheduled increase to 67 years for both women and men to the pre-2013 level of 60 years for females and 65 years for males (Chłoń-Domińczak, 2016, 2019). The law was legislated in November 2016 and came into force in October 2017.

some extent; however, they are strongly dependent on the implementation of the recommended policy actions.

From the individual perspective, a longer life span is accompanied by more time spent in each of life phases such as education and training, work and retirement, and also by changes in time lived in different family positions (a child, a partner, a parent and a grandparent). Moreover, family roles of individuals are overlapping during their life course as the number of coexisting generations is increasing. That affects the whole life course of individuals who should account for that when planning and organising own professional career and family life. Additionally, functional loss and decreases in autonomy, social isolation and loneliness, poor living conditions, single living and income issues are concerning risks at old age. It is thus important to enhance individual life satisfaction, counteract unequal ageing (OECD, 2017) and promote the path of successful ageing (Rowe & Kahn, 1987) over the life course. Active ageing concept (WHO, 2002) is instrumental towards achieving these goals which define implications for policies.

1.2 The family model and care provision

1.2.1 Family changes in developed countries

Before discussing family changes in developed countries some definitions need to be introduced. Firstly, my focus is on a family nucleus that comprises a couple without or with children and a lone parent with children living in a private household while a private household is defined as people living together in a housing unit and sharing the costs of maintenance.[15] This family concept limits relationships between children and adults to direct (first-degree) relationships, that is, between parents and children (UN, 2015; UNECE, 2015). An extended family is constituted by a family nucleus and relatives living in a private household, who do not form a separate family nucleus. Family households consist entirely of persons related by blood, marriage or adoption contrary to non-family households which refer to one-person households and multiperson households, that is, comprising two or more people who do not form a family nucleus (GUS, 2020d). In addition, I will refer to the evolving family structures/ kinship networks (often described as complex families) to account for within and intergenerational relationships between members of different families.

---

15   The Statistics Poland define the private household as a group of people living together in a housing unit and jointly maintaining themselves (GUS, 2020d).

Therefore, the term 'family changes' refers to both nuclear families and family networks, however, the former is fundamental for the latter.

Demographic and societal processes that began in the 1960s in the developed Western countries have led to deep changes in demographic structures of population (population ageing), but have also revolutionised the institution of family. They sparked a universal tendency that individuals started moving away from marriage and parenthood, fundamental for the nuclear family, which changed the structures of households and family networks as well as the organisation of the family life.

Changes in family-related behaviours refer to all stages of family life from the union formation, through the transition to parenthood and childrearing to the family dissolution (Abramowska-Kmon, 2011; cf. Kotowska, 2010; Lesthaeghe, 2014). An important change in the family formation process is the deinstitutionalisation of family and marriage[16] which is reflected by a diminishing role of marriage in starting partnership throughout the second half of the 20th century in the United States, Canada and western European countries (Cherlin, 2004). Modern generations are less willing to marry which manifests itself in falling proportions of married. Instead of starting a family with marriage they more often either resign from marriage or delay a marital contract and form a consensual union/Living-Apart-Together (LAT) relationship. As a consequence, LAT partnerships started to be on the rise and cohabitation began to supplant marriage as both the before marriage and persistent cohabitation became a more frequent choice. In addition, the 'pre-conception' cohabitation has been increasing more quickly (Perelli-Harris et al., 2012) Also, alternative unions (other than marriage) are increasingly more relevant to subsequent (postmarital) partnerships with accompanying decline in remarriage rates. Lastly, a raising acceptability of the same-sex unions has been observed.

Changes in partnership patterns are interrelated with a decline in fertility, its postponement and a rise in the number of births outside marriage. Births

---

16 Cherlin (2004) defines deinstitutionalisation as the weakening of the social norms that define people's behaviour in a social institution such as marriage. In the same article he also summarises a process of transition from the *companionate* marriage to the *individualised* marriage. The roles of spouses within marriage are more flexible and negotiable and personal choice and self-development gain on importance. Marriage is more treated as a union providing individualised rewards, while traditional rewards of being a good parent or a supportive spouse are less appreciated. Still, marriage is important on a symbolic level as it is perceived to increase the prestige of the union, especially among the higher educated.

out-of-wedlock have become more prevalent and less stigmatised, in some countries becoming even more numerous than births from within marriage (e.g. the proportion of births outside marriage exceeds 50 % in Bulgaria, Denmark, France, Estonia, the Netherlands, Portugal, Slovenia, Sweden or Norway). The contribution of childlessness by choice is considerable, too. Less children within families coincides with less families with children inducing declines in the average household size. There is also a decrease in the number of multiple-generations households in favour of two-generation households with nuclear families and an increase in one-person households, with a lot of them formed by older women.[17] Increasing instability of marriage (and unions in general) reveals itself in a rise in divorce and separation rates. Higher union dissolution contributes to growth in the number of one-parent families (mainly lone mothers) and patchwork families too.

Profound changes in fertility and marital perceptions that were underpinned by changing norms from materialism to post-materialism and attitudes from altruistic to individualistic have been framed into the second demographic transition theory (SDT) (Lesthaeghe, 2010; van de Kaa, 1987, 1994, 2002). According to Lesthaeghe (2010, p. 216), "the second demographic transition started with a multifaceted revolution, and all aspects of it affect fertility." Contraceptive revolution, sexual revolution (disagreement with "notions that sex is confined to marriage and mainly for procreation only"), gender revolution and ideational reorientation are enumerated as the foundation of the transition. The theory relates demographic changes observed in developed western European countries to changes in the value orentation of the population and a shift towards greater 'progressiveness'. Changes in the family formation and fertility are linked to socio-economic and technological developments as well. The importance of technological change cannot be overstated because the spread of effective contraception helped to initiate and to advance the transition with accessible and affordable possibility to postponing and spacing births. It is in line with Hakim's preference theory (2003) which assumes women are heterogeneous in their lifestyle preferences for family and employment. The contraceptive revolution gave women independent control of their fertility. The use of contraception led to lower fertility but was not the only cause of it.

---

17   The number of households with older persons is increasing with a greater presence of women. Men, if surviving to old age, live mostly together with their (usually also old) partners. More detailed description of trends in living arrangements of older people can be found in Chapter 2.

The family model and care provision 41

A focus on individual autonomy and self-realisation was accompanied with the trend toward gender equity (McDonald, 2000, 2006). A change in the household labour division towards more equity between men and women has been originally driven by the increased female labour force participation. Women's higher activity on the market that improved their incomes altered the traditional (female) homemaker and (male) breadwinner division of work advocated in Gary Becker's specialisation model. It is argued that fertility was influenced by social liberalism and economic restructuring that provided opportunity to engage women beyond the household and increased the risk aversion among young people due to labour market deregulation and increased competitiveness (McDonald, 2006). Both rising women's labour market participation and economic aspirations as well as market-imposed prolonged stay in educational system delayed childbearing and brought fertility to even lower and long-lasting levels.[18]

The more and more diverse forms of the family have become the new normal. From the life-course perspective, individual family careers are more dynamic and de-standardised. Throughout one's life a person may experience many family transitions and, with higher fragility of couple relationships, may be a member of multiple families, which alters family networks. Oláh et al. (2018, p. 42) recognise that the family is a dynamic entity and the decision-making processes regarding transitions over the family life course and organisation of family life are becoming increasingly complex. The changes in the family model relate to both demographic behaviours as well as to 'doing family' which refers to patterns of housework and care division between men and women in different family models classified by labour market involvement of men and women.

Changes in family-related behaviours accompanied by longer lifespans exert influence on interrelations between and within generations. The rising life expectancy leads to kinship networks becoming more vertical, while low fertility affects the size of subsequent generations to reduce horizontal ties (slimming of kinship networks). The new trends in timing of demographic events, for example, driven by longer education for men and women that postpone marriage and childbearing, induce additional changes in family structures. Later parenthood

---

18 According to Lesthaeghe (2014, p. 18115): "SDT theory formulated in 1980s was correct about anticipating: (i) the unfolding of very different patterns of partnership formation; (ii) the shift in value orientations in many spheres that emerged as central driving forces in childbearing decisions; (iii) the emergence of subreplacement fertility as a structural and lasting feature."

often means less years spent in certain family roles and increased spacing between generations. It also entails some economic and social consequences which pertain to the issue of inheritances, the types of intergenerational exchanges among kin and division of tasks within the family that members would consider helping each other with. From one side the increased longevity allows for more generations coexisting, but from the other side later parenthood pushes towards larger age gap between generations living together. The traditional intergenerational support for the elderly may be, therefore, affected by the change in values and norms, while more frequent marital disruption and higher female involvement in professional careers may put additional demands and restrictions on potential family caregivers (Agree & Glaser, 2009). In other words, the evolving structure of kin networks puts pressure on the intergenerational ties and norms of filial obligations which govern the exchange transfers (up and down) between generations.

Together with the increased longevity individual relationship careers can also be more heterogeneous allowing single marriages to last longer, but also to spend more years unmarried or in multiple unions over the life course (Agree & Glaser, 2009). Contemporary adults are more likely to have more complex couple histories because they form and end relationships more frequently and re-partnering could mean the arrival of stepchildren (Dykstra & Hagestad, 2007). That affects the family networks that will become much more diverse and complex in the future than those experienced by previous generations.

More conscious decision-making about offspring results in lower total fertility rates and smaller families. Consequently, declining fertility determines the future availability of children for caregiving. Studies show that there is no clear association between reduced fertility and reduced support towards older people. The study by Dykstra and Hagestad (2007) reveals that childless people face support deficits only toward the end of life. For example, in Italy the elderly nonparents and older people with children have similar likelihood of receiving support (Albertini & Mencarini, 2014). But, it is important to note that lower fertility may be a result of both having less children within the family and the increased prevalence of childlessness. As long as having at least one child leaves the possibility for receiving care from descendants in the future, the increased presence of people having no children makes more future seniors subject to receiving care outside families, including formal care (Agree & Glaser, 2009). A qualitative study on care for childless elderly people in Poland shows that seniors without children facing temporary health deterioration can rely on members of their social networks (neighbours, friends, distant relatives). In the event of serious illness or loss of independence, institutional support appears to be the only – although not desirable – solution for such people (Abramowska-Kmon & Mynarska, 2020).

Esping-Andersen and Billari (2015) argue that the trend towards less family observed in the second half of the 20ᵗʰ century has recently reversed. They put forward three arguments against further family erosion. Firstly, they find stability of family preferences with respect to marriage, motherhood and the ideal family size. Secondly, a reversal of the relationship between fertility rates and economic indicators is observed. Now, economic development, income and female employment rates are positively correlated with fertility. Thirdly, they spot a micro-level change in the relationship between education and family behaviour as higher educated women have been characterised by increasing fertility rates recently. The spread of gender-egalitarian norms is argued to be the main driver of change. That statement coincides with argumentation of Goldscheider et al. (2015) who argue that "the entry of women into the labor force might indeed have stressed family relationships, but as the second half of the gender revolution slowly emerges – with men joining women in the private sphere of the family – we argue that the revolution is actually strengthening families" (p. 208). Oláh et al. (2018) note that more egalitarian approach toward gender roles within families as well as greater women's engagement in paid work is expressed in increasingly prevalent transition from the male breadwinner model to the dual-earner – dual-carer model in Europe. The latter indicates greater involvement of fathers in family responsibilities and childrearing which follows mothers' higher participation in the labour market. The spread of the transition is argued to affect the family life substantially, but its progression varies across and within welfare regimes, reflecting the importance of institutional, cultural and economic settings for the evolution of the family.

1.2.2 Family changes in Poland since 1989

Changes in fertility and family formation behaviours that were observed in Western Europe have finally, even though with some delay, reached Central and Eastern Europe. Notably, the later had the transition began, the more rapid and turbulent it has been progressing. The higher intensity of behavioural changes is attributed to the economic and political transformation that was taking place in those countries at the turn of 1980s and 1990s, including Poland (Kotowska & Jóźwiak, 2012). Kotowska et al. (2008) find a lot of similarity of family developments in Poland with those observed in Western Europe. The main directions of changes, namely the declining propensity to marry, decreasing desire to rear children as well as the postponement of both decisions, were common.[19] However, there have also been dissimilarities – they concern diffusion of cohabitation and marriage dissolution. Poland belongs to countries with low levels of divorce with a delayed but increasing trend in divorce rates (Styrc, 2016). However, marriage is still considered as a relatively stable institution as compared to other European countries.

Another element of change in the family model pertains to popularity of cohabitation unions. Even though the prevalence of cohabitation has been rising since the 1970s, it has still been marginal until the end of millennium (Fihel, 2005). However, more recent studies show that Poland has already reached the second stage in the process of cohabitation diffusion (Mynarska & Matysiak, 2010) and the scale of the phenomenon is underestimated (Kotowska et al., 2016; Matysiak, 2009). Cohabitation is more a trial period before marriage for young Poles and possibility to live in a union for the divorced. Consensual unions are mostly formed by least educated but also become more attractive for higher educated groups as an alternative form of living arrangement to marriage. It is perceived to offer freedom to leave a union at any time without consequences, but does not provide secure conditions for childbearing (Mynarska et al., 2014). Additionally, there has been observed a rise in the number of births outside marriage and higher marital instability indicated by a systematically rising total divorce rate but both characteristics are still relatively low in comparative perspective (Abramowska-Kmon, 2011).

The advancement of ideational change in Poland was lagged and much less relevant, at least in the beginning, than in developed countries. In the 1990s the structural component (the labour market changes that led to uncertainty about jobs and income, deterioration of household welfare) as well as the institutional component, that is, deficient labour market policies and family policies (above all, poor access to care services and facilities, quality and cost of services and their match to one's need) that did not address the problems of reconciling work and family responsibilities faced by Polish families, were of much bigger importance (Kotowska et al., 2008; Kotowska & Wóycicka, 2008).

The family-related behaviours in Poland might also be depicted from the transition to adulthood perspective framed by the sequence and timing of life events leading to adulthood. The study of the life-course developments in early

---

19   A deep reduction in TFR, change in age-specific fertility pattern and postponement of fertility in Poland has already been mentioned. The most detailed and up-to-date information is available in Fihel et al. (2017), Tymicki, Zeman and Holzer-Żelażewska (2018) and Kotowska (2019b).

adulthood based on the second wave of the Generations and Gender Survey shows that pathway to adulthood in Poland has been prolonged and become increasingly diverse (Kotowska, 2018; Rybińska, 2016). From the comparison of male and female cohorts born in 1950–54 and 1975–1979 it arises that younger cohorts spend more years in education, start working before completing education, but also had more periods of unemployment than older ones. From the union formation perspective, marriage is increasingly preceded by a period of cohabitation which also delays the decision to conceive first child. In summary, the transition to adulthood in Poland has been stretched over a longer time-period and consists of a greater number of events than in the past. It is much in line with the ideal-typical pattern of 'late, protracted and complex' pathway formulated by Billari and Liefbroer (2010).

Changes in family formation and dissolution patterns influence the structure of households and families.[20] Abramowska-Kmon (2014) reports an increase in the number of households between censuses in 1988, 2002 and 2011 and a drop in the average household size. One can observe a growth of the percentage of one-person households, a decline in the share of family couples without children and a significant rise of single parenthood. From the marital status perspective, there is higher share of unmarried males and females and more divorced and widowed persons. Consequently, the share of married persons went down which may indicate a slow retreat from marriage.

The structure of households in Poland is also evolving due to ageing. In 2011 almost every fifth household (19.3 %) was populated exclusively by persons aged 60 or more, while another 22.1 % of households included at least one person of that age. It is a growth from 18.9 % and 17.2 % in 2002 respectively. The increase in the share of households with two or three generations reflect the corresponding increase in the two-family households. When it comes to solitary living, the comparison of data from recent censuses shows that in 2011 nearly half (48 %) of all one-person households were formed by people aged 60 and over. This share was higher than in 2002 by 2 percentage points (p.p.) but lower by 4 p.p. than in 1988 (which can be explained by improvements in mortality, in particular of men's mortality). Women constitute most of all one-person households (61.2 % in 2011) and the share of one-person households lived by women aged above 60 was 37 %. Improvements in longevity contributed to the increase in the number of households with the oldest-old persons. In 2011,

---

20   More information on the living arrangements of older people in Poland can be found in Chapter 2, section 2.1.4.

almost one-third of people aged 80 and more lived in households represented by a person in 35–65 age group compared to one-fourth in the previous census. Co-residence of older persons with younger generations is important from the care provision perspective discussed in the following section.

1.3 Care arrangements for older people

The interrelationship between values about care and institutions that take part in organisation of care, such as welfare state, the family, the labour market and the non-profit sector, constitutes care arrangements (Pfau-Effinger, 2005). It deserves attention, however, that care arrangements operate in a certain population context. One of the consequences of population ageing is the distortion of the age structure of populations from an expanding shape of population pyramid to a more constricted one. It affects relations between generations, which raises questions about the future of care provision for older people (Agree & Glaser, 2009). The size of the cohorts that reach the old-age threshold as well as their incidence of disability determine both supply and demand of care. Additionally, changes in the family structure, that is, a decrease in the number of children per family, as well as an increase in geographical mobility affect the family care reservoir due to reduced number of potential caregivers and their unavailability because of distance (World Health Organization, 2011). On top of declining fertility rates and migration, there has been an increase in women's involvement in the labour market, which also affects the family care resources and the subjective well-being of caregivers.[21] In the European context, taking the changes altogether, there is a 'care deficit' identified that poses a major challenge to most European societies (European Commission, 2014). Dependency and the consequent reliance on other people resulting in the increase in demand for various forms of health care, nursing care and ongoing support by others in activities of daily living are becoming a challenge for social policy and health care in Poland as well (Błędowski & Maciejasz, 2013). Given that providing care and support for older dependants is a prerequisite for achieving a good quality of life, meeting the current and future care needs becomes a concern of a growing part of population.

---

21   Caregiver's full-time employment reduces time spent on caring for others (Glauber, 2017; Henz, 2009). However, some caregivers, mostly women, do not trade off time in paid work with time in caregiving, but they provide care at the expense of their leisure time. The trade-off of the time spent on caring responsibilities and time for leisure is especially significant for intensive caregivers (Stanfors et al., 2019).

1.3.1 Characteristics of care

Care is a complex concept with multiple layers and meanings which understanding in academic debate has evolved for many years, from invisible domain of women's housework into political and public concern (Anttonen & Zechner, 2011). Care is broadly defined as "the provision of daily social, psychological, emotional, and physical attention for people" (Knijn & Kremer, 1997, p. 330). In this work I focus on long-term care (LTC) defined as "the care for people needing support in many facets of living over a prolonged period of time" (Colombo et al., 2011, p. 39) that is dedicated to older people. Here, I concentrate on personal care, for which the need of support stems from a reduced degree of functional capacity, either physical or cognitive, that leads to limitations in basic activities of daily living (ADL). Therefore, less attention is paid to emotional care or practical help that deals with limitations in instrumental activities of daily living (IADL). In a review of various definitions of long-term care, Iparraguirre (2018a, p. 206) highlights the concept of LTC is about *care, not cure*. It is repeatedly stressed that the aim of long-term care is to maintain the maximum/optimal level of functional independence (personal functioning). At the same time, LTC recognises possibility of deterioration of person's condition over time. In contrast to acute/curative health care, *caring* is compensating for a lasting inability, while *curing* aims at improving the person's medical condition (Iparraguirre, 2018a). However, from the point of view of spending, long-term care is as a mix of both health and social care services that refer both to health care and social care sectors and are strongly intertwined (Colombo et al., 2011).

Long-term care can be characterised by various distinctions. Most importantly one can distinguish between formal and informal care work (Triantafillou et al., 2010), although some other types are also identified, for example, semi-formal care work (Geissler & Pfau-Effinger, 2005). Informal care is provided mainly by family members but also by other relatives or non-kin such as friends or neighbours who usually are not trained to provide care.[22] Providing informal care is not bound with any contract regarding care responsibilities and is unpaid, however, some financial transfers following informal care services are possible. On the contrary, formal care services are paid for and are usually supplied by qualified professionals with specified care responsibilities. Formal care is an activity belonging to the labour market either under the responsibility of the

---

22   It is worth remembering that help from close family (spouse, children) is usually more prevalent and more continuous, while help from other relatives and friends is rather ad hoc (Błędowski, 2012).

welfare state or through the private provision (Triantafillou et al., 2010). It is noteworthy that informal LTC consists only of personal care services, while formal LTC additionally includes assisted living, respite care, nursing care and hospice care (Iparraguirre, 2018a). Consequently, informal care is home-based while formal care is more diverse as it can be provided at home (domiciliary care), in community (e.g. day centres) and in institutions (e.g. nursing homes, palliative care). From the point of view of funding, LTC can be financed publicly, privately, or both (more details, for example, in Iparraguirre 2018a, p. 211). Lastly, long-term care services can be provided in-kind or as a cash benefit (Colombo et al., 2011). In-kind services are providing direct care for eligible recipients in need while cash payments allow care recipients to choose care services and providers individually according to their preferences.

1.3.2 Care regimes in Europe

Caregiving is often based on the legal obligations between generations. However, it becomes less a solely family domain to emerge more as a public issue. The actual care practices are mostly a mixture of private and public actions that depend on social values, norms and institutional settings such as social policies and civil law (Anttonen & Zechner, 2011). Welfare policies towards care within care arrangements are mainly based on family values and welfare values. Family values are related to the structure of the family and the division of labour by gender while welfare values pertain to perceptions about the provision of welfare in society. Both types of values imply how caring tasks are distributed within the family and between the family and societal institutions (Pfau-Effinger, 2005). The level of engagement of the family and the state (or the market) is differentiating countries with respect to the existing care arrangements (Anttonen & Sipilä, 2005; Pfau-Effinger, 2005).

European countries significantly differ with respect to care arrangements for older people. Some studies find evidence for a North-South gradient in Europe with northern countries characterised with 'weak' family ties and southern countries with 'strong' family ties (Reher, 1998). The strength of family ties is usually discussed using categories of familial loyalty, obedience, authority, but also demographic models of intergenerational co-residence (living arrangements) and models of support for older people (Bolin et al., 2008; Kohli et al., 2005). For example, strong family ties are characterised by higher co-residence of young adults with parents, predominance of collectivistic values and care provision for frail and dependent supplied by the family. In contrast, countries with weak family ties have young adults leaving home relatively early, representing individualistic attitudes and relying more on private and public institutions to cover the care needs of family members. As noted by Dykstra (2018, p. 2), the studies on intergenerational ties in Europe provide support for Reher's weak family–strong family dichotomy depending on the measure used. However, some empirical research advocate a more complex view on family life in Europe. Glaser et al. (2004) agree that variation across countries is explained mostly by attitudes, reflecting cultural norms and values about intergenerational obligations of care, and by policy arrangements, that is, the availability, costs and quality of public service provision. However, when taking into account different dimensions of support for older people it is difficult to categorise European countries according to the clear North-South divide. Glaser et al. (2004) point at the central European countries that are much more difficult to characterise. Ogg and Renaut (2006, p. 740) find that the pronunciation of the gradient depends on the definition of care used. Providing any care (practical, paperwork or personal) to ascendants is most prevalent in the Northern countries and least prevalent in the Southern countries. But when a frequency of providing care is accounted for, the North-South gradient is reversed with much higher rates of regular and almost daily help in Southern Europe and lower rates in Northern Europe. In the same vein Brandt et al. (2009) observe that receiving help by the parents (including practical help with the housekeeping) is more likely in the Northern states. In southern European countries though, where institutional support from welfare state is lower, there is higher likelihood of children providing informal care and taking up more demanding tasks, that is, personal care. In other words, the larger the social service sector in a country, the lower the proportion of physical care provision by informal carers (e.g. help with bathing, dressing or eating). Haberkern et al. (2015) point at the influence of the welfare state characteristics on the division of family care by men and women and find that the geographical division of intergenerational care is relevant for daughters only. The so-called familialistic countries that offer few alternatives to family care augment the gender gap as women are much more likely to be involved in caring responsibility than men. Additionally, a lower provision of formal services in the familialistic regime makes it more difficult to help more than one generation, in case the caring children are grandparents themselves. That forces caregivers, usually daughters, to select which generation to help (Herlofson & Brandt, 2019).

As the most care for older people is provided by family members (Colombo et al., 2011), there is an ongoing discussion on how much institutions can support or even replace informal caregivers in providing specific care tasks. In general, there are examples of studies that were successful in finding that informal care is a substitute for formal care, but there are also examples that failed to prove it or even shown complementarity between both types of help. In a review by Iparraguirre (2018b, pp. 270–276), it is concluded that the informal care services can partially substitute formal home and institutional care, yet "particular informal services are closer substitutes for particular formal services but not as strong replacements for other formal services" (p. 275). Additionally, there is a country variation in whether informal care is substituted or complemented by formal care. In the European context of support for older people living alone, regions with strong family ties (Southern Europe) are more likely to substitute formal care with informal care (Bolin et al., 2008).

The concept of care arrangements overlaps with the welfare regime division framed by Esping-Andersen (1990) who established a classification of countries based on the degree of decommodification of workforce through public transfers and services. The original welfare state typology that identified conservative, liberal and social democratic types of regimes became an inspiration and a reference for further international comparative research, but also underwent many modifications. For instance, the typology was extended to isolate another regime type for the Mediterranean countries (Ferrera, 1996) and revised to accentuate the family and household economy (Esping-Andersen, 1999). Additionally, the regime of central and eastern European countries was included (Fenger, 2007). The concept of integrating social care services into the welfare state regimes classification has been presented by Anttonen and Sipilä (1996). It has been a starting point for Saraceno and Keck (2010) to establish a grouping of countries with regard to intergenerational obligations to care for children and the old separately. They have offered a conceptual framework that distinguishes four different patterns with respect to underlying dimension of familialism. At one end of the spectrum there are countries that offer no public alternative to family care ('familialism by default' or 'unsupported familialism') and at the other end there are countries that reduce the responsibilities and dependencies of the family ('de-familialisation') by individualisation of social rights (e.g. entitlement to receiving care, minimum income provision). 'Supported familialism' refers to policies supporting family carers in their financial and care responsibilities mainly through financial transfers (including taxation and paid leaves). The last pattern, and the most rare, offers an option in-between supported familialism and de-familialisation alternative (Saraceno & Keck, 2010). By use of data on the 27 EU Member States regarding both downward (towards children) and upward (towards the old) obligations several clusters of countries in Europe have been identified. In this framework Scandinavian countries and France represent a high degree of de-familialisation towards both generations. In opposite, a high degree of familialism characterises Poland, Italy, Spain, Greece and Bulgaria with Latvia, Slovakia and Portugal being close to this group. The highest degree of supported familialism is found in Hungary, the Czech Republic and Estonia, while other countries are profiled as a mixture of degree in familialism dimensions with regard to both set of obligations (Saraceno & Keck, 2010). The established framework enables cross-national comparisons of international family obligations and enhances our understanding of the influence of macro-level factors on care relations within families. It is, however, equally important to be aware of possible within-country variability in family solidarity patterns (Dykstra & Fokkema, 2011).

1.3.3 Predictors of care provision in developed countries

When discussing care provision, it is important to take a closer look at the population of older people who require care services as well as at care providers. First of all, a need for care is bound with a functional status of an individual and may occur at different ages. The remaining lifespan of the population of older people is heterogeneous with respect to health and life circumstances. Therefore, the diversity of care strategies adopted to address functional needs has to "reflect not only variability in the nature and severity of functional health, but also the availability of family members, as well as economic and social resources and individual preferences" (Agree & Glaser, 2009, p. 658). For example, due to mortality differentials between men and women there is an imbalance of care needs by sex. The female's advantage in mortality has created a gender gap in life expectancy that led women to outnumber men in the oldest age groups and wives outlive their husbands. On the one hand, more women become unpartnered at older ages than men and, therefore, are more reliant on support from others than their husbands or partners. On the other hand, such disproportion leads also to the gender distribution of care as older men depend a lot upon their surviving wives (Agree & Glaser, 2009).

Along with a variety of caring needs of older people there is a diversity in countries' organisation of care which is reflected in a mix of formal and informal care provision. The following considerations refer to the modes of care provision that is presented in this order: firstly, formal care mode is discussed, then informal care mode (supplied mainly by families) is described, and finally, transitions between formal and informal modes are demonstrated. However, it is necessary to note that it is sometimes difficult to compare statistics on care internationally because definitions of care and the reference population used may not be compliant.

From the global point of view, most support comes from family members or social networks. Supply of formal services is generally underdeveloped, coverage of not-for-profit organisations is limited and private markets usually cannot offer sufficient and affordable provision of help (World Health Organization, 2011). In the developed countries the use of formal long-term care services is diversified in terms of financing and availability. Among the population age 65 and over, on average 10.8 % adults receive long-term care (lowest 0.9 % in Poland[23] and highest 22.4 % in Switzerland) and almost 70 % of care services is received at home[24] (OECD, 2019a). On average, the total spending on LTC is equal to 1.7 % of GDP. It varies from 0.2 % (Estonia and Hungary) to 3.7 % of GDP (the Netherlands) (OECD, 2019a, fig. 11.28) with a dominance of public over private source of funding. On average, the private share of the total LTC spending is equivalent to about 15 %, although there are some exceptional countries, for example, Switzerland (60 %), the United States (40 %), Germany (31 %) or Spain (27 %). In Poland, long-term care is almost fully public-funded (Colombo et al., 2011).

Informal care provision is more widespread. Verbeek-Oudijk et al. (2015, fig. 3) using the 2011 Survey of Health, Ageing and Retirement in Europe data (SHARE, wave 4) on people aged 50+ who live independently find out that in twelve European countries studied the majority of home care delivered was unpaid (informal). The share of informal carers[25] among the population aged 50 and over in 2017 (SHARE, wave 7) ranged between 6.5 % in Greece to 19.7 % in the Czech Republic with an average of 13.5 % (OECD, 2019a). In another study using the European Social Survey data from 2014, the average prevalence rate of informal caregivers in Europe amounts to 34.3 % (7.6 % for intensive caregivers[26]) (Verbakel et al., 2017). Variation of informal care provision between

---

23 Data for Poland is underestimated as it refers only to recipients of LTC in institutions, while for the majority of the countries compared care received at home is also included.

24 Between 2007 and 2017 in the OECD countries, the proportion of LTC recipients aged 65 and more who received care at home rose by 6 %, from 64 % to 68 % (OECD, 2019a).

25 Informal carers are defined as people providing any help (at least weekly) to older family members, friends and people in their social network, living inside or outside their household, who require help with everyday tasks.

26 Intensive caregiving is defined as providing care for minimum 11 hours a week. Sample data is representative for population aged 25–75 years from 20 European countries based on the special module on the social determinants of health in European Social Survey, Round 7 collected in 2014.

countries is large, from 43.6 % in Finland to 8.2 % in Hungary, with the higher prevalence in Nordic countries and the lower in Southern, Central and Eastern countries. With regard to intensive care provision, the geographical gradient is reversed (ranging between 3.5 % to 11.6 %). Verbakel et al. (2017, p. 93) argue that this regularity observed at the macro level is related to the effect of the welfare state. The generous welfare states encourage providing help to others (crowding in) but simultaneously relieve the necessity to provide intensive care (crowding out). At the micro-level this observation is supported by van den Broek and Dykstra (2017). In their study on relations between residential care availability and care provided by adult children to single-living parents, they conclude that in countries that offer more beds in residential care adult children are more reluctant to help their impaired parents. They explain it by referring to the 'diffusion of responsibility' hypothesis that argues the responsibility for care provision is more diffused between the welfare state and the family when residential care settings are more available.

The state systems of support are at different stages of development worldwide, yet even the countries with the highest formal care coverage rely heavily on the family and friends' support. World Health Organization reports that across high-income countries families meet around 80 % of the support needs of older people (World Health Organization, 2011). Care provision is more and more perceived as a team effort that involves multiple family (and non-family) members coordinated by a primary caregiver. Although individual caregivers may provide care continuously, the care networks of older adults are inherently dynamic as nearly half of older parents experience a change in their care networks over time (Szinovacz & Davey, 2013). The family's decision on the level of engagement in care provision depends on the individual characteristics of the care-takers and caregivers, the family composition and kinship networks, cultural norms, and welfare state institutions (Abramowska-Kmon, 2015; Haberkern & Szydlik, 2010; Haberkern et al., 2015).

Within families, the most common source of care for older people is spouses followed by adult children (e.g. Silverstein & Giarrusso (2010) for the United States, Geerlings et al. (2005) and Jacobs et al. (2018) for the Netherlands, Pickard et al. (2000) for the UK, Błędowski (2012) for Poland). The research on the US data shows that not only are spouses the primary caregivers, but they are also more likely to serve as the sole caregiver (68 %) than others (34 %) (Wolff & Kasper, 2006). Similarly, in the Dutch study authors conclude that spousal care largely excludes care from other informal caregivers (Jacobs et al., 2018). Children play more important role for a parent who lives alone. Bolin et al. (2008) based on SHARE data from 2004 (Wave 1) estimated that for people aged 50+ living alone, children accounted for 83 % of all informal care provision. The adult's children partners (children-in-law) provide less support to their parents-in-law especially when the care needs are limited (Henz, 2009). The greater number of children in the family provides opportunities to share care duties for old parents among brothers and sisters. The greater number of siblings allows individuals to postpone care provision entry and to quit or exchange caring responsibilities within the family networks (Szinovacz & Davey, 2013). From the gender perspective, women are more likely to provide care for parents in their role as a daughter than men (Ogg & Renaut, 2006; Patterson & Margolis, 2019), especially in families with brother only (Vergauwen & Mortelmans, 2019). In the recent examination of care provision by gender to the older people by adult children in sibling groups and their spouses it is evident that male children have much lower likelihood of providing care to their parents than female children (Grigoryeva, 2017; Luppi & Nazio, 2019). Men shift the caregiving responsibilities for elderly parents to their sisters rather than to their female partners, especially in the southern European countries. In fact, it is not the presence of sibling that facilitates sharing the burden of elderly parent care across the adult children but whether there is a sister or not (Luppi & Nazio, 2019). Vergauwen and Mortelmans (2019) conclude similarly that sons enter caregiving roles more in the absence of sisters. The study in the US context give likewise results, the amount of care provided by sons is lower if they have sisters, whereas daughters provide relatively more care if they have brothers (Grigoryeva, 2017). Additionally, the gender of the parent matters. The positive effect of being a caregiver found for women is stronger when caring for a mother than a father (Abramowska-Kmon et al., 2015). Sons provide relatively more care if the parent-in-need is a father, while daughters provide relatively more care to mothers, which underlines the importance of gendered norms about receiving care (Grigoryeva, 2017). Leopold et al. (2014, p. 315) highlight the importance of this phenomenon for women as "the primacy of the mother-daughter tie in transitions to parent care".

Glauber (2017) examined gender differences in spousal care among married adults across the later life course. Drawing on the Health and Retirement Study representative of the U.S. population over the age of 50, she found a large gender gap in care among adults aged 50–65 that decreased as they moved from mid-life to older age. As women provide much more hours of care to their husbands than receive from them, this gap is the most wide in middle ages and gets narrower in older ages. The study showed that gender differences are explained by employment differences as working full-time impedes the amount of spousal care provided by men; the effect was not found for women. The importance of employment status is also found for siblings. Vergauwen and Mortelmans (2019) point out that having no time constraints due to being out of paid work increases the likelihood of starting a care-providing role within families. The effect of children's employment is found not uniform across Europe. In countries representing 'mixed' and 'supported familialistic' regimes in Central Europe there is the employment effect for daughters. Those who work full-time have lower propensity to support parents compared to the non-working. In countries with high 'de-familialisation' (e.g. Scandinavian countries), neither daughters nor sons are affected by their employment status (Herlofson & Brandt, 2019).

Chances to receive personal care from social networks are best predicted by current family structures (e.g. presence of a coresident partner, the number of living children and siblings) (Nazio, 2019). Albertini et al. (2007) argue that differences in social support are reflected in the rates of co-residence of elderly parents with adult children. Co-residence is much more prevalent in Southern countries than in Northern and Continental Europe as it is a way of transferring resources across generations. A greater geographical proximity is also an important factor to be involved in helping parents in need. Children that live close-by are more regularly involved in providing care for parents (Ogg & Renaut, 2006). Becoming a caregiver is facilitated by close residence, but is impacted by the distance of siblings' residence as well – the farther away siblings live, the higher the chance to commence care provision (Vergauwen & Mortelmans, 2019). Parent's co-residence is also associated with a higher provision of caring and increases involvement in parent care by children-in-law (Henz, 2009).

Provision of care is a multidimensional and complex process. Care may be provided and received in different circumstances which are not necessarily permanent. For instance, care may be considered from the point of view of its stability. For older adults who just started receiving care, more than half was informal home care. The transition from no care to informal home care is triggered by the immediate need for care that is associated with a chronic physical disease and functional limitations. Additionally, some predisposing and enabling variables are also significantly associated, for example, higher age, low education, having no partner and low urbanisation (Geerlings et al., 2005). Informal care is highly unstable as there is a substantial share of older adults who experienced transition from receiving informal home care to not receiving any care three years later. Transitions from professional care to informal or no care are also observed; however, they are very seldom (Geerlings et al., 2005).

Transitions between types of care depend on objective factors, such as health status, but also on preferences. Most of older people prefer to receive informal care rather than formal care, but more often formal care is obtained as a complement to existing informal care networks (Agree & Glaser, 2009). On the one hand, the use of formal services may support informal care to keep the older person in the community by providing a respite for the caregiver (Tennstedt et al., 1993). On the other hand, informal care has a protective effect from relying on formal services. Having a partner decreases the probability of using formal care only (Suanet et al., 2012), while having no partner predicts transition to private home care and institutional care (Geerlings et al., 2005). The availability of siblings and adult children also reduces the risk of formal care use (Freedman, 1996; Kemper, 1992). The primary source of care is proved to be retained for long time and is usually substituted with informal caregiver in the next generation (Jette et al., 1992). A permanent substitution of informal care for formal services is usually determined by the loss of the primary caregiver, usually due to death or illness rather than competing demands or interpersonal conflict (Jette et al., 1992; Tennstedt et al., 1993).

Luppa et al. (2010) provide a systematic review of predictors of institutionalisation in the general population in developed countries. The key point is that nursing home placement is basically caused by cognitive and/or functional impairment, and dementia is considered the most common cause. Once an older person suffers from any impairment, the likelihood of admission to a nursing home increases due to lack of support in daily living needs. Indeed, functional limitations, depression and cognitive impairments are associated with the transition to institutional care (Geerlings et al., 2005). The move to professional care is also predicted by age, education level and partner status, however the effect varies by the source of care. The fact of receiving informal help versus receiving no care before increases the chance of institutional care use as well (Geerlings et al., 2005, pp. 120–121). In another meta-analysis, based on the US studies only, Gaugler et al. (2007) report an increased risk of nursing home admission for men and low income of persons in need. However, Luppa et al. (2010) argue, based on a broader number of studies, that the effect of gender and income on institutionalisation is inconclusive, and if any, then only of slight value. Broese van Groenou et al. (2006) do not find any differences in the use of formal help among older people by socio-economic status once need of care (defined by health) is controlled for. In the European-level analysis of the nursing home admission in the last year of life, Stolz et al. (2019) confirm that the need factors, for example, functional impairment, are crucial in the admission process, but also highlight the major role of the country of residence. In countries which provide extensive public institutional care services such as Sweden or the Netherlands, chances for the nursing home admission in the last year of life are almost 2.5 times higher than in countries with restricted public spending on institutional care such as Poland (Stolz et al., 2019). From the geographical perspective, a clear North-West/South-East gradient emerged.

1.3.4 Care provision for older people in Poland

Provision of care for older people in Poland is determined by cultural, that is, relatively strong intergenerational ties, and institutional factors, that is, the low formal care availability. In the typology by Saraceno and Keck (2010) Poland is classified as a country with a high degree of familialism. With respect to intergenerational responsibilities towards children and the old family ties in Poland remain strong. Among Poles, the family, next to health, is declared the most important value in life, preceding other values such as a professional career or friendship (Czapiński, 2015; Titkow & Duch, 2004). The strong family orientation is also reflected in high scores in the index of filial obligations (Muresan & Hărăguş, 2015). In the study on Polish migrants in the Netherlands, the strong commitment to family life, even in detached ties, is evident (Karpinska & Dykstra, 2019). Among adults aged 45–65 years asked about preferences towards care provision for older people, 89 % of respondents agreed or strongly agreed that it is children's responsibility to provide help to the old. The study also revealed an aversion to institutionalisation as 70 % of respondents claimed an older person should reside in a social assistance house only in case the family cannot meet the caring need (Bojanowska, 2009). Among caregivers, the dominant motivation to provide care to older people (82 %, mostly children of care recipients) is conviction that it is one's responsibility (Kałuża-Kopias & Szweda-Lewandowska, 2018). In a summary of the available research on the scale of care needs of older people in Poland, Błędowski (2012) concludes that the family role in care provision cannot be overestimated. The high level of informal care provision can be attributed to filial norms, but also to the relatively frequent co-residence of older people with their offspring (Golinowska & Sowa-Kofta, 2018). Poland is standing out as having some of the largest households in Europe with extended intergenerational co-residence (Iacovou & Skew, 2011). The most recent Eurostat estimates from 2019[27] show that the share of young people aged 25 to 34 who were living with their parents in Poland (44 %) is well above the EU average (29 %). Living with parents in Poland is becoming more prevalent (36 % in 2004) and is much more widespread among men (51 %) than among women (37 %).

---

27   https://ec.europa.eu/eurostat/web/products-eurostat-news/-/EDN-20200812-1 [accessed 10 October 2020].

As regards informal care provision, 8.4 % of population aged 50+ in Poland provides daily or weekly help with everyday tasks informally to people living inside or outside their household (estimate for 2017 based on SHARE wave 7)[28] versus 13.5 % of the OECD average, of which almost two-thirds are women (OECD, 2019a, fig. 11.20). According to the European Health Interview Survey (collected in 2014), 16 % of the population aged 15 and more is engaged in care provision for older and dependent people on a daily basis with women being more frequent care providers than men (18 % and 13 % respectively). Most of care transfers (76.4 %) are directed towards own family networks' members only (21.1 % of people care for persons outside the family network). Caring for both relatives and non-family members is rare (2.6 %) and mostly prevalent among inhabitants of urban areas. In terms of care intensity, 25.3 % of carers provide care for 20 hours or more per week, 16.8 % spend weekly at least 10 but less than 20 hours on caring activities, while the most (57.8 %) devote less than 10 hours to providing care or assistance (GUS, 2016c). Other survey data (the European Social Survey, Round 7 from 2014) show that among Poles aged 25–75 years 36.3 % provide any informal care to others because of long-term physical and/or mental ill health or disability, or problems related to old age and 9 % provide intensive care, that is, spend 11 hours a week or more on care (Verbakel et al., 2017). The estimate of the monetary value of informal care based on time use survey data by Francavilla and Giannelli (2019) revealed that the value of adult care was 0.2 % of GDP in Poland.

In the representative study on older people aged 65 and more years in Poland – PolSenior (Mossakowska et al., 2012), the overwhelming majority of respondents (93.5 %) who declared support needs from others pointed at family network members as the care providers (Błędowski, 2012). The structure of support provision is age-related. The higher age of the person in need is accompanied by the gradual change in the structure of people who provide help to others. Table 2, based on the results of the PolSenior study, shows the change in the share of family members providing help to persons with limitations as they are getting older. The drop of family care is compensated by the increase in proportion of caregivers from social services as it quadruples for the oldest age groups. The role of other informal caregivers such as friends and neighbours is diminishing

---

28   Estimates based on SHARE wave 4 collected in 2011 and 2012 inform that around 8 % of people aged 50 or more in Poland provided regular care to members of their households with women (9 %) providing more support than men (7 %). Also, more than 18 % respondents declared providing help to people from outside their households (20.5 % of women versus 15 % of men) (Abramowska-Kmon et al., 2014).

as well. Błędowski (2012, p. 461) argues that there are two factors reducing the help provided both from the family network and close non-relatives. Firstly, the providers of care – children, friends, neighbours – are getting older which makes them less mobile or even less independent and, therefore, less capable of supporting others. The second factor is related to the health condition of the person in need. The advancing frailty of a care-receiver leads to increasing dependence on support from others in terms of the range of activities and professional skills. This change in demand for care is depicted by the rise in the share of others who provide care, including those providing for a fee. Błędowski (2012, p. 461) concludes that among caregivers supporting the older age groups two main shifts are in place: family carers are getting more skills through training by professional caregivers – on the one hand – and informal carers are replaced by skilled formal carers and other persons – on the other hand.

Table 2. Persons providing help by respondent age (%)

Age group	Family members	Carers from social assistance centre	Neighbours, friends	Other persons
65–69	95.3	1.5	11.8	4.1
70–74	94.7	3.5	8.9	3.1
75–79	92.9	4.8	10.0	3.9
80–84	93.4	2.6	9.3	6.5
85–89	91.9	7.9	6.2	6.6
≥ 90	91.0	7.1	6.7	8.9

Source: PolSenior results (Błędowski, 2012, p. 461).

The financing of long-term care in Poland follows the pattern observed in other central and eastern European countries with social protection beyond kin and non-kin networks being far less developed than in other parts of Europe (Österle, 2012). The context of care provision in that European countries is characterised by lower employment rates for men and women in general and among older persons, less part-time employment opportunities and higher availability of earlier retirement than in western European countries (Österle, 2012). In fact, there is no legally defined long-term care sector in Poland and the LTC services are provided through health care and social assistance sectors[29]

---

29 Home care services supplied by health sector are financed by the Polish National Health Fund (Narodowy Fundusz Zdrowia – NFZ) and delivered by community

(Golinowska & Sowa-Kofta, 2018). A lack of clearly separated long-term care system in Poland introduces ambiguity in its description (Czepulis-Rutkowska, 2016).

Golinowska and Sowa-Kofta (2018) highlight the existent imbalance between the rapidly growing demand for care services and their insufficient supply in Poland. The access to formal (institutional) care services in Poland compared to other European countries is very low. Both formal home care services and residential care facilities for the elderly remain strongly underdeveloped (Spasova et al., 2018). The overall public expenditure on long-term care in Poland is estimated at about 0.5 % of GDP in 2016 with the average of 1.3 % of GDP in the European Union. It is also projected to increase to around 0.7 % in 2030 and 1.3 % of GDP in 2070 according to the Ageing Working Group reference scenario, yet never to reach the European average (European Commission, 2018). Based on the OECD data (OECD, 2019a), the total government spending on LTC that covers both the health and social care components accounts for 1.7 % of GDP on average across OECD countries in 2017. Poland is one of the lowest spenders with expenditure on LTC of 0.4 % of GDP. In comparison, the Netherlands allocates the highest share of GDP equal to 3.7 %. Also the share of adults aged 65+ receiving long-term care is consistently the lowest[30] (0.9 %) in the OECD area (average for 25 countries – 10.8 %) (OECD, 2019a, fig. 11.17). The availability of nursing and residential care facilities is highly underdeveloped as there are only 12 care beds in facilities per 1,000 population aged 65+, which is four times less that the OECD average (OECD, 2019a, fig. 11.26). Comparing the nursing home admission in the last 12 months of life for adults aged 65+ among 16 European countries, Poland reported the second lowest percentage

---

nurses on the basis of the primary care physician's decision on individual's health status. The social sector provides home care services to dependent people due to their age, illness or disability, unable to live independently in everyday life. Usually, they are in poor economic circumstances, living alone and without adequate assistance from their family. Care is provided by non-specialised employees of social assistance houses (dom pomocy społecznej – DPS) and is associated with a fee. Care services are also provided by semi-residential facilities, such as day-care centres for older people, but the number of facilities is low and their long-term sustainability questionable (Golinowska & Sowa-Kofta, 2018).

30   Data for Poland and five other countries is underestimated as it includes only recipients of LTC in institutions, while for most countries data for both institutional and home care recipients is used.

equal to 3.5 % versus 14.3 % for the total sample and the highest observed 27.9 % in Switzerland and 29.7 % in Denmark (Stolz et al., 2019).

The Supreme Audit Office report on care services for older people in place of residence provided in 2015–2017 concludes that this form of help in Poland is poorly accessible and unstandardised. In 23 local authorities audited, on average only 1.5 % of the population aged 60 years or more used this type of service. Almost 20 % of local self-governments constituting basic territorial units in Poland (gmina) did not provide any care services for older people in place of residence even though their organisation and provision is the role of the local authority (Najwyższa Izba Kontroli, 2018).

According to the legal definition, care services provided in place of residence are in-kind benefits that incorporate help in addressing the everyday necessities of life, hygienic care, nursing advised by a doctor and, if possible, contact with the environment. Services are directed to lone persons who require support from others due to age, illness or other reasons and cannot be provided by their close ones (Najwyższa Izba Kontroli, 2018). Care services provided in place of residence are more senior-friendly than a stay in constant care facilities. They are also four times cheaper than a stay in residential homes and are not limited to residential resources of the local government. The number of older people (here aged 60+ years) who receive care services in place of residence is growing systematically, yet it is very little. In 2014 such services were provided to 84.5 thousand dependent people, while in 2016 it was 94.2 thousand. Data from the Ministry of Family, Labour and Social Policy shows that the share of older people provided with care services nationally amounts to about 1 % of population of 60+ (increase from 0.99 % in 2014 to 1.04 % in 2016). At the same time the population of older people in Poland grew by almost 6 % from 8.5 million in 2014 to almost 9.1 million in 2016 (Najwyższa Izba Kontroli, 2018).

Care provision is also affected by migration flows. On the one hand, Poland's accession to the European Union in 2004 unleashed the unprecedented volume of emigration of young adults that pushed population ageing in Poland forward and affected the structure of informal caregivers. According to the data from the Statistics Poland,[31] during the 2004–2018 period the number of Polish residents' temporary abroad increased from 1 million to 2.5 million. The vast majority of Polish migrants choose Europe as their destination with Germany and the United Kingdom as primary directions. Taking up employment was the main

---

31 Statistics Poland is the current English translation for *Główny Urząd Statystyczny (GUS)* previously called the Central Statistical Office.

motivation to emigrate (GUS, 2019). These trends have not yet expired as in 2017 Poland still remained in the fourth place in the ranking of countries of origin of new immigrants to OECD countries only behind China, Romania and India (OECD, 2019b). Fihel and Okólski (2017) argue that mass return migration of Poles is unlikely. Given that emigration is a factor that may weaken family relationships and the age selectivity of migrants, the future potential of informal support provision, especially personal care by family members, is to be reduced.

Recent years have brought a substantial increase in immigration inflows to Poland that could diminish care deficit. For the second year in a row, Poland was the top OECD destination for temporary labour migrants taking in 1.12 million temporary migrants in 2017. More than 90 % of new temporary labour migrants registered in Poland came from Ukraine, mostly to fill vacancies in agriculture, construction and industry (OECD, 2019b). Immigrants are also taking up jobs to care for older adults replacing the unavailable family caregivers, yet there are no official statistics about the number of legal foreign workers in the care services sector. Additionally, many of them work unregistered in grey economy which hinders estimations even more (Sobiesiak-Penszko, 2015). Migrant care services are an alternative to limited home care services, though they are paid for fully by users (Sowa-Kofta, 2018). Kałuża-Kopias (2018) predicts an increase in the employment of immigrants as caregivers for older adults based on the projected increase in the number of households with adults aged 80 and above. Szweda-Lewandowska and Kałuża-Kopias (2019) drawing on a study of persons aged 75 or more and their caregivers, carried out in 2016 in big Polish cities Łódź and Warsaw, find out that 24 % of the elderly persons and 37 % of family caregivers would be willing to use the help of an immigrant, with Ukrainians being the most preferred nationality.

From the financial situation standpoint, older people have on average lower incomes than the average income of the total population. In Poland the average income of all aged over 65 amounts to 88.7 % of average income of total population (OECD, 2019c, pp. 184–185). It puts the older people in a disadvantaged position to cover the costs of care services in case of a reduced functional capacity. Especially, high costs of private residential care services are perceived to be difficult to cover from retirement pensions (Golinowska & Sowa-Kofta, 2018). Even though there is a nursing benefit universally granted to all individuals aged 75 or more, irrespective of their need for care, it is relatively small (Spasova et al., 2018). Women and persons living in single households are comparatively in the worst financial situation with usually the lowest disposable incomes (Błędowski et al., 2012). A group with a higher risk of financial problems are older widows who constitute a relatively large subpopulation in Poland and are exposed to a higher risk of poverty than older married women (Timoszuk, 2017). From the household perspective, the presence of persons requiring care and aged at least 65 years does not affect negatively the level of household income because usually care recipient contributes to the household budget with their own relatively stable source of income (mainly pensions) (Kotowska & Wóycicka, 2008).

1.3.5 Demand for care and provision of care in the future

Any statements about the future population developments are based on population projections. It also pertains to the outlook for demand for care among older people. Population projections refer to the future size of a population and its composition by age and sex.[32] Usually the projected number of people above certain age is treated as the simplest proxy of the future demand for care which is often adjusted by the prevalence ratio of age-specific dependency measure. Population projections by age and sex and additional characteristics relevant for risks of dependency are prepared much less frequently because of much higher data requirements. The future demand for care, that is, the projected number of persons in need, is primarily considered in the projections of expenditures on health care and long-term care (Comas-Herrera et al., 2006; European Commission, 2018; Kalbarczyk & Mackiewicz-Łyziak, 2019; Pickard et al., 2007; e.g., Schulz et al., 2004). There are also population projections that focus solely on health status, for example, by estimating the number of people with disability, chronic diseases or limitations in activities of daily living (Lutz & Scherbov, 2005; van der Gaag et al., 2015). Projections that next to health are extended by the family situation of older adults are rare but particularly interesting in the context of older people's care demands and supply of care potentially available within the household. Among the most advanced projections of demand for care including both dimensions and referring to European countries one needs to mention studies of (Eggink et al., 2016) for the Netherlands, the PACSim model for the UK (Kingston et al., 2018) and the projection by Gaymu et al. (2008) concerning nine European countries as part of the FELICE project ('Future Elderly Living Conditions in Europe'). The latter one integrated the information about the marital status and the household composition but did not include Poland. In study by Geerts et al. (2012) Poland was one of the countries analysed yet due to data limitations the projection on home care use was skipped, only the basic projection on residential care use was prepared.

---

32   More insight about population projections is presented in Chapter 4.

To the best author's knowledge there are only few elaborations related to projections of disability and demand for care in Poland to date (Abramowska-Kmon, 2011; Bonneux & van der Gaag, 2012; Szukalski, 2004; Szweda-Lewandowska, 2016). All of them show the increase in the overall number of old people in need of support in the future.[33] The projected number of dependent older people is driven by the advancement of population ageing expressed by the growth rate of the older population and their health status. The high dynamics of the older population in the coming two decades are affected by ageing of the post-war baby-boom cohorts. Additionally, it is in line with the research on the impact of the age-specific disability trends on long-term care needs that shows the number of older people with functional limitations is projected to increase even assuming falling disability rates (Jacobzone et al., 1998). One should not expect that reductions in severe disability among older people will offset increased demands for long-term care (World Health Organization, 2011).

The projections of old dependents are also prepared for the European Commission in the scope of the economic and budgetary projections for the EU Member States by the Ageing Working Group (AWG). The final report presents results of the macrosimulation model for the expenditure on long-term care in the future. The rudiment of the LTC expenditure projection is a demographic component that estimates the size of the dependent population using the Eurostat population projections and the prevalence rates of dependency.[34] In the most recent version of the report (European Commission, 2018) the number of dependent older people (age 65 and above) in Poland in the AWG reference scenario is expected to grow by 70 % from 1,344 thousands in 2016 to 2,287 thousands in 2030. At the same time, the number of dependent people receiving institutional care and receiving home care is projected to grow by 31 % and 30 %, respectively. Therefore, the proportion of older people in need of care that receive in-kind formal care will diminish (Table 3).

---

33 The work by Abramowska-Kmon (2011) stands out because it complements the health status analysis with the family situation using a static projection model with prevalence rates.

34 The prevalence of dependency is based on EU-SILC data on "self-perceived longstanding severe limitation in activities because of health problems [for at least the last 6 months]". In order to improve the reliability of the data, a four-year average is used (European Commission, 2018, p. 136).

Table 3. The Ageing Working Group projections of LTC needs in Poland, 2016–2070.

	2016	2020	2025	2030	2070
Number of dependent people (in thousands)	1,344	1,987	2,129	2,287	3,217
of those receiving institutional care	86	94	103	113	172
of those receiving home care	122	132	145	159	245
Proportion receiving institutional care (in %)	6.4	4.7	4.8	4.9	5.3
Proportion receiving home care (in %)	9.1	6.6	6.8	7.0	7.6
LTC spending as % of GDP (in %)	0.5	0.5	0.6	0.7	1.3

Note: The AWG reference scenario.
Source: European Commission (2018, pp. 258, 264–265), own elaboration.

The growth of the number of dependent older people is substantial and raises questions about covering the needs of the vulnerable. Colombo et al. (2011, p. 70) notes that the projected growth in frail elderly greatly outweighs that of potential caregivers. In case of Britain, cohorts born after 1950s will include increasing proportions with no or few children (Grundy & Murphy, 2007). According to the FELICE projections the potential family support available to older (western) Europeans will tend to increase until 2030 due to decreasing proportion of childless people among those aged 75 and over, especially among women. Longer-term prospects are much less favourable. The authors stipulate that the demographic availability does not, however, necessarily correspond with actual provision of support (Tomassini et al., 2008). Murphy et al. (2006) find for France, Finland and Great Britain that the proportion of people aged 60 with a mother alive will be increasing substantially for at least the next 30 years. It indicates that adult children, who enter age of increased care needs, will more often still have an older parent than themselves whose care needs will probably be even higher. At the same time, a higher proportion of older people will be likely to have a surviving child that extends the period of reaping the benefits of intergenerational exchanges. From a more optimistic perspective, older people are not only the main recipients of formal and informal long-term care services but also the main providers of informal care (Iparraguirre, 2018a).

The future of populations is characterised with a marked increase in the demand for care among older people. On the one hand, it is clear that most of care is and will be provided informally by families. On the other hand, the pool of potential care providers is shrinking. Experts from the Population Europe network point that "a growing demand for care in the social context of smaller social networks could create tensions between generations and expose the most vulnerable groups of older individual to a significant care deficit if public support is not ensured" (Nazio, 2019, p. 2). However, public support, especially long-term care, involves high organisational and monetary costs and is not widely available. It is therefore important to take advantage of technology to aid independent functioning. Agree and Glaser (2009) provide some examples of success stories. For instance, an increase in the use of assistive technology helped to decrease the personal care required over the 1990s in the United States of America. Portable devices and home modifications can help older persons with some level of physical disability to regain some independence and put the concept of ageing-in-place in practice. Also, the use of assistive technology for ADL limitations was found associated with fewer hours of help. Surely, this kind of help is not able to fully substitute personal care, but it can complement it by facilitating the use of self-care strategies aided by technology.

Chapter 2. Living arrangements and health of older people in Poland

After discussing population ageing together with changes in family formation patterns and their impact on care arrangements, I now focus on how those trends affect living arrangements and health of older people. According to the United Nations, the distribution of individuals within private households is used to determine the living arrangements of families (United Nations, 2015). Van Imhoff and Keilman (1991, p. 9) refer to private households and their members, whose characteristics like a family type they form and their marital status are used to operationalise the concept of living arrangements. Therefore, the household classification (one-person vs multiperson households, family vs non-family households) along with the composition of household members (either belonging to a family nucleus or not) are applied to describe living arrangements. Sandström and Karlsson (2019, p. 1648) underline the life-course perspective of living arrangements which are often temporary stages linked with various life-course events, such as leaving home, forming a new union, having a child or divorce. Living arrangements of older adults are focused on in this study, that is, following the definition by de Jong Gierveld et al. (2001, p. 193) I refer to the composition of the households in which older persons live. The term 'living arrangements' is used interchangeably with terms 'household structure/composition' and 'family situation'.

The goal of this chapter is to explore living arrangements and health status of old-aged people with special attention given to Poland. The analysis is descriptive to illustrate the up-to-date situation of seniors and to explore past trends where possible. Living arrangements of older persons is described first. Next, health status of older people follows with some introductory remarks about basic definitions. General trends and determinants of changes are reviewed. More detailed information on the population of interest in Poland is presented, extending the data source used by selected survey data. At the end of the chapter, relationship between living arrangements and health is examined.

2.1 Living arrangements of older persons

2.1.1 Trends in living arrangements of older persons in a comparative perspective

The research on living arrangements of older people is gaining on importance as the number of older people is growing all over the world and the family formation patterns are evolving. The consequences of the trends attributed to the Second Demographic Transition (presented in the previous chapter), inter alia, fertility postponement, deinstitutionalisation and de-standardisation of family life and the greater instability of relationships, affect family networks and intergenerational relations, and thus also influence the households in which people live. The final outcome – living arrangements – is relevant from the older people's perspective, especially in the light of potential care demands in case of independency loss. Tracking changes in the prevalence of living alone[35] among older people is particularly socially relevant as this living arrangement is becoming more and more widespread and potentially important for the health and well-being of seniors in single living as well as social policy in general (Reher & Requena, 2018). Here, I review the trends in living arrangements of older people in private households in the developed countries, with special attention to solitary living, and put applicable statistics in a comparative perspective.

Firstly, the average household size has been following a global declining trend since at least 1970s (except some high-fertility populations in Africa or Asia) which is associated mostly with smaller share of households that include children (UN, 2017). Europe and other developed countries have been continuously recording the lowest levels of this indicator due to the reduced family size, but also because of a great increase in the number and proportions of persons living alone (Keilman, 2006). In parallel, in some countries the proportion of co-residence between parents aged 65 and older and their adult children has dropped enormously (Gratton & Gutmann, 2010; Ruggles, 2007). The average household size in Poland has followed the same trend to decline from 3.39 in 1970 to 2.82 in 2011[36] and is forecasted to go down further to 2.50 in 2050 (GUS, 2016b). The main driver of the decline is the predicted ongoing decrease in the average number of children in households. However, the inevitable increase

---

35 The term 'living alone' will be used interchangeably with 'solitary living', 'single living' and 'one-person household' throughout the text.

36 A high drop in the average household size in Poland was observed between 1988 and 2002 when the respective averages amounted to 3.1 and 2.84 (GUS, 2013a).

in the population of older persons will contribute to either. According to the United Nations Database on Household Composition and Living Arrangements of Older Persons the average size of households of people aged 65 years or over is 1.8 persons in France and Switzerland, 2.0 in Hungary and 2.1 in the United States of America and Italy[37] (UN, 2019a). The corresponding average for Poland is 2.67 persons in 2011 (2.51 persons in 2002) which is still higher than in other developed countries but already lower than the overall national average (2.84 in 2002 and 2.82 in 2011) (GUS, 2014a).

Population ageing brings an increasing proportion of households that include older persons. In countries of Europe and Northern America, where more than 15 % of the total population is aged 60 years or over, the households with at least one older person among their members constitute a third of the total households (UN, 2017). At the same time, intergenerational households, that is, with both a member under age 20 and a member aged 65 or over, remain unusual. The living arrangements of older people in developed countries have changed dramatically in the end of the previous century, with increases in the proportions living alone, and decreases among those living with others, that is, children, siblings and parents (Grundy, 2001). According to the United Nations, living with a spouse only is the most common arrangement in Europe among persons aged 65 years or older that is followed by living alone (UN, 2019a). Household statistics from the European Union Labour Force Survey (EU-LFS) confirm this pattern (Figure 9). In 2019 in the European Union, 50 % of adults aged 65 or over were estimated to live in a couple without children, while 31 % were estimated to live alone. It is especially relevant for males as in all the EU Member States living solely with a partner is a dominant form of living for men. The situation of women is much more diverse – in about half of the EU countries living with a partner is the most prevalent living arrangement for older women. For the remaining EU countries the top living arrangement among females is living alone. As regards the household composition, living alone is indeed very much a living arrangement that is concentrated at older ages (Fokkema & Liefbroer, 2008). It is a very popular form of living of older persons even the increase in life expectancy and declining gender gap in the average lifespan cause many couples to live a joint life longer (Puur et al., 2011; Tomassini et al., 2004). On the other hand, for people who dissolve their partnerships and do not enter any new relationships, the mortality decrease may imply more life years without

---

37   The most recent estimates refer to the year 2011 for France, Hungary, Italy and the United States of America, and 2000 for Switzerland.

a partner (de Jong Gierveld et al., 2001). That would be an argument for the potential increase in the proportion of older people living alone. Also, higher levels of childlessness observed currently may determine higher prevalence of living alone among the older population in the future (Agree & Glaser, 2009).

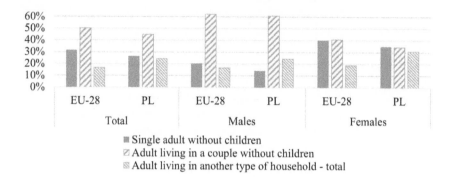

Figure 9. Household composition in the EU and Poland among people aged 65 and over by sex, 2019.

Note: Selected (top 3) household composition categories included only, does not sum up to 1. Data refer to people living in private households; people living in collective or institutional households are excluded.

Source: Eurostat online database [lfst_hhindws], own elaboration.

The description for Europe cannot be uniform as there has been a geographical division in variability in trends of older people's living arrangements and the current household structures.[38] Living alone among older adults is much more common in Northern and Western Europe than in Eastern and Southern Europe. It is a natural consequence of the fact that the northern European countries are characterised with the highest rates of living alone in the working-age population (Sandström & Karlsson, 2019). There are differences in the rates of co-residence of elderly parents with their children (and other relatives) with much higher rates observed in southern and eastern European countries as compared to northern and continental European countries (Albertini et al., 2007; Tomassini et al., 2004). Central and eastern European countries are more similar to the southern European countries with a lower proportion of older people living alone which is

---

38   As nicely put by Kuijsten (1999, p. 102): "Variation in living arrangements occurs at all ages, and the elderly are no exception."

attributable to the relative high frequency of households with extended families in these countries (Liu & Esteve, 2020).

The age pattern of solitary living is a common feature. In all European countries, more people live alone when they are in the older age groups, aged 70–79 and particularly 80 and over, than at younger ages. It is mainly driven by widowhood of women who are around twice as likely to live alone at the oldest ages as men due to their life expectancy advantage (Iacovou & Skew, 2011). In a comparative European perspective Poland is classified into the group of countries distinguished by, among others, having some of the largest households in Europe, later home-leaving patterns and extended intergenerational co-residence, leading to a high percentage of extended-family households[39] (Iacovou & Skew, 2011). These results find support in SHARE data which depict Poland as having the highest share of population aged 50 and over that lives in extended families – couple with other people (children, relatives, others) (Kurkiewicz & Soja, 2015).

Another characteristic of living arrangements of older people is a gender gap in living alone. Living alone at older ages is much more prevalent among women than men (Fokkema & Liefbroer, 2008; Gierveld et al., 2012; Iacovou & Skew, 2011; Liu & Esteve, 2020). The main causes of gender differences are: the lower life expectancy of men, differences in spousal age gaps, the higher prevalence of widowhood among women, and higher remarriage rates among men after widowhood or divorce (Sandström & Karlsson, 2019; UN, 2019a). It is also found that, with the exception of Germany and France, the probabilities of living alone are quite similar between men and women up to the age of 50–54 years. Notably, in all European countries the share of women living alone increases more rapidly than among men for those aged between 50 and 64 years. The shift to a surplus of women living alone tends to be somewhat more pronounced in the less gender-equal countries, which also pertains to Poland (Sandström & Karlsson, 2019).

2.1.2 Understanding the determinants of living arrangements of older persons

The determinants of living arrangements formed of older people can be summarised with the following statement: "Living arrangements of older persons are the result of individual preferences and available resources, as well as the social, economic or health constraints that people face as they grow older" (UN, 2019a, p. 1). In the same vein, but slightly more generally, the older people's choice

---

39   On the opposite side of the spectrum are Nordic countries with small households, early home-leaving patterns, and a very low proportion of extended families.

of living arrangements is described by Kuijsten (1999, p. 102) as "determined by the objectives of the elderly themselves on the one hand and by the opportunities and constraints with which they are confronted on the other hand". The aim of this section is to take a deeper look into the constitutive elements that formulate those statements.

First of all, it is important to note that living arrangements in old age are strongly affected by the (demographic) events that had taken place earlier in the life course (Kuijsten, 1999). Therefore, individual trajectories to certain living arrangements at old age are heterogeneous. For example, the pathways into living alone have been proven to differ by gender, partnership histories, parenthood, and socio-economic resources (Sandström & Karlsson, 2019). The key factor is marriage which has been (at least for older cohorts) a trigger and a precondition for long-lasting relationships and a parental career. Both having a partner and children broadens the variety of household configurations that a person can experience in old age, and thus affects the informal and formal exchanges of support (Kuijsten, 1999). On the contrary, there are events such as death of a spouse, divorce, loss of functional independence or abrupt changes in income or employment (e.g. retirement) that have a strong destabilising effect on households (Hays, 2002).

Preferences for living arrangements at older ages are considered as a point of departure for individual household decisions. Mutchler and Burr (1991) refer to the preference for independent living that says individuals in later life, *ceteris paribus*, prefer to live either with nuclear family members (i.e. spouse and minor children) or alone. The choice of living arrangements is conditioned by the available resources, but, in general, older persons are reluctant to relinquish headship, live with extended-family members or stay in nursing homes. Molina-Mula et al. (2019) in a qualitative study on the attitudes and beliefs of families in Spain regarding their family members aged 75 years and over living independently find out that the older family members' choices to live alone is interpreted as an effort to retain the ability to make their own decisions. Furthermore, older people consider home as a space which provides autonomy that allows them to retain accessibility and social networks (Kurkiewicz, 2007). Therefore, in case of worse health conditions, there is a strong preference to receive assistance at home rather to leave it for assistance. In most European countries co-residence of older parents with their children is the preferred living arrangement once parents lose their ability to live independently. But, in the north-western part of Europe (Denmark, Sweden, the Benelux countries) there is quite strong preference for institutionalisation irrespective of state of health, even among older people themselves (Kuijsten, 1999).

Occupying a certain living arrangement is related to the life-course stage and single-person households are typical for older people. However, in order to realise one's privacy norms, adequate income resources are needed (Richards et al., 1987). The importance of economic resources is also underlined by Gratton and Gutmann (2010) who argue that a sharp shift from intergenerational co-residence to establishing autonomous households observed from 1940 to 1970 in the U.S. was largely possible thanks to extraordinary improvement in the economic situation. Mutchler and Burr (1991) discuss three major types of resources needed to realise one's preferences. Health is needed for retaining independence and autonomy. Poor health, usually stemming from limitations in physical activity, but also more general health problems, is often accompanied with the insufficient level of independence that in more severe cases requires co-residence or even institutionalisation. Kinship, that is, the availability of close relatives, foremost adult children, is important with relation to the risk of being institutionalised. For example, in the study of the British context in the 1970s and 1980s, being single was a major predictor of moving to an institution for men (Breeze et al., 1999). Reduced kinship networks limit the choice of living arrangements and constrain potential family care supply.[40] Last, but not least, are the economic resources. Higher income means higher likelihood to sustain the living alone setting.[41] Meeting this requirement can be difficult for older people who rely mostly on pensions and have reduced chances to diversify their income. In a similar vein, de Jong Gierveld et al. (2001) point at the economic and financial situation, standard of living, and quality of social security and health care systems as factors affecting older person's types of living arrangements. The latter are institutional factors that differ by country and are shaped at the macro level, yet influence the attitudes and decisions of individuals. The availability of residential care is among the determinants that influence older adults and their adult children on selection of the optimal living arrangements in the context of intergenerational family caregiving. With better availability of the institutional care setting the likelihood of sharing household with impaired parents is lower (van den Broek & Dykstra, 2017).

---

40 Noteworthy, intergenerational exchanges may be beneficial not only for the senior generation. Older individuals may serve as resources to their adult children by providing free or reduced-cost housing, contribute their stable pension income to the common household budget or provide childcare services.

41 Co-residence of older and younger generations may be also imposed by the inadequate economic resources of younger generations (who may be in poor situations and are helped by older generations).

Another factor that impacts living arrangements is education. Sandström and Karlsson (2019, p. 1646) find the educational gradient of living alone related to gender equality by country that pertains to the working-age population, but which has its consequences on the older population as well. Authors of the study note that educational level is an important proxy of income and sociocultural resources at the individual level which affects personal chances for partnering and family formation. They also find out that in the more gender-equal countries (Northern Europe) one observes a negative educational gradient of living alone, especially for men. In the least gender-equal countries, including Poland and Italy, a positive educational gradient, especially for women, is found. That means living alone is more common among highly than low-educated groups. One of the explanation is the difference in access to resources. Highly educated women are in better position to stand alone economically and refrain from traditional family behaviour (Sandström & Karlsson, 2019) .

2.1.3 Living arrangements of older people in Poland

Changes in living arrangements are indirectly related to age as they reflect changes in unions' histories but also changes in health trajectories (de Jong Gierveld et al., 2001). As noted by Szatur-Jaworska (2012, p. 50), age and sex are the two essential factors that differentiate their living arrangements. In the book I focus on private households but in this section I additionally take a glimpse at institutional households to outline the complete picture of how older people in Poland live.

The source of importance of age and sex on living arrangements of older adults is related to mortality differentials, that is, the excess male over female mortality and the age-related differences in mortality overall. Both age and sex are two dimensions that will be focused on when presenting different aspects of living arrangements of older people in Poland. Firstly, a closer look at older people living in private households is given. After marital status of the elderly is described, household composition of older Poles is highlighted. Then, some insights into the older population living in institutional households is provided. Primarily, the description of older peoples' living arrangements is based on the recent 2011 census.[42] Additional insights come from the PolSenior study which is the representative study on older people aged 65 and more years in Poland

---

42   In the scope of the 2011 Population and Housing Census there were established several research topics including 'Households and families'. Within the 'Households and families' topic the following characteristics were collected: the size and composition of household and family, nuclei and reconstituted families, single-parent families, family status, household status (GUS, 2013b).

(Mossakowska et al., 2012). At the end of the section, to collate the census results, I look into living arrangements of Polish seniors with the use of survey data.

The elderly population by marital status

According to the 2011 Population and Housing Census, 55.7 % of the population aged 15 and more is married *de jure*. Among persons aged 60 years and more, 56.8 % are married, of which 78 % of males and 42 % of females, while among seniors aged 65 years and more, 49.9 % are married (76 % of males and 34 % of females). When looking at *de facto* marital status of the population aged 65 and more this percentage amounts to 48.8 %, while 1 % live in cohabitating unions (which corresponds to 53.8 thousand older men and women) (GUS, 2012; Szatur-Jaworska, 2012).

The prevalence of marriage is decreasing with age in favour of widowhood. While among persons aged 60 years and more 33.7 % were widowed, the proportion of widows and widowers increases to 42.2 % for 65-and-more-year-old persons and 66.1 % for 80-and-more-year-old persons. The data from the 2011 Census indicate remarkable gender differences in proportions of married and widowed persons that unveil with age (presented in Table 4). Most of older men are still married until age 90, while widows become the major group for women once they reach their 70s. These differences mainly stem from sex differences in mortality but also from the re-partnering patterns. These gender differences are accompanied by differences in the duration of family life phases. Szatur-Jaworska (2012) points out that today's older women on average have got married earlier than men as well as got divorced or widowed earlier too. Therefore, knowing that women live as married couple less often at old age than men of the same age – they become single (once divorced or widowed) at earlier age and have higher life expectancy than men – their periods of living alone in old age are longer than for men.

When it comes to other marital statuses, one can observe a relatively stable pattern of never-married men among the older age groups and a significant increase of their percentage among the younger elderly. The proportions for females are similarly stable but slightly higher than for males in older age groups. Although not as spectacular as for men, there is also a rise in percentage of never married among women in younger ages which indicates the proportions of never married will (probably) be higher in the future (for men in particular). Being divorced is not widespread among older people, especially among the oldest-old but it is more prevalent in younger age groups and for women than for men.

Table 4. Legal (*de jure*) marital status of persons aged 50 and over by age and sex, Poland (in %).

Age	Never married		Married		Widowed		Divorced	
	Male	Female	Male	Female	Male	Female	Male	Female
50–54	13	7	78	75	2	9	7	9
55–59	10	6	80	71	3	15	7	9
60–64	7	6	82	64	5	23	6	8
65–69	5	5	83	54	8	35	4	6
70–74	4	4	81	42	12	49	3	4
75–79	3	4	76	30	18	63	2	3
80–84	3	4	67	17	28	76	2	2
85–89	2	5	55	8	42	85	1	2
90–94	2	5	41	3	56	90	1	1
95–99	3	5	29	1	67	93	1	1
100+	5	6	34	2	61	92	0	1

Note: Marital status *unknown* excluded.
Source: 2011 Census Hub, https://ec.europa.eu/CensusHub2, own calculations.

The structure of older population by marital status was stable in the years 2002–2011 (GUS, 2014b). The proportion of persons married or widowed remained high for both males and females between 2002 and 2011. The small share of divorced persons in the population aged 65 years and more increased to 3.5 % from 2.7 % in 2002. The proportion of never married remained relatively small too. It increased by 0.5 p.p. to 3.8 % among males and decreased by less than 1 p.p. to 4.3 % among females.

The majority of older adults who experienced later-life marital dissolution (either through bereavement or divorce) remain single (Brown et al., 2018). The studies conducted in the United States and the Netherlands show that for adults aged 50 years and over the rates of re-partnering are negatively associated with age meaning lower chances of forming a new relationship after marital dissolution at later age (Brown & Lin, 2012; de Jong Gierveld, 2004). Noteworthy, consensual unions and Living-Apart-Together relationships are competing with remarriage after widowhood or divorce, which is becoming an increasingly widespread alternative even for older adults (de Jong Gierveld, 2004). Re-partnering behaviours of women aged 35 to 55 examined in 11

European countries with the Harmonised Histories[43] data show that age at union dissolution is negatively associated with re-partnering in almost all countries (Gałęzewska et al., 2017). Poland is among the countries with the lowest probabilities of re-partnering observed. Thus, if the number of divorces at ages close to 50 years increases, there is a higher risk that more women will remain unpartnered.

In 2019, males aged 60 and more contracted 6,112 marriages, while females of this age – 3,686. Marriage rate among men aged 60 and more was 1.5 (1.8 in urban and 1.0 in rural areas). Senior women were getting married less often than senior men – the marriage rate for them accounted for 0.7 (0.8 in urban and 0.4 in rural areas).[44] Between 1980 and 2019, marriage rates for both women and men aged 60 and more (per 1,000 females/males aged 15 and more) decreased proportionally to marriage rates of the total population (by about a half) but at the same time the share of contracted marriages by senior males and females in total new marriages more or less doubled (GUS, 2020a). Still, marriages of senior persons accounted for only a small fraction of total marriages (3.3 % for males and 2.0 % for females).

When it comes to divorces, in 2019 there were 3,028 divorces involving women aged 60 and more (at the moment of filling petition for divorce) which accounts for 4.6 % of all divorces.[45] There were significantly more divorces involving men of that age (4,378 divorces, i.e. 6.7 % of the total number) (GUS, 2020a). In the last ten years (between 2009 and 2019) the proportion of divorces involving females aged 60 and more doubled and divorce rate (per 1,000 females aged 60 and more) increased from 0.4 to 0.5. The respective proportion for males nearly doubled and divorce rate for males increased from 0.8 to 1.1 (divorces of males aged 60 and more per 1,000 males aged 60 and more).

Widowhood in Poland can be thus considered as a relatively stable marital state. Marriage (or remarriage) and divorce at old age are still relatively seldom events with forming new unions outnumbering union dissolutions. In fact, changes in marital status of seniors are driven mostly by mortality.

---

43 A cross-national comparative database of union and fertility histories harmonising data from existing surveys into one common format (for more information, see www. ggp-i.org/data/harmonized-histories/ or www.nonmarital.org).

44 For comparison, in 2019 in Poland there were almost 183.4 thousand new marriages overall. The marriage rate (the number of newly contracted marriages per 1,000 population aged 15 and more) amounted to 5.6.

45 There were 65,341 legally valid court decisions in actions for divorces in 2019.

Household composition of older people

According to the 2011 Census, there were 13,568 thousand private households, of which 5,634 thousand included persons aged 60 and above. Private households that included senior persons constituted 41.5 % of all private households in Poland, which is more than the corresponding 36.1 % observed in 2002. The increase in the share of households with older people refers both to urban and rural areas. This share is higher in rural areas (45.5 % versus 42.6 % in 2002), but the growth is more dynamic in the cities (39.6 % as compared to 32.8 % in 2002) (GUS, 2014a). The average household size with persons aged 60 and above is equal to 2.7, with bigger households in rural than in urban areas.

Among private households in general, there were 2,623 thousand households exclusively constituted of persons aged 60 and more. They represented 19.3 % of the total number of households and nearly a half (46.6 %) of households that included persons aged 60 and more. Such households existed more often in urban (21.0 % of the total urban households) rather than rural areas (15.8 %) and their average size was 1.4 persons per household, which is much lower than the country average (compare Table 5) (GUS, 2020b). Indeed, households of older persons tend to be small. Drawing on information about the household size by age of household heads one can observe an increase in the proportion of one-person households with age. Among people aged 60 and more who are running a household 37 % are one-person households, while for seniors above age 80 the proportion reaches almost 60 % (compare Table 6).

Table 5. Average number of persons per household, 2011

	Total	Urban areas	Rural areas
Total	2.8	2.5	3.4
including persons aged 60 and more	2.7	2.3	3.4
including exclusively persons aged 60 and more	1.4	1.4	1.4

Source: 2011 Census, GUS (2018, Table 2.1.4).

Table 6. Households by number of household members and age of household head, 2011

	Total		60–69 years old		70–79 years old		80 and more years old	
	ths.	%	ths.	%	ths.	%	ths.	%
Total	13,568.0	100.0	2,123.1	100.0	1,407.2	100.0	685.6	100.0
One-person household	3,254.7	24.0	567.0	26.7	591.3	42.0	409.6	59.7
Two-or-more person household	10,313.3	76.0	1,556.1	73.3	815.8	58.0	276.1	40.3

Source: 2011 Census, MRPiPS (2016, p. 34, Table 17).

Nearly a half (49.3 %) of all older people stay in one-generation households. Such households comprise of either one-person households or two-person households run usually by married couple that belong to the same generation (Błędowski et al., 2012). Relatively many older people co-reside with younger generations as the share of households with persons aged 60 and above and having at least two generations has increased between the 2002 Census and the 2011 Census from 17.2 % to 22.1 % (GUS, 2014a). Findings from the PolSenior study show that one-generation households are typical for urban areas while three-generation households are much more frequent in rural than in urban areas (Szatur-Jaworska, 2011).

Most older people residing in private households in Poland live in a family nucleus, especially in married couples until their seventies (compare Table 28 in the Appendix). However, the composition of households is changing with age. With the decreasing proportion of persons in married couples, more persons live in other forms of private households that contain a family nucleus of which they are a member, mainly a parent with children. The older age groups, above age 75, most frequently live in non-family households with most of them living alone.

The proportion of older people living alone in Poland is strongly related to age and sex. The first and most important observation is the increasing proportion of living alone with age for both men and women. As nearly every tenth adult aged 50–54 in 2011 lived alone,[46] the proportion is increasing (for women especially to reach a peak in the 80–84 age group and then to decline gradually) and triples for older adults aged 80–95 (Figure 10). The second important observation is a wide disproportion by sex. The share of solitary living is much greater for women in almost all age groups and it disappears only for the oldest-old age group (100 years and above). When comparing

---

46 Considerations of living alone are extended to younger ages (from age 50) because this living arrangement is accentuated in the longitudinal analysis in Chapter 3 that is following individuals from age 50 onwards.

the time trend between 2002 and 2011 living alone occurs to have become slightly less prevalent. Historically, the proportion of elderly living alone and in two-person households (with partner) was increasing (Abramowska, 2006), however, the 2011 Census data show that the pace of growth is slowing down. The latest household projections for years 2016–2050 in Poland suggests a dynamic increase in the number of single households up to year 2030 and a drop afterwards (GUS, 2016b). Together with an increasing proportion of people aged 80 and more from the year 2028 onwards, an overall increase in the number of seniors living alone can be expected.

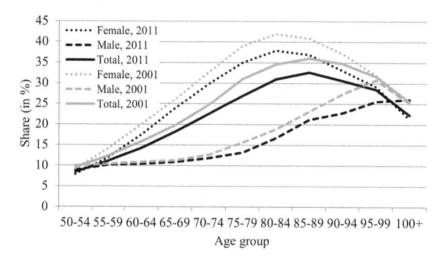

Figure 10. The share of persons living alone in Poland by age and sex, 2002 and 2011 Census.
Source: Eurostat online database [cens_01nhtype]; 2011 Census Hub, https://ec.europa.eu/CensusH ub2, own elaboration.

Data from the PolSenior study confirm the increasing share of older adults living alone with age. The share of solitary living rises from 17.7 % in the 65–69 age group to 26.9 % in the 85–89 age group with a small decline to 24 % in the oldest-old (aged 90 years and over). The study shows also a gender gap in living alone among adults aged 65 years and more as 11 % of males versus 29 % of females is reported to live alone.[47] Also, there are differences in forms of family life by place of residence: higher proportions of living alone is found among elderly living in cities as compared to rural areas (Szatur-Jaworska, 2011).

---

47   The high share of one-person households led by women inflates the proportion of female household heads. Poland is one of nine out of 153 countries with an estimate of more than half of all households (54 %) being headed by women (UN, 2019b).

According to Tomassini et al. (2004), the trend towards more independent living arrangements of older people derives from the increases in human longevity, declines in the prevalence of disability among older population (e.g. Schoeni et al. (2001)) as well as improvement in the financial situation of the elderly. As noticed by Kurkiewicz (2007), the emergence of one-person households formed by older people in Poland may be treated as an effect of their pursuit of maintaining privacy and autonomy which is an expression of the ongoing acceptance of individualistic attitudes. The efforts of older people to stay independent are favoured by higher education and living in urban areas.

Taking a closer look at the older persons living alone allows us to notice that up to their seventies, the marital status distribution is more diverse, especially for men (Table 7). A lot of individuals living alone are either never married or divorced. With age increasing, the dominant position is taken by widowers and widows. Szatur-Jaworska (2011), drawing on the PolSenior study, highlights the differences between widowed and divorced or separated older persons. In aggregate, older divorced persons more frequently than widowed person are living alone and less often belong to two or three generations households. Actually, census data shows that living alone is a living arrangement prevailing in varying degree by marital status. It is predominant among the never married and the divorced (compare Table 8). With the increase in the number of divorces as well as growth among the never married the number of living alone at older ages can accelerate too.

Table 7. Marital status of persons living alone, aged 50 and over by age and sex, 2011 (in %)

Age	Male – Living alone				Female – Living alone			
	Never married	Married	Widowed	Divorced	Never married	Married	Widowed	Divorced
50–54	47	18	6	30	32	16	23	29
55–59	40	18	11	31	24	12	37	26
60–64	32	18	21	29	18	8	53	21
65–69	26	16	34	23	13	5	69	14
70–74	21	13	49	16	8	3	80	9
75–79	13	9	67	10	6	2	87	5
80–84	8	7	79	6	6	1	90	3
85–89	5	4	88	3	7	0	91	2
90–94	3	3	92	2	6	0	92	2
95–99	4	3	93	1	6	0	94	0
100+	12	18	70	0	6	0	94	0

Source: 2011 Census Hub, https://ec.europa.eu/CensusHub2, own elaboration

Table 8. Household status by age and legal marital status, 2011 (in %)

Household status	Total	Legal marital status			
		Never married	Married	Widowed	Divorced
65 to 84 years					
Persons in a family nucleus	61	7	97	22	20
Persons not in a family nucleus: Living alone	24	59	2	47	59
Persons not in a family nucleus: Not living alone	14	27	1	30	18
Persons in an institutional household	1	7	0	1	3
85 years and over					
Persons in a family nucleus	33	4	95	19	15
Persons not in a family nucleus: Living alone	32	47	2	39	47
Persons not in a family nucleus: Not living alone	33	35	1	40	27
Persons in an institutional household	3	14	1	2	10

Note: Columns may not sum up to 100 % due to rounding.
Source: 2011 Census Hub, https://ec.europa.eu/CensusHub2, own elaboration.

Institutional households

Here, the proportion of adults living in institutional households is investigated. At first, one has to note a drop in the prevalence of institutionalisation between censuses carried out in 2002 and 2011 in Poland despite the growth in total number of institutionalised persons (from nearly 91.5 to 104.7 thousand aged 50 or more and from 58.9 to 61.9 thousand aged 65 or more) (GUS, 2013b, p. 172). The share of persons aged 50 and more living in an institutional household fell from 0.83 % in 2002 to 0.78 % in 2011 (the share of persons aged 65 and more amounted to 1.21 % and 1.18 % respectively). The drop is visible particularly for the oldest age groups as the growth among people above age 75 outperformed the respective growth in the number of institutionalised. At the same time, the proportion of adults aged 50 and more in the total population in institutional households increased from 21.8 % to 28.5 % (among population aged 65 and more the respective numbers were 14.1 % and 16.8 %). Figure 11 presents more detailed view on the institutionalisation prevalence by age and sex. Very low proportions of institutionalisation for both sexes are maintained for people below 80 years old.

Once individuals reach their eighties, the proportion is on the rise. Women are nearly twice as much prevalent in institutions as men, but the highest proportion barely exceeds 7 % for the oldest reaching their nineties. In aggregate, neither in 2002 nor in 2011 the share of men aged 65 and more in institutional households reached 1 %. For women the respective numbers are 1.4 % and 1.2 %.

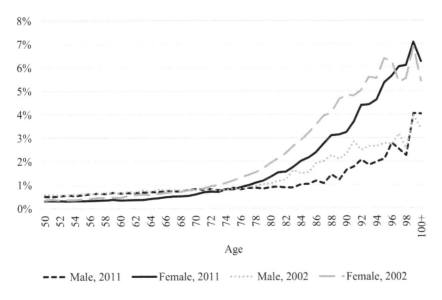

Figure 11. The share of persons in institutional households in Poland by age and sex, 2002 and 2011 Census.

Source: Eurostat online database [cens_01nhtype]; 2011 Census Hub, https://ec.europa.eu/CensusH ub2, own elaboration.

The institutionalised population of older people in Poland restricted to residential care only gives a similar picture. The inhabitants of nursing residential long-term care homes in the health sector,[48] social assistance homes (domy pomocy społecznej – DPS) and mental health care account for the majority of the institutionalised older population, yet the prevalence rates get naturally lower (compare Figure 12). The age distribution of adults living in residential care is maintained; that is, relatively more people are institutionalised at older ages. The share of adults aged 65 and above receiving long-term care in institutions

---

48   There are three types identified: (i) chronic medical care homes / care and treatment facilities (zakład opiekuńczo-leczniczy – ZOL), (ii) nursing homes / nursing and care facilities (zakład pielęgnacyjno-opiekuńczy – ZPO) and (iii) palliative care homes.

decreased between 2002 and 2011 by 0.1 percentage point. No change was reported later as this share amounted to 0.9 % in 2017 (OECD, 2019a). The latest information from the administrative sources show that in 2018 there were 1,831 stationary social welfare facilities, of which there were 876 social assistance houses and 364 centres providing full care to disabled, chronically ill or older persons. These facilities provided 118.9 thousand places, with the majority (82.8 thousand) in social assistance houses. The share of seniors in in-patient health care facilities was 62.9 % of the total number of patients in these facilities (GUS, 2020b).

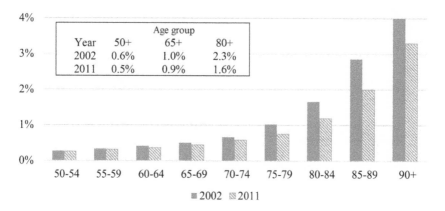

Figure 12. The share of persons in residential care in Poland by age group, 2002 and 2011 Census.

Note: Residential care includes nursing care homes, social assistance homes and mental health care.

Source: GUS (2013b, p. 172), own calculations.

In summary, it is rare for seniors to live in institutional households in Poland. It is related both to supply-driven factors (low availability of institutional places) and the demand side (e.g. relatively high costs of living in institutions, especially in private entities, and cultural factors). This form of living is relatively more prevalent among the oldest-old (above age 80) and women, which is strongly associated with health status and dependency level.

2.1.4 Living arrangements of the older people: The EU-SILC-based picture

The previously discussed data concerning living arrangements of older people originated from the population census. Their indisputable advantage is completeness and a display of wide cross-section of population characteristics. On the side of disadvantages, there is a 10-year interval between subsequent censuses. The European Union Survey on Income and Living Conditions (EU-SILC) is a survey that allows its users to track a household composition in yearly intervals, however, does not allow to track household relationships in detail.[49] I use data from the 2005–2014 period to analyse living arrangements in Poland (pooled data) and their changes over time (yearly data) selecting four basic categories: living alone, living with partner/spouse only, living with partner/spouse and others (non-relatives and/or other relative) and living without partner/spouse but with others.

Some regularities in living arrangements by age in the 2005–2014 period are illustrated in Figure 13. The proportion of living alone at the age of 60 does not exceed 20 % overall. For the older people who reached age 80 this proportion more than doubles and exceeds 40 %. The share of people living with partner/spouse is strongly diminishing. The share of seniors living without partner or spouse but with others is gaining importance as every third of living arrangements among the oldest-old is constituting this type of household. Figure 14 shows the gender-specific patterns. Solitary living is dominant for women: actually, more than 90 % of females live without their partners once they reach age 80. The picture for men is quite different as less than half of them when reach age 80 live without their spouses or partners.

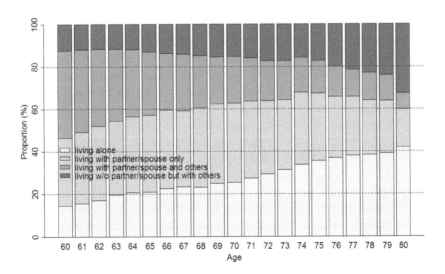

Figure 13. Living arrangements by age, averages for years 2005–2014.

Source: Own elaboration based on EU-SILC cross-sectional data, weighted.

---

49   More information on the EU-SILC dataset can be found in the Appendix.

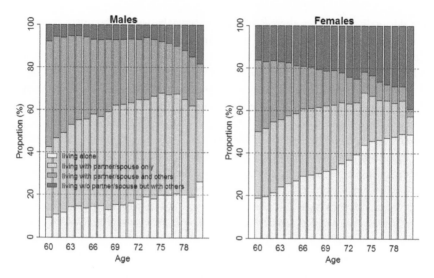

Figure 14. Living arrangements by age and sex, averages for years 2005–2014.
Source: Own elaboration based on EU-SILC cross-sectional data, weighted.

While the pattern of living arrangements is subject to change with age, one can observe that living arrangements over calendar years are relatively stable. In the analysed period between 2005 and 2014 the proportion of people aged 60 and more living with partner/spouse only and living without partner/spouse but with others was unchanged and amounted to 31 % and 19 % respectively. The other categories of living arrangements evolve over time. The proportion of living alone decreased by 7 percentage points with the corresponding increase in the proportion of living with partner/spouse and others. The drop in solitary living was pronounced in the oldest age groups, in (75, 80) and 80 and above in particular (Figure 15). These findings are in line with the tendency depicted between 2002 and 2011 on census data (compare Figure 10) and may indicate a trend of lower prevalence of living alone for the future. Arguably, this tendency reflects the improvement in life expectancy of males in Poland that allows more older women to live with their partners longer. However, it does not imply less households of older persons living alone which absolute number is forecasted to increase (GUS, 2016b).

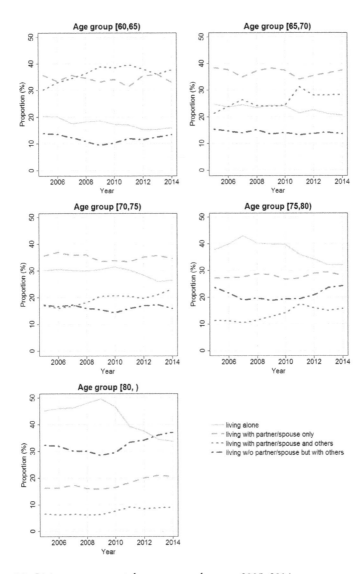

Figure 15. Living arrangements by age groups by years 2005–2014.
Source: Own elaboration based on EU-SILC cross-sectional data, weighted.

2.2 Health status of older people

2.2.1 Disability and health: The concept and measurement

The need for care at old age is above all related with one's health status (e.g. Czekanowski & Bień, 2006; Doblhammer et al., 2008). For this reason health is in the centre of attention when investigating care provision.[50] One of the basic challenges in health research is that health can be understood in many various ways and, therefore, measured differently. The World Health Organization (1948) defines health with no changes since 1946 as "a state of complete physical, mental and social well-being and not merely the absence of disease or infirmity". This definition is very broad and general, and allows for various operationalisation for research purposes.

There are many ways to measure health outcomes.[51] The routinely collected and commonly used data on health services (containing information about, e.g., discharges from a hospital by the patient's diagnosis) as well as traditional clinical outcome measures (e.g. a length of survival, symptoms, biochemical tests) are now more often supplemented with measures of a broader health status and a health-related quality of life. These measures are referred to as patient-based measures because they refer to individuals' rating/evaluation of their own health status and the impact of their health on various aspects of their lives (Bowling, 2005).

The most widely used indicator describing the disablement process with ageing is the ability to perform the daily life activities related to self-care (Deeg et al., 2003). The Katz Activities of Daily Living (ADL) scale is a graded measure of functional independence that assesses six basic functions related to personal care: bathing, dressing, going to toilet toileting, transferring (moving in or out of chair or bed), continence, and feeding (Katz et al., 1963). Another measure is the ability to perform Instrumental Activities of Daily Living (IADLs) which refers

---

50 In the study I do not discuss health needs that are covered by the health system in general. My focus is on the functional limitations of older people that create a need of care, and a need of instrumental care in particular. Therefore, I do not provide any description of the health system in Poland. A review of recent developments in organisation and governance, health financing, health care provision, health reforms and health system performance in Poland is discussed in great detail by Sowada et al. (2019).

51 The wealth of health indicators can be grasped in many demographic and epidemiological readings (e.g. Lamb & Siegel, 2004; Bowling, 2005; Wróblewska, 2008; Siegel, 2012a).

to household-level activities required to live independently such as shopping, housekeeping, laundry and cooking (Lawton & Brody, 1969). Both measures are used to assess the functional status of individuals, but also can help in objective evaluation of ageing populations (Fuentes-García, 2014). Within the broader concept of a functional ability there are social models of disability that attempt to explain what disability is and how it is experienced (Bowling, 2005). In the latest update and revision by the International Classification of Functioning, Disability and Health (ICF) disability is perceived as problems with human functioning categorised in three interconnected areas:

- impairments are problems in body function or alterations in body structure – for example, paralysis or blindness;
- activity limitations are difficulties an individual may have in executing activities – for example, walking or eating;
- participation restrictions (previously called handicaps) are problems an individual may experience in involvement in life situations – for example, facing discrimination in employment or transportation.

Disability is therefore an umbrella term that refers to difficulties encountered in any or all three areas of functioning. It denotes the negative aspects of the interaction between an individual (with a health condition) and that individual's contextual factors (environmental and personal factors) (WHO, 2011).

In most uses, disability is understood as the inability to perform usual daily activities (Deeg et al., 2003). In Poland, the official statistics differentiate between two definitions of disability which is examined on two criteria: legal (formal) – disability with a legal confirmation, and subjective (self) – biological disability. The legal disability status is connected with an appropriate judgement issued by an authorised body (GUS, 2016c). It is determined by legal assesment of disability in order to establish a right to social protection, disability benefits in particular (Golinowska & Sowa-Kofta, 2018). The biological disability is based on a subjective declaration. The biologically disabled person is a person, who does not necessarily have a legal judgement but feels constrained in the ability to perform basic activities for his/her age.

The mutlidimensionality of health and disability concepts results in many indicators and consequently raises difficulties to navigate through all of them. Scientists make efforts to harmonise measures that would allow monitoring disability over time and space consistently and comparatively. The successfully adopted health indicator for the European Union is the Global Activity Limitation Indicator (GALI). GALI examines activity limitations as the presence of long-standing activity limitation due to health problems. It is considered a single disability question with a broad activity coverage (Verbrugge, 2016). GALI is one of three global health questions (next to self-perceived health and chronic morbidity) contained in the Minimum European Health Module (MEHM) that became a baseline to monitor progress in various policy domains[52] (Bogaert et al., 2018; Deeg et al., 2003). Due to the MEHM availability and proven reliability this measure will be central in the following health analyses. GALI is particularly of interest because it measures functional capacity of the individual that determines independence in everyday functioning. Dependency includes individual perceptions of ability to live independently. Importantly, it is dependency rather than disability that initiates the need of care. Having some forms of disability does not necessarily translate into a need of care. Limitations in activities of daily living measured via GALI instrument are considered a reasonable proxy for a need for care, personal care especially. Additionally, GALI is used to generate the disability-free life expectancy which is the most common health expectancy. The health expectancy measures a length of life spent in different states of health and is the most suitable (and increasingly used) indicator to measure and monitor population health[53] (Giudici et al., 2013).

2.2.2 Trends in health of older persons

The best single measure of improvements in human life duration is the massive increase in life expectancy from around 40 years in the beginning of the 19th century to around 80 years on the verge of the new millennium (Oeppen & Vaupel, 2002; Vaupel, 2010). People do not only live longer, but also live longer in better health than their predecessors. The explanation of those improvements has been formulated in the epidemiologic transition theory (Omran, 1971, 1998; Wróblewska, 2012). In a nutshell, it argues that the infectious diseases that cause death at a young age have been replaced by chronic diseases that make people die at an older age.[54] In this section I briefly discuss major determinants of health,

---

52   The questions asked within the Minimum European Health Module as well as studies examining their reliability are referenced in the Appendix.

53   Population health integrates the concepts of mortality, morbidity, and disability and looks into the linkages between them at the population level. Understanding population health necessarily involves understanding the interaction of these major health processes (Warner & Hayward, 2019).

54   Omran's epidemiologic transition that corresponds to the vanquishing of infectious diseases is seen as the first stage of health transition. The second stage of health transition refers to the reduction of cardiovascular disease, while the third one aims at slowing the ageing process (Vallin & Meslé, 2004).

review hypotheses on morbidity and provide a closer look into recent trends in health, both in general and in Poland. For this purpose, I mainly use the healthy life years indicator (HLY, also called disability-free life expectancy – DFLE) that is defined as the number of years that a person is expected to continue to live in a healthy condition, that is, without limitation in functioning and without disability.[55] It is widely accepted macro-level indicator to summarise population's functional health.

Determinants of health

Health status is subject to a change over time. Studies consistently report that while physical and mental functions change gradually with age, they decline most sharply in the older age groups (Andersen-Randberg et al., 1999; Chatterji et al., 2015; Vestergaard et al., 2015; Wizner et al., 2012). Higher disability rates among older people reflect an accumulation of health risks across a lifespan, such as diseases, injuries, or chronic illnesses (WHO, 2011). Older persons are more exposed to the risk of multimorbidity (comorbidities), that is, the presence of multiple chronic health conditions that coexist in individuals (Siegel, 2012a). The prevalence of multimorbidity increases substantially with age and is common among people aged 65 years and older (Barnett et al., 2012; Salive, 2013). The coexistence of chronic diseases translates into greater care needs, higher health care utilisation and costs (Glynn et al., 2011). Moreover, the presence of multimorbidity is expected to continue its rise (Tucker-Seeley et al., 2011). Some researchers are identifying an age-related hierarchy of loss of functional ability, but they represent it with the time between stages of progress of disability rather than at specific ages (Gore et al., 2018). The need for care and dependency on others is thus a consequence of deterioration in health rather than the ageing itself.

Health status is related to age but it also varies according to other individual characteristics. The most evident disparities in health are associated with gender and socio-economic status (e.g. education, income), but also with health-related behaviours. For example, there is a clear gender gap in survival and health expectancy showing a female advantage in mortality but a disadvantage in disability and other health outcomes relative to men (e.g. Newman & Brach, 2001; Nusselder et al., 2019; Oksuzyan et al., 2010; Verbrugge, 1984; Wizner et al., 2012). This phenomenon is known as the male-female health-survival

---

55 https://ec.europa.eu/eurostat/statistics-explained/index.php?title=Glossary:Healthy_life_years_(HLY) [accessed 15.10.2020 r.].

paradox. The reasons for the paradox of women living longer than males but in worse health are not unambiguously identified but among potential explanations biological and behavioural factors are advanced (Oksuzyan et al., 2008). In Poland the male-female gap in life expectancy is prevalent as well, however, since the 1990s it has been diminishing (GUS, 2020c; Muszyńska, 2011).

Educational and income differences that determine a social class and human capital are also major predictors of healthy life with higher education and better economic resources having a beneficial effect (Rubio-Valverde et al., 2019). Unhealthy behaviours lead to health inequalities – smoking has proved to be fatal, while obesity disabling (Majer et al., 2011; Reuser et al., 2009). On the contrary, physical activity is associated with better health outcomes and a physically active lifestyle is important even in very old age (Rise et al., 2019).

The beforementioned factors are not isolated from each other and their effect on health should often be considered cumulatively. Let us reflect on the education gradient. As pointed by Ross et al. (2012) higher education has a beneficial influence on health. The beneficial effect is reflected in better health and lower mortality thanks to accumulation of advantages throughout the life course. The advantages cumulate on different levels, from socio-economic (e.g. flexible resources such as employment, money, prestige, beneficial social networks, access to modern health technologies), through behavioural (e.g. quitting smoking faster once the health danger of smoking became known, resisting obesity more successfully, having more regular exercise) to physiological ones (blood pressure, cholesterol levels) (Miech et al., 2011; Mirowsky & Ross, 2005). Qualitative studies show that higher educated men and women seek for information that helps them to interpret and understand health issues they face (Flandorfer & Fliegenschnee, 2010). In other words, higher education gives better chances to accumulate higher human capital during the life course which allows for pooling economic resources for better access to health care and using information more effectively to avoid risky health behaviour and to adopt healthier lifestyles (Hayward et al., 2006).

The European cross-country comparison confirms that educational disparities in health and disability exist, but there are notable differences in their magnitude between and within welfare regime groups (Cambois et al., 2016). The reduced disability disadvantage of low-educated groups was found in Nordic countries, while the larger advantage of high-educated groups was prevalent in Baltic and eastern European countries. Those effects are attributed to differences in policies and health systems which can be more protective and publicly grounded (Nordic) or more privately grounded (Eastern). In Poland, the advantage of the high-educated is relatively large, especially for males, but it is smaller among the older people (the 65–79 age group). On a positive note, trends in health inequality in Europe, contrary to the ones observed in the United States, show improvements in health of the low-educated and the narrowing gap between the high-educated[56] (Mackenbach et al., 2018).

The positive effect of education is especially important for Poland as the socio-economic and political transformation after 1989 resulted in sharp increases in education attainment (Antonowicz, 2012; Jakubowski et al., 2010) manifesting itself in the highest enrolment rates in tertiary education in Europe in 2010 (Kwiek, 2013). The increasing demand for the elderly care would be therefore mitigated to some extent by the effects of better education in the future. It is clearly visible in the context of the association of education and care demand among older people. The results of Polsenior study on older population corroborate this observation in the Polish context. They show that 42.2 % of low-educated respondents declared they definitely or rather need help, while only 19.5 % of higher educated persons made such declaration (Błędowski, 2012). However, the benefits of lower care needs because of education-driven health improvements among the elderly should be considered in a long-term perspective.

On the future of morbidity: Selected theoretical concepts and some empirical findings

In the context of demand for care, the question about the future development of health status of the elderly plays a prominent role. The discussion on the future change of morbidity,[57] whether it is expanding, compressing or remaining proportionally stable, is ongoing. Fries (1980, p. 135) advocated the compression of morbidity referred to as a shorter span between the increasing age at onset of morbidity and the fixed occurrence of death. In his original considerations Fries assumed a fixed maximum of human lifespan, approximately 85 years, and a rectangularisation of the survival curve that began with elimination of premature deaths. The morbidity curve would follow the same trend as mortality and become more rectangular, mainly thanks to the postponement of chronic illnesses. Less chronic diseases, indicating less disability, could be postponed or prevented by promoting changes in lifestyle (e.g. avoiding overweight, quitting

---

56 It is worth noting that the prevalence of activity limitations and educational inequalities in European countries differ between the surveys used (Rubio-Valverde et al., 2019).

57 The term morbidity refers to a manifestation of ill health (Mamun, 2003).

smoking and doing exercise) to modify the ageing process. As a result, the disability-free life expectancy should be increasing faster than the life expectancy.

Taking the opposite perspective, some researchers supported the hypothesis of expansion of morbidity (Gruenberg, 1977; Olshansky et al., 1991). In epidemiologic transition they saw a trade-off of a lower risk of death from fatal diseases at older ages for an extension of disabled years because the progression of the diseases themselves is assumed to remain unchanged. It leads to a shift in the distribution of causes of disability from fatal to non-fatal diseases associated with ageing. Therefore, the increase in total life expectancy is accompanied by an absolute and relative increase in years with disability.

The concept of 'dynamic equilibrium' advanced by Manton (1982) suggested counterbalancing effects of two phenomena leading to a stable proportion of disability in the additional years gained. According to Manton, the severity and the rate of progression of chronic disease are directly related to mortality. As mortality improvement produces extra years with morbidity, changes of lifestyles and medical progress reduce the rate of progression of chronic diseases keeping the proportion of years with disability constant. Life expectancy in industrialised countries may grow at advanced ages not only by intervening in chronic disease processes but also by developing interventions for other aspects of senescence such as Alzheimer's disease (Manton et al., 1991).

The discussed competing concepts have framed the debate on health and ageing for a long time. However, the general theory on population ageing advocated by Robine and Michel (2004) assumes that all three hypotheses, though perceived as mutually exclusive, can be combined in a single theory. The authors argue that they can be categorised as the successive phases of demographic and epidemiologic transitions. Another possibility is, with the increasing numbers of very old people, that within the same population both trends – compression and expansion – may be possible, but for different age groups.

Some current research provide mixed evidence for these different hypotheses of morbidity. Many researchers argue that the final conclusion depends on the health indicator used. Mostly, these are questions on chronic illnesses or activity limitations but other measures are also used (e.g. the debate on the compression or expansion hypotheses was also extended to cardiovascular morbidity; Mamun, 2003). For example, Rosen and Haglund (2005) challenge the compression-of-morbidity hypothesis reporting the prevalence of long-standing illness is increasing among the old in Sweden. On the contrary, Schoeni et al. (2001) find evidence for a decline in disability among elderly persons in the United States. Christensen et al. (2009) drawing on data from the last two decades of the 20th century from the United States, Japan and France concluded that the proportion of people with activity limitations in daily living went down. The data from three population censuses in Poland of 1978, 1988 and 2002 show that the prevalence of disability among older people has been increasing in the years 1978–2002 (Szukalski, 2008).

Other researchers find some heterogeneity in their results. Martin and Schoeni (2014) reveal that between 1997 and 2010 in the U.S. for middle-aged persons, most limitations/disabilities increase, while for older persons, most limitations/ disabilities decrease. In a similar vein, Crimmins et al. (2016) argue that in the U.S. context there was no compression of morbidity across the life course, but some compression at older ages (65 years) was observed. Kassebaum et al. (2016) point out that compression can be interpreted in both absolute and relative terms. The study of the 1990–2015 span using Global Burden of Disease Study allows the authors to conclude that for the past 25 years health has progressed but not universally. As people spend more years with reduced functional status it is argued that the absolute expansion of morbidity has occurred. However, the proportion of years in bad health has been relatively constant since 1990. Similarly, the results for the Netherlands are also inconclusive (Nusselder, 2007). From the perspective of advances in development, high-income countries show patterns of morbidity compression, while for low- and middle-income countries there is no reliable evidence of compression, and morbidity might be even expanding (Chatterji et al., 2015). Finally, Abeliansky and Strulik (2019) find a steady progress in human health that implies substantial delays in human ageing, which is attributed to medical progress.

Essentially, different hypotheses propose contradictory directions of morbidity developments but neither can be treated as definitely verified. Yet, the possibility that extra years of life gained will be unhealthy years is also feasible. In such a scenario the demand for care in the future would be even more inflated.

Trends in healthy life expectancy

So far healthy life expectancy is rising along with life expectancy increases (Kassebaum et al., 2016; Mathers et al., 2001). Most importantly, gains in healthy life expectancy across countries exceed gains in total life expectancy, suggesting that reductions in mortality are accompanied by reductions in disability. Even though women live longer, more of their years of life is spent with disability relative to men. Women's mortality advantage contributes to more healthy life years, but their larger disability disadvantage reduces the difference in healthy life years between sexes. The male-female gap in healthy life expectancy is global, but shows substantial variation across countries that is related to the length of life expectancy itself as well as the GDP and the expenditure on elderly care (Van Oyen et al., 2010, 2013). Another important finding is that increments in healthy life expectancy are positively related with average levels of health expenditure per capita and their growth rate is higher than for total life expectancy gains. Thus, population-level investment in health boosts the overall length of life, but it has even stronger effect for healthy life years increases.

The healthy life years indicator for Poland shows a steady increase for both sexes since 2009 (GUS, 2020c). A male born in 2019 is expected to live 59.7 years without disability (HLY_0) conditional on mortality rates and health prevalence remaining constant. Women born in 2019 should expect 63.3 years without any limitations in functioning. It is an increase of 2.2 years for both sexes between 2009 and 2019. Compared to increases in life expectancy at birth in the same period (+2.6 years for males and +1.8 years for females), the relative improvement was stronger for women as the growth of proportion of healthy life years in total life expectancy at birth was 0.2 percentage points for men and 1.1 percentage points for women (compare Table 9 and Figure 16). Still, the proportion of total life expectancy spent in good health is higher for males (81 %) than for females (77 %).

Changes observed for both discussed indicators at age 60 are also positive. Men at age 60 in 2019 are expected to live additional 19.3 years, of which 10.3 years (53 %) are free of disability. That is more than in 2009 by 1.4 and 1.5 years in LE and HLY, respectively. Women at age 60 in 2019 on average live longer than men (24.2 years, 1.1 years more than in 2009) and more of their extra years of life are lived without disability (11.4 years, 1.3 years more than in 2009). However, in relative terms, less than half (47 %) of their additional years of life is expected to be healthy, that is, less than for males.

The mortality and disability differences between males and females still persist. The gap in life expectancy at birth – favourable for women – in 2009 amounted to 8.5 years and decreased to 7.7 years in 2019. The gap in life expectancy at age 60 also went down, from 5.3 years in 2009 to 4.9 years ten years later (see Table 9). The gender differences in HLY show less convergence. Despite the improvements in gender gap represented as proportion of HLY at birth between men and women, the absolute gender difference remains stable (3.6 years). The gender gap in HLY at age 60 reduced slightly (from 1.3 to 1.1 years) but in relative terms it increased (by 0.8 percentage points). Differences by gender in HLY at birth are higher in absolute terms, but at the same time smaller in relative terms when compared to respective gender differences in HLY at age 60 (Figure 16).

Table 9. Life expectancy (LE), healthy life years (HLY) and proportion of HLY (%HLY) at age 0 and 60 in Poland, 2009–2019

			2009	2019	Δ (2009, 2019)	Δ (Male, Female)₂₀₀₉	Δ (Male, Female)₂₀₁₉
at age 0	Male	LE0	71.5	74.1	2.6	-8.5	-7.7
		HLY0	57.5	59.7	2.2	-3.6	-3.6
		% HLY0	80 %	81 %	0.2 p.p.	4.1 p.p.	3.1 p.p.
	Female	LE0	80.1	81.8	1,8	8.5	7.7
		HLY0	61.1	63.3	2.2	3.6	3.6
		% HLY0	76 %	77 %	1.1 p.p.	-4.1 p.p.	-3.1 p.p.
at age 60	Male	LE60	17.9	19.3	1.4	-5.3	-4.9
		HLY60	8.8	10.3	1,5	-1.3	-1,1
		% HLY60	49 %	53 %	4.2 p.p.	5.5 p.p.	6.3. p.p.
	Female	LE60	23.2	24.2	1,1	5.3	4.9
		HLY60	10.1	11.4	1.3	1.3	1,1
		% HLY60	44 %	47 %	3.5 p.p.	-5.5 p.p.	-6.3. p.p.

Note: p.p. stands for percentage point.
Source: Statistics Poland, own elaboration.

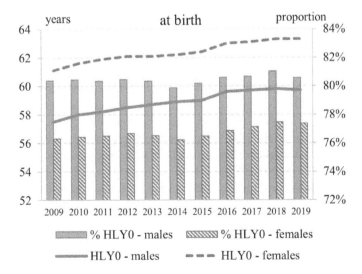

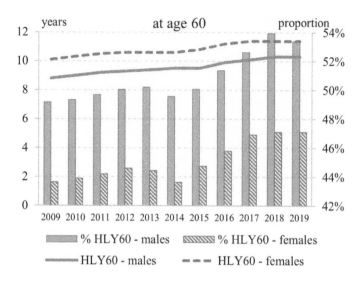

Figure 16. Healthy life years (HLY) and proportion of HLY (%HLY) at birth and at age 60, Poland, 2009–2019.

Source: Statistics Poland, own elaboration.

The survey-based health evaluation

According to the European Health Interview Survey,[58] late in 2014 nearly every second person aged 60 years and over was classified as persons biologically disabled according to EU, that is, as a person who had limitations in activities of daily living due to health-related problems. Almost two-thirds of the mentioned population are people with some limitations, but not severe, while the remaining one-third experiences severe limitations (GUS, 2016a). The possibility of performing personal care activities is decreasing with age and three out of five oldest persons declare problems. The scale of the needs can be also pictured by the fact that nearly 45 % of older people having problems with performing personal care activities have to be on their own because they do not receive any help. Nearly 28 % of older people, who declare limitations in running households, do not receive any help as well (GUS, 2016a).

To analyse health at the individual level I compare the three dimensions of health: self-perceived health, chronic morbidity, and activity limitations, available in the European Health Interview Survey (EHIS) and the European

---

58   More information on the dataset is provided in the Appendix.

Union Statistics on Income and Living Conditions (EU-SILC) surveys in 2009 and 2014. A separate check for consistency of results between the two surveys is performed and presented in Table 10. I compare both surveys to validate whether the EU-SILC health questions provide similar picture as the EHIS which is a dedicated study for health analyses.[59] The biggest differences between both surveys are amongst the answers to the chronic morbidity questions. The gap between results amounts to 20 percentage points and makes comparison hardly possible. The other two health outcomes get similar level of responses, however in self-perceived health question the EU-SILC results seem to be lower at 'good' and 'very good' responses at the cost of 'fair' and 'bad' responses. The question on activity limitations yields most comparable results between the analysed surveys. Still, international comparisons show discrepancies in GALI responses between countries and the surveys used (Rubio-Valverde et al., 2019).

Table 10. Comparison of the MEHM measures among population aged 60 and more between EU-SILC and EHIS in 2009 and 2014.

	Self-perceived health			
	EU-SILC 2009	EHIS 2009	EU-SILC 2014	EHIS 2014
Very good	1.0	1.9	1.3	2.0
Good	13.0	18.6	18.1	24.4
Fair	43.9	44.6	48.4	43.5
Bad	33.3	27.4	25.9	23.4
Very bad	8.8	7.5	6.3	6.6
	Chronic morbidity			
	EU-SILC 2009	EHIS 2009	EU-SILC 2014	EHIS 2014
Yes	67.4	85.6	65.4	88.7
No	32.6	14.4	34.6	11.3
	Activity limitations			
	EU-SILC 2009	EHIS 2009	EU-SILC 2014	EHIS 2014
Yes, strongly limited	18.8	22.5	17.4	18.3
Yes, limited	33.2	33.2	32.6	32.1
No, not limited	48.0	44.3	50.0	49.6

Source: Own elaboration based on EHIS and EU-SILC cross-sectional data, weighted.

---

59 EU-SILC data, because of having the panel component, will be used in the analyses of health dynamics in subsequent chapters.

The annual distributions of activity limitations[60] (GALI question) asked in the EU-SILC questionnaire to adults age 60 years and above are steady (Figure 17). Throughout the analysed years around half of the older population reports no limitations. Among the other half of the older population, of which people feel limited, around 40 % declare having severe limitations.

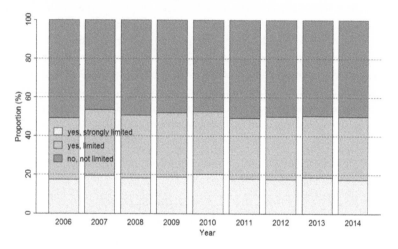

Figure 17. Activity limitations among adults aged 60 years and above by years.
Source: Own elaboration based on EU-SILC cross-sectional data, weighted.

The frequency of reporting long-standing activity limitations is increasing with age and the severity of limitations is stronger (Figure 18). While around 60 % of people in their sixties report no limitation, this proportion drops to 25 % among people aged 80 and above. Among people, who declare suffering from activity limitations, the proportion of those having severe limitations is increasing with age. At the age of 80 every third person is severely limited in activities of daily living. When it comes to gender differences, older women tend to report slightly more limitations that older men, especially after reaching their seventies (Figure 19). There are some differences in reporting severe limitations, however. The proportion of males reporting severe limitations is actually higher than of females up to early seventies. In older ages it is women who report relatively more severe limitations than men.

---

60   The results for GALI are reported since 2006 rather than 2005 because of the change in the question wording between the two time points that make direct comparison inappropriate or even impossible.

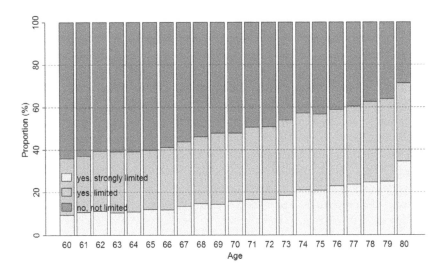

Figure 18. Activity limitations by age, average for years 2005–2014.
Source: Own elaboration based on EU-SILC cross-sectional data, weighted.

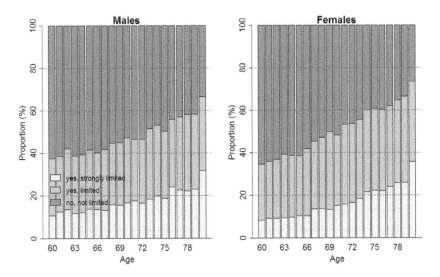

Figure 19. Activity limitations by age and sex, average for years 2005–2014.
Source: Own elaboration based on EU-SILC cross-sectional data, weighted.

The same conclusions can be drawn when analysing self-rated health (Figures 47–49 in Appendix). Against the cross-sectional comparison for limitations in activity, the distribution of self-perceived health between 2005 and 2014 is much less stable showing same differences in proportions of each category. There is the increase in the proportion of individuals reporting fair or better health. In the span of 10 years this increase amounts to 10 percentage points. On the contrary, the proportion of 'bad' or 'very bad' responses has been going down. It would suggest that either the health of population of people aged 60+ improved or perception of their health changed. The distribution of self-perceived health by age and by sex depict common phenomenon of health deterioration with age. The average results for women are also somewhat worse than for men. In each age group the proportion of women perceiving their own health as 'very bad' or 'bad' is higher than for men.

2.2.3 Relationship between living arrangements and health

Hypotheses on the impact of demographic (changes in kin availability and the timing of fertility), cultural (adherence to family norms and values affecting the likelihood of multiple generations co-residence) and economic factors (resources allowing achieving independence and privacy) on changes in household structure have been examined (Glaser, 1997; Grundy, 1992). The relationship between living arrangements and health is another complex dimension. On the one hand, the question about the extent to which changes in living arrangements have been facilitated by improvements in the health status of the older population is discussed. On the other hand, it is difficult to assess the impact of living arrangements on health because of the strong association between health, and changes in health, and transitions between different types of households (Grundy & Murphy, 2007). For example, there is considerable evidence indicating that increases in disability among older people lead to changes in their living arrangements, in particular to moves into institutions or to the households of relatives (Breeze et al., 1999; Grundy, 2001; Smits et al., 2010).

Living with others might have beneficial effects on health. First of all, the presence of a partner in the same household is associated with lower mortality risk, especially among 50–64-year-old men in Southeast Europe (Zueras et al., 2020). Living with a partner or a spouse has a protective effect against the depressive symptoms reported. The stronger effect is found for men rather than women and for eastern than western European countries (Grundy et al., 2017). Co-residing persons may bring material advantages (pooling of incomes and resources), which is especially important for older women, but also support and companionship that are important for practical and mental health. Furthermore, in her literature review, Grundy (2001) finds some evidence that living alone may be associated with various health-related disadvantages, for example, higher rates of poor health among older people living alone or a higher risk of a functional decline than others. However, she also refers to even more numerous studies of older people that show seniors living alone to be healthier than older persons living with adults other than a spouse, or in some cases, even than married adults. It is underlined that living alone at very old age is possible, or attractive, only for persons in satisfactory health condition. So good health might be a prerequisite of solitary living for many. It can be thus argued that there is a health-related selection in particular types of living arrangements. It is related to the observed associations between marital status and health that the married enjoy the best health, followed by the single, the widowed and then the divorced, which holds even in the oldest age groups reporting limiting long-term illness (Murphy et al., 1997).

Coming back to living alone and its potential adverse effects on health of some older persons, Grundy (2001) concludes that the empirical evidence does not unambiguously support such reasoning and, probably, such 'true' effects cannot be ever quantified. Possible effects of living alone on health might vary depending on individual- and population-level characteristics. For example, living alone might have a negative psychological effect if it is perceived as stigmatising (e.g. among lower educated in Japan) or a positive/neutral effect when it is valued as a sign of independence and autonomy (e.g. among highly educated in Northern Europe or the United States). Indeed, in Nordic countries no association between living alone and low levels of well-being is found (Young & Grundy, 2009). Living alone might have negative economic consequences for low-income elderly who lose opportunities for economies of scale, and therefore lose opportunities for better health care, but at the same time may have no effect for older people with high incomes. From the domestic services and care provision perspective, individuals who lack skills allowing them to perform domestic tasks such as cooking or cleaning may be disadvantaged when living alone. However, there will be no effect on older adults who are able to run households on their own that are able to care for themselves (Grundy, 2001).

Chapter 3. The multistate model for estimation of health and living arrangements transition rates of older people

This part of the monograph investigates two main processes of interest: changes in health status and changes in living arrangements (family situation) of older adults in Poland. In contrast to the previous, more descriptive chapter that illustrates the current and past situations of seniors in Poland with cross-sectional measures, this chapter aims to model the dynamics of both processes using longitudinal data. At the first stage, changes in health status and changes in living arrangements are modelled separately. Their relationships with age, sex and education with each of the variables of interest are examined. At the next stage, a joint model of changes in health and living arrangement is formulated. For that purpose, multistate models are proposed. They allow representation of the dynamics of both processes in terms of transition intensities between defined health states and living arrangements states. The estimated parameters of the multistate models are the input information to the final population projection model, necessary to prepare population projections of older people by their health status and living arrangements.

I start from presenting the general framework for population projections modelling that defines the structure of the application part of the book, that is, Chapter 3 and Chapter 4. Afterwards, a distinction between prevalence and incidence measures of health statuses is discussed. Then, an introduction to multistate models is provided. Following is the section on the data sources considered and ultimately used for the analysis. Next, I discuss results of modelling each of the two processes separately, starting from the evolution of health with age and next moving to changes of living arrangements. Finally, I estimate and discuss the full multistate projection model of changes in health and living arrangements of older people. Discussion closes the chapter.

3.1 The general framework of population projections

Population projections of the older population by health status and living arrangements are achieved in a two-stage modelling process. At the first stage a micro-level study is conducted, while the second stage involves a macro-level analysis. This sequence of modelling is crucial as the results of micro-modelling are the input data to obtain the macro-level output. The framework of the population projection procedure is summarised in Figure 20.

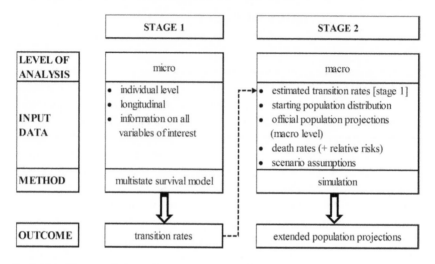

Figure 20. The extended population projections scheme.
Source: Own elaboration.

The first stage concerns modelling changes in health and living arrangements of older people as they age. For this purpose, individual longitudinal data are required. The main outcome of this stage is transition rates between the states defined for both processes. Transition rates are a summary description of the dynamics of health and living arrangements of older individuals derived from the use of multistate methods.

The second stage of the projection procedure is based on two types of data. The transition rates estimated at the first stage are the elementary input information to be used in a microsimulation model. Another key information are the official population projections from Eurostat. Population projections determine the population's size and its composition by age and sex and their future developments. Additionally, Eurostat's assumptions about mortality are crucial. The initial data on transition probabilities together with prospective mortality rates according to the Eurostat's assumptions supply the microsimulation model to generate individual health and living arrangements life histories over the future. Individual trajectories are then aggregated to redistribute the official population projections across health and living arrangements statuses. The final product of the modelling are the population projections by age, sex, health status and living arrangements of people 65 years old or more.

This general modelling framework is depicted in the two subsequent chapters: this chapter describes in details the first stage of the modelling while the simulation model and the outcomes of the second stage are the subject of Chapter 4. Both chapters are structured similarly: firstly, the theory underlying the respective models is introduced along with both data requirements and necessary assumptions. Next, the model and its estimates are presented. Finally, the output of the modelling is discussed in the context of other research results.

3.2 Incidence and prevalence measures in the population description

The basic idea behind an analysis of any process is the way how the process is represented. Here, I focus on changes in health and living arrangements depicted as trajectories of older individuals which constitute their life histories or careers. Trajectories are defined by the sequence of states and transitions between states (Willekens, 2014). When considering health trajectories (but other trajectories as well) it is important to make distinction between two analytical approaches: one is based on the prevalence of some health conditions and the other is based on the incidence of health conditions. The *incidence* is the number of new (or recurrent) cases of a condition (disease, dependence, disability, etc.) in a population in a given period of time, whereas the *prevalence* is the total number of people affected by that condition in a given population at a point in time (Gourbin & Wunsch, 2006). In case of prevalence, one distinguishes the *point prevalence* when referring to a specific point in time, the *period prevalence* if the number of affected individuals in population is considered in a defined period of time, and the *lifetime prevalence* if the condition occurred anytime during one's life until time of study (Rothman, 2012). In summary, the incidence refers to events (flows) while the prevalence to a status (stock) in the considered moment or period. Both types of information allow calculation of population health measures and can be applied to population projections. However, they have advantages and drawbacks in different applications and differ in data requirements (Murray et al., 2000).

Historically, researchers worked on the development and application of methods that would combine mortality and morbidity data into a single measure providing a summary of the population health. In their review Robine and Jagger (2006, pp. 290–291) list three methods of calculation of the health state expectancy: the Sullivan method (method of observed prevalence tables), the method of double extinction tables (Katz's active life expectancy) and the multistate model. The Sullivan method (Sullivan, 1971) is a modification of the conventional life table model that adds the prevalence of a given health condition of interest into calculations. Its main advantage is simplicity and the use of data on mortality and disability that may be collected independently. In this method standard mortality tables can be used together with disability prevalence data collected from cross-sectional surveys. However, a change of the health status, so a re-entry into the life table population, is not possible, which is a serious limitation of that approach. The active life expectancy proposed by Katz and colleagues (Katz et al., 1983) should be based on double decrement life tables referring to individuals who can move into two absorbing states: a limited function and death. However, this method assumes that the health condition under study is irreversible and the recovery of lost functions is negligible. This assumption is valid for some applications (e.g. dementia) but might not be met for other definitions of disability (Robine & Jagger, 2006). The multistate tables Rogers et al. (1989) allow transitions from an independent to a dependent health status and back again. Taking the return transitions into account is the main advantage of this method. However, it requires longitudinal data that historically had been relatively scarce and thus not always available. Noteworthy, the multistate methods imply that the data on mortality and disability are collected in the course of the same study which requires a sufficient sample size to maintain a desired precision (Robine & Jagger, 2006).

When it comes to health projections, Siegel (2012b, p. 761) outlines two general types of analytical approaches: (1) general analytic methods and (2) statistical methods, which also may come in combination. Statistical methods exploit time-series techniques and regression/econometric/structural equation models and they will not be discussed here. The approach based on analytic methods distinguishes demographic and epidemiological methods. Both groups of methods use prevalence ratios and incidence rates but they differ in the data employed and a way of taking risk factors and covariates into consideration. Demographic methods directly employ data on the health condition or disability to be projected with no reference to data on related factors that could contribute to a particular health condition. In contrast, epidemiological models rely on data on diseases and disabilities from repeated cross-sectional surveys or longitudinal surveys and are often extended with additional risk factors and covariates.

From a methodological point of view functional projections may differ in the mechanism that allocates people in a given age and sex into functional states. The distribution method, also known as static, uses a distribution function (e.g. headship rates, education enrolment rates or health prevalence rates) to impose the population structure by functional states. On the contrary, the dynamic method is based on transition (incidence) rates that govern the transitions people make in life. In this method the distribution of people among functional states is the outcome of their life trajectories (Willekens, 2007). The basic demographic projection method for health status is the prevalence-ratio method. It relies on the availability of population projections for age-sex groups and the past age-sex-specific prevalence ratios of disability. In order to estimate the future number of disabled one needs: firstly, to project historical age-sex specific shares of persons with disability in the population in the subsequent years and secondly, to apply them to population projections disaggregated by age and sex (Siegel, 2012b). The procedure provides the future number of disabled, however, it does not take into account the interaction between changes in mortality and changes in disability. Van der Gaag et al. (2015) accentuate that disability and mortality are interrelated in at least three ways. "First, trends in medical progress that affect mortality may also be expected to affect disability. Second, risk factors that affect both mortality and disability, such as the prevalence of obesity or smoking, may be expected to change over time and may affect mortality and disability in a different way. Finally, mortality rates may differ between non-disabled and disabled persons" (van der Gaag et al., 2015, p. 77).

To accommodate all the above interdependencies in the projections scholars recommend to utilise multistate projection models (a dynamic method). Mamun (2003, Chapter 2) in his dissertation points out that the relaxation of the assumption of unidirectional health changes over the life course in the multistate methods allows individuals to experience different health events as they age, both the onset of health problems but also recovery from them. Additionally, there is no condition either on the number of events occurrences (repetition of events) or their time sequence (a chronological order). It makes the method attractive due to a possibility of reconstruction of an individual biography and flexibility to define the structure of the functional states considered.

3.3 Multistate models as a tool for modelling demographic processes

3.3.1 A theoretical review

The traditional cohort-component model projects a population by age and sex. In order to extend it to project a population by age, sex and other characteristics a multistate model is introduced. A multistate model allows changes of the population structure to be presented according to the distinct states which an individual can occupy. The states are defined by population attributes to be selected. The first formulations of the multistate model in demography concerned a population classified by geographical regions (Rogers, 1975; F. Willekens & Drewe, 1984), but since then many other individual characteristics been considered, such as marital status (Belanger, 1989; Kotowska, 1994; F. J. Willekens et al., 1982), education level (Stonawski, 2014; Strzelecki, 2007), labour force participation (Willekens, 1980), a household position (Van Imhoff & Keilman, 1991) or a health status (Crimmins et al., 1994; Mamun, 2003). In epidemiology, multistate models are useful to depict the evolution of subjects/individuals through different statuses, generally including clinical statuses and death. They are a generalisation of survival and competing risks models (Commenges, 2003). Moreover, an inclusion of other attributes than age and sex allows accounting for the population heterogeneity and to generate a cohort biography giving for each age the distribution of cohort members among functional states. In other words, biographic models provide a description of how state occupancies and events evolve with age (Willekens, 2007).

The multistate model can be applied to a single individual and generates an individual biography – a life history. A life history can be viewed as a realisation of a stochastic process that is modelled with probability models. The theory of stochastic processes is well-established (e.g. Kulkarni, 2011) and is successfully used in a multistate modelling framework (Schoen, 1988; van den Hout, 2017). The fundamental assumption of the model is that life histories are realisations of a continuous-time Markov process (Willekens, 2014). The underlying Markov model is defined by a state space, which is a set of possible states that individuals can occupy. The states originate from the categories of personal attributes of individuals (e.g. education is an attribute, while 'low', 'medium' and 'high' levels are its categories). Depending on the research questions, the key attributes define the state space while other attributes may be included as covariates. The states within the state space that are intercommunicated are characterised by possible transitions between them. One can distinguish *transient states*, which subjects/individuals can move in and out back and forth, and *absorbing states*, which can be entered but not left (e.g. 'dead' state). Following the notation by Kalbfleisch and Lawless (1985) and van den Hout (2017), I define a stochastic process $\{Y(t): t \geq 0\}$, where variable Y_t is the state of the process at time t by a randomly chosen individual (i.e. a state occupancy). Then, for $0 \leq t_1 \leq t_2$, and k being the number of possible states, a transition probability matrix $P(s,t)_{k \times k}$, incudes following entries/transition probabilities:

$$p_{rs}\left(t_1,t_2\right)= P(Y_{t_2} = s\,|\,Y_{t_1} = r\}, \text{ for } r,s = 1,2,\ldots,k \qquad (1)$$

where $p_{rs}(t_1,t_2)$ denotes the probability that individual being in the state r at the exact time t_1 will be in the state s at the exact time t_2. The transition rate between two states r and s at the exact time t is defined as:

$$q_{rs}\left(t\right)= \lim_{\Delta t \to 0} p_{rs}\left(t,t+\Delta t\right)/\Delta t, \quad r \neq s. \qquad (2)$$

Both transition rates and transition probabilities characterise a Markov process because the probability that an individual will leave a state during $\left(t_1,t_2\right)$ time period depends only on the state occupied at time t_1. It is the basic assumption that the future evolution depends only on the current state while the previous trajectory can be ignored (Schoen, 1988). Transition rates reflect the collective experience of similar individuals under observation and describe the dynamics of the process under study (Willekens, 2014). The transition rates for a continuous-time Markov chain are also called transition intensities or transition hazards and will be used interchangeably. It is worth noticing, that contrary to the transition probability, hazard may take values greater than one.

In modelling Markov processes the choice of time scale is important as the process can be analysed with different measures: age, calendar time or time since a reference event (e.g. time since the birth of a first child, time since the labour market entry, time since the onset of a disease, etc.). In the analysis and modelling of life histories age is the main time scale and, therefore, cannot be treated as a personal attribute (Willekens, 2014). It also means that the process is time-inhomogeneous (or, precisely, age-inhomogeneous). In the time-homogeneous Markov process transitions rates are constant over time, while introducing a time dependency in the model lets transition rates to vary within time (age) intervals (Schoen, 1988). The time dependency in multistate models is allowed to be transition-specific and can be modelled using both parametric and non-parametric methods (van den Hout, 2017). Continuous-time processes may be approximated with discrete-time models, however, in this setting at most one transition is possible for each time interval. Continuous-time models allow changes of a state at any time and there are no restrictions on the number of transitions between transient states within a time interval.

Singer and Spilerman (1976) highlight the attractiveness of multistate mathematical formulation in social sciences as it permits a researcher to focus upon the dynamic properties of a social process. They notice that "Markov models provide a convenient framework for analysing the structural mechanisms which underlie social change and for extrapolating shifts in the state distribution of a population" (Singer & Spilerman, 1976, p. 1). As previously noted, calling a multistate process Markovian informs that the future depends on the current state only and is independent of the past trajectory. That Markovian assumption is appealing to researchers due to its simplicity, although in most applications it is an oversimplification. It ignores the influence of duration in the state (duration dependence), which in some applications affects the intensity of transition. It also neglects the effects of 'origin dependence', where the initial state affects future behaviour, for example, in return migration (Schoen, 1988). The multistate models allow the Markovian assumption to be somewhat relaxed and let other factors play a role by inclusion of the explanatory variables (Commenges, 1999). As pointed out by van den Hout (2017), "although many processes in real life are not Markovian, a statistical model based upon a Markov chain may still provide a good approximation of the process of interest. (…) By linking age and values of covariates to the risk of a transition, information about the future is contained not only in the present state, but also in current age and additional background characteristics."

Including covariates into the model is possible with the use of hazard regression models. The transition-specific hazard regression models can be defined for all those states designed in the state space between which a transition is feasible in line with the considered multistate process (van den Hout, 2017, sec. 4.3). The model is a combination of a baseline hazard with a log-linear regression and is given by

$$q_{rs}(t) + q_{rs}(t \mid x(t)) = q_{rs.0}(t)\exp\left(\beta_{rs} x(t)\right) \qquad (3)$$

for the parameter vectr $\beta_{rs} = (\beta_{rs.1}, \beta_{rs.2}, ..., \beta_{rs.p})^{\mathsf{T}}$ and the covariate vector $x(t) = \left(x_1(t), x_2(t), ..., x_p(t)\right)^{\mathsf{T}}$, which has no intercept. The expression $q_{rs.0}(t)$ stands for a baseline hazard.

The general formulation of the log-linear regression model with a baseline hazard allows many statistical regression methods to be incorporated in the analysis of multistate data. Van den Hout (2017) provides some examples of parametric baseline hazards:

$$\text{exponential}: q_{rs.0}(t) = \exp(\beta_{rs.0}) = \lambda_{rs} \quad \lambda_{rs} > 0 \qquad (4)$$

$$\text{Weibull}: q_{rs.0}\left(t\right)= \lambda_{rs}\tau_{rs}t^{\tau_{rs}-1}\lambda_{rs}, \tau_{rs}>0 \tag{5}$$

$$\text{Gompertz}: q_{rs.0}\left(t\right)= \lambda_{rs}\exp\left(\xi_{rs}t\right)\lambda_{rs}>0 \tag{6}$$

$$\text{log-logistic}: q_{rs.0}\left(t\right)= \frac{\lambda_{rs}\rho_{rs}(\lambda_{rs}t)^{\rho_{rs}-1}}{1+(\lambda_{rs}t)^{\rho_{rs}}}\lambda_{rs}, \rho_{rs}>0. \tag{7}$$

This method is flexible as alternative definitions of the baseline hazard may be used for different transitions. Additionally, the restrictions on parameters can also vary across transitions according to transition characteristics and the availability of information on certain transitions in the data. Time-dependent covariates in the $x(t)$ vector are also allowed.

Transition rates are estimated by relating transitions to exposures (Willekens, 2014). Estimation of model parameters is undertaken by maximising the log-likelihood. The contribution of each individual to the likelihood is conditional on the first state and is differentiated by the fact whether at the observation time a living state, a right-censored state or death is observed (the relevant formulae for the contribution of the individual to the likelihood can be found in van den Hout (2017, sec. 4.5) and Jackson (2011, p. 3)). Methodological details on multistate model estimation can be found in Jackson (2011), Kalbfleisch and Lawless (1985), van den Hout (2017). The Akaike's information criterion (AIC) and the Bayesian information criterion (BIC) are criteria which can be used for models' comparison and selection when the estimation is performed by maximum likelihood. For nested models, a likelihood ratio test is complementary.

A model assessment for panel-observed multistate models is rather a complicated task. Titman and Sharples (2009, p. 647) point at the unknown transition times between states and the irregular nature of the observation scheme as the main difficulties. There are only a few studies that provide recommendations on model checking (Jackson, 2011; Lawless & Nazeri Rad, 2015; Titman & Sharples, 2009; van den Hout, 2017). Some recommendations of formal ways of assessing a general model fit as well as simpler alternative methods are provided in a comprehensive review by Titman and Sharples (2009); however, they focus mostly on time-homogeneous multistate models. They argue that the problem of irregular observation times can be overcome by comparing the observed state occupancies at a fixed set of times with those expected by the fitted model, however this method is not free of difficulties (Lawless & Nazeri

Rad, 2015). Still, comparing expected and observed frequencies is highlighted as a heuristic tool to assess the model fit (van den Hout, 2017).

A model validation is very important though, especially when a multistate model is used for prediction and the extrapolation of the model goes beyond the age range in the data (van den Hout et al., 2014). Next to the goodness-of-fit assessment, the external validation of a multistate model is considered as an independent method. It relies on comparing inference from the model with results or data from other studies. It usually pertains to summary statistics provided by national bureaus of statistics, that is why the population underlying the longitudinal study must correspond to the existent population for comparison purposes.

3.3.2 Selected empirical research

Multistate models allow defining a state space and transitions between states in a flexible way which makes the multistate representation attractive for researchers. Multistate models often provide a relevant modelling framework for event history data (Andersen & Keiding, 2002) and are common to describe the development for longitudinal failure time data (Hougaard, 1999). Therefore, they can be adapted in many research settings including demography[61] and epidemiology.

Modelling transitions in health with multistate models is well established. For example, Crimmins, Hayward and Saito (1994) show effects of changing mortality and morbidity rates for changes in the prevalence of health problems in the older population with a five-state multistate life table (based on independence and ability to provide self-care indicator). Hardy et al. (2005) use a multistate representation of disability to model transitions between two states of disability (mild and severe, defined with limitations in ADL) and functional independence among persons aged 70 years or older, and death using a U.S.-based prospective cohort study. Drawing on the same dataset, Gill et al. (2005) use multistate life table techniques to compute active and disabled life expectancy. Hanewald et al. (2017) develop the multistate Markov model of health transitions at older ages using the Chinese Longitudinal Healthy Longevity Survey as an input for further

---

61   For instance, Willekens (2014) provides two modelling examples related to demography. The first is an example of a multistate analysis of a path between leaving parental home and motherhood among women in the Netherlands. The second is an example of life table method used to estimate transition rates between job and unemployment representing employment careers in Germany.

research on population aging and retirement financial planning in China (an ADL limitation-based definition of disability is used as well). The non-parametric multistate model for transitions in health is also estimated for Poland using the EU-SILC data (Łątkowski, 2015).

The presentation of some other applications of dynamic multistate models in epidemiology (for infectious and chronic diseases) can be found in a review by Van Den Berg Jeths et al. (2001). Mamun (2003) estimates the multistate life table model of cardiovascular disease. Multistate survival models have also been successfully applied to describe change in cognitive function in the older population (van den Hout et al., 2014) as well as disability and multimorbidity among nonagenarians (Hoogendijk et al., 2019). Multistate life tables are also used to assess changes in duration of ADL disability (Reuser et al., 2009) or duration of cognitive impairment (Reuser et al., 2011) by self-reported BMI (for obesity), smoking status and levels of education. Multistate models of functional disability are also employed for actuarial purposes (long-term care insurance applications) (Fong et al., 2015; Rickayzen & Walsh, 2002). Also, van der Gaag et al. (2015) project future trends of ADL-disability prevalence among the elderly in the Netherlands using the multistate projection model

Next to examples of multistate models in health research, there are also prominent applications of these models for living arrangements. Raymo et al. (2019) use multistate life tables to summarise information on the transitions between different living arrangements between ages 65 and 90 from the Health and Retirement Survey in the United States. They define four categories of living arrangements (based on the proximity of residence of older parents' children plus institutional living) that are interwined with each other. The recognised example is the LIPRO ('LIfe style PROjections') model used for family and household projections (Van Imhoff & Keilman, 1991). It is based on the methodology of multistate demography that allows incorporation of family and household positions to freely define living arrangements states and estimate transitions between them (Keilman, 2019). Another important example is the ProFamy model (Zeng et al., 1997) which strongly relies on a multistate accounting model for transforming the living arrangement statuses (based on marital/union statuses and co-residence with children and parents statuses) as well as ADL-based disability status transitions on a year-to-year basis (Zeng et al., 2014).

3.3.3 The analytical strategy for modelling changes in health and living arrangements

In this study I focus on the health status and the living arrangements status of older individuals. Those two attributes and their categories define the state space. Firstly, each attribute serves to formulate a separate state space of a multistate model and then both attributes account for a broader state space of a joint model. These multistate models are applied to describe and later mimic the underlying processes of health change and shifts in living arrangements of adults age 50 and over. The estimation of multistate model parameters, that is, transition rates, is a key outcome.

As stated in the previous chapters, the literature on changes both in health and living arrangements confirm their relationship with age and sex. The human physical and mental functions change with age and they reportedly decline most sharply in the older age groups (Andersen-Randberg et al., 1999; Vestergaard et al., 2015). Changes in living arrangements are indirectly related to age as they reflect changes both in family biographies and health trajectories (de Jong Gierveld et al., 2001). Knowing the dependencies above, one may expect the rates of transitions between health states as well as living arrangements states vary with age, therefore I will model them as the time-inhomogeneous Markov process. By estimating separate models, I inspect what is the relationship of each attribute with age and later – in the final model – of attributes taken jointly. Information on sex is also included to grasp differences between males and females. I also investigate the effect of education on the studied processes. Education is a covariate of special interest as its association with both health and living arrangements is well documented. Estimation of the effect of education is considerable also in the context of the increasing higher education attainment of the current middle-aged cohorts who will be reaching old age in the medium-term future.

I start out modelling with an exponential hazard model and then I extend it by adding time dependency and compare it with piecewise-constant models. Next, I examine the effects of risk factors which leads to estimating regression models for the transition intensities. I also put some restrictions on parameters due to sparse data on certain transitions. In the selection of best models I refer to Akaike's information criterion (AIC) and the likelihood ratio (LR) test.

3.4 Data

The topic of the study and the choice of an analytic approach imply certain data requirements. Multistate models require longitudinal data, either retrospective or prospective (panel) data. The data about the same individual in at least two points in time is a prerequisite to learn about the number of events of interest and the number of corresponding exposures in the considered time period. This is the basis for the calculation of transition rates. Keeping in mind that the estimated transition rates will serve as input for a population projection model, the spacing between observations is desired to be as narrow as possible. Preferably, the spacing between observations should amount to at most one year to match the exogenous population projection structure that provides yearly changes by single age groups. The other condition of the dataset that needs to be met is providing at the same time the data on the health status and the living arrangements status of individuals, which are main variables of attention. Since I focus on older people in the population, I impose a restriction of being 50 years or older at the baseline observation. Additionally, I require the data to include the sex of respondents. I review the available datasets for Poland to conform to these specifications and select the best one for the purpose of the study.

3.4.1 Datasets considered for the analysis

The dataset that was found appropriate for the analysis is the European Union Statistics on Income and Living Conditions (EU-SILC) dataset. The EU-SILC is the European Union reference source for comparative statistics on income distribution and social exclusion at the European level. From the point of the analysis it covers information on the household composition and basic questions on self-rated personal health. It offers longitudinal data pertaining to individual-level changes over time, observed once a year over a four-year period. The reference population of the EU-SILC is all private households and their current members residing in the territory of the Member States at the time of the data collection. Collective households residents and institutionalised individuals are excluded from a target population (European Commission, 2016). The data is collected from individuals aged 15 years old and older. However, the age of the oldest individuals is described in a single open age group 80+ once they reached 80 or more years. More detailed information on age of the oldest respondents is restricted due to confidentiality reasons and thus unavailable. The longitudinal data available for Poland for this study cover years 2005–2015. Even though individuals are observed in different chronological time periods, they are followed on the same age scale which allows grouping them into a synthetic cohort. The population of adults aged 50 years or more gives the effective sample size equal to 43,962 respondents that are observed in at least two points in time and have no missing information on their health state and living arrangement. The number of recorded transitions depends on the defined state space but there are 1,667 transitions to death observed.

The other longitudinal dataset that would meet requirements of the analysis was the Survey of Health, Ageing and Retirement in Europe (SHARE) dataset. The SHARE is a panel database of micro data on health, socio-economic status and social and family networks focusing on adults aged 50 years and above (Börsch-Supan et al., 2013). It covers multiple European countries; however, their number varies across different waves. To date, seven waves of the SHARE have been collected. Poland is a member of the SHARE consortium, however it missed data collection in Wave 1 and Wave 5. The first wave that Poland took part in was Wave 2 conducted in 2006/07. Since then Poland participated in the following waves: 3 (2008/09), 4 (2011/12), 6 (2015) and 7 (2017). It is important to note that the design of Wave 3 (SHARELIFE) differed from the design of other waves. It focused on retrospective life histories and could not be used for the modelling purposes of this study because of lack of health questions asked in other waves. The main advantages of the SHARE over the EU-SILC are no constraints on the information about age of the oldest respondents and a much broader array of questions referring to both physical and mental health. However, it has much smaller sample size and therefore less records of transitions made. In the four waves conducted in Poland that could be considered for the analysis (2, 4, 6 and 7) there were 7,558 main interviews released. It gives a maximum of 4,727 respondents interviewed at least twice plus 567 respondents whose death was captured (Bergmann et al., 2019). Additionally, there is the longer and irregular spacing (at least two years, but also 4–5 years) between waves. It is a disadvantage as longer time distance between waves implies limitations in modelling transitions (Wolf & Gill, 2009). Compared to annual collections of the EU-SILC and its larger sample size, the SHARE ranks inferior to the EU-SILC for this particular study.

Another longitudinal dataset that was examined to perform multistate modelling of health and living arrangements under the population ageing in Poland is the Social Diagnosis (Diagnoza Społeczna, www.diagnoza.com) (Czapiński & Panek, 2015). The survey investigates households and their members aged 16 and above on their objective and subjective quality of life in Poland. The project is a panel study with eight waves conducted (2000, 2003, 2005, 2007, 2009, 2011, 2013, 2015). In all the waves, 26,685 households with 84,479 members and 62,541 individual respondents (aged 16 and above) were interviewed (Panek et al., 2015). Despite a long time span covered by the study and a large sample, the questions on respondents' health status were found unsatisfactory because of changes in the wording of questions on health status between subsequent waves (a lack of coherence). Also, the two-year spacing between waves was found less favourable in comparison to the EU-SILC.

The other longitudinal study considered for the analysis was the Generations and Gender Survey (GGS). There were two waves of the GGS conducted in Poland, the first in 2010/2011 and the second in 2014/2015. In contains a panel sample of 12,419 respondents aged 18–79 years with broad information on demographic, social and economic characteristics (Kotowska, 2017). Similarly to previous studies, it ranked lower than the EU-SILC due to the greater spacing between waves and the lower number of observations.

Lastly, it is worth mentioning the database originating from the study *Medical, psychological, sociological and economic aspects of elderly in Poland* ('Aspekty medyczne, psychologiczne, socjologiczne i ekonomiczne starzenia się ludzi w Polsce', PolSenior) (Mossakowska et al., 2012). It is a representative sample of population of older people in Poland from the research conducted from 2007 to 2012 covering 5,695 individuals in total (4,979 respondents aged 65 and more, and 716 respondents just about to enter old age (55–59 years)). The aim of the study was to examine medical, psychological and socio-economic aspects of ageing in Poland (Błędowski et al., 2011). This database is very interesting in terms of the questions asked and the age of respondents, as it was the first broad study that covered the assessment of health, social and economic situation of seniors. The study was initiated as the first nationally representative research on the older people population and as a first step toward longitudinal analysis (Błędowski et al., 2011). However, no panel continuation of the study was performed within subsequent years which unfortunately imposed a rejection of this dataset from the set of viable options.[62]

3.4.2 Details on the selected database

The ultimate choice for the multistate model estimation is the EU-SILC longitudinal database. The choice of the dataset was driven mainly by the fact the longitudinal data are produced annually and contain information on

---

62   The fieldwork of the second wave of the study – PolSenior2 – was conducted between September 2018 and December 2019, and the monograph describing the results of the study has been published in 2021. Still, the results could be only used for the cross-sectional comparisons. More information about PolSenior2 can be found here: https://polsenior2.gumed.edu.pl/.

individual's health and the household structure. Individuals observed in different chronological time periods but on the same age scale are grouped into a synthetic cohort. The effects found in the estimated model should be then interpreted as average effects observed for the 2005–2015 period.

The EU-SILC data is based on a nationally representative probability sample of the population residing in private households within the country. The representative probability samples are achieved both for households, which form the basic units of sampling, data collection and data analysis, and for individual persons in the target population (European Commission, 2016). The reference population of the EU-SILC is restricted to private households, therefore persons living in collective households and in institutions are excluded from the analysis. The longitudinal component of the database pertains to individual-level changes over time and is realised through a rotational panel.[63] Figure 21 illustrates the idea of the rotational design after the system is fully established. The sample for every single year consists of four replications, which have been in the survey for one to four years. Any particular replication remains in the survey for four consecutive years. Each year, one of the four replications from the previous year, the one with the longest history in the sample, is exchanged for a new one. Consequently, the sample overlap between year T and T+1 is 75 %. For every additional year the overlap is reduced: between year T and year T+2 it is equal to 50 % and from year T to year T+3 amount to 25 %. For longer intervals there is no overlap at all (European Commission, 2016).

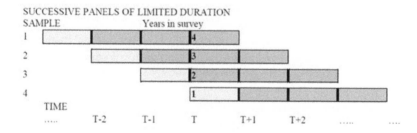

Figure 21. Rotational design in the EU-SILC longitudinal data.
Source: European Commission (2016, p. 21).

---

63   As per EU-SILC methodological guidelines: "Rotational design refers to the sample selection based on a number of subsamples or replications, each of them similar in size and design and representative of the whole population. From one year to the next, some replications are retained, while others are dropped and replaced by new replications" (European Commission, 2016, p. 19).

The main time variable is age in years at the time of interview available directly in the survey. Due to confidentiality reasons the oldest age group available in the EU-SILC is 80 years and over which is a limitation from both research and technical standpoint. The oldest individuals are classified as having the same age over the four years of observation. To overcome the technical problem, it is possible to extend age in years into age in quarters using information on year and quarter of birth and year and quarter of a personal interview or year and quarter when a person died. Therefore, dataset allows analysing age with one-year age groups with the last (open) age group being 83 years and more. More information on the calculations and the data preparation assumptions can he found in the Appendix. This transformation allows multistate modelling techniques to be applied to the data, however, does not solve the problem of the last aggregated age group that still has to be treated as an average for the oldest individuals.

The interviews take place at yearly intervals for up to four years. There is some variation in time between interviews since some individual interviews have not been conducted in exactly one-year intervals and some respondents missed one or more planned interviews. For example, the following ages: 60, 60.75, 62 and 63 years may have been recorded for a person followed for four years. In such a case, the intervals between subsequent interviews were 0.75 (three-quarters), 1.25 (one year and a quarter) and 1 year, respectively. The distribution of the length of time intervals in the sample is presented in the left panel of Figure 22. Interval equal to 0.25 means that there was a time distance of one-quarter between the last interview and the next encounter (death in this case). The mean length of interval was 1.01 years as 89 % of all length of intervals was equal to one year. The other 9 % amounted to either 0.75 or 1.25 years. The longest time interval observed in the sample was 3.25 years (two respondents missed two middle interviews). The total number of respondents in the database was 43,962. More than half of them, that is, 22,718 were interviewed four times, 9,784 were interviewed three times and 11,460 were interviewed twice (compare the right panel of Figure 22). There were 1,667 transitions to absorbing state ('dead') recorded.

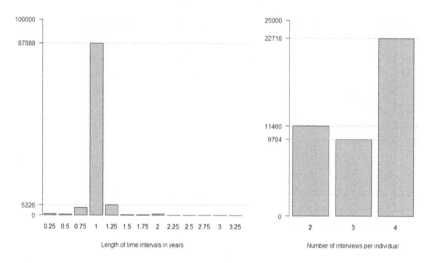

Figure 22. Description of the final EU-SILC sample.
Source: Own elaboration based on the EU-SILC data.

3.5 The multistate models for health and living arrangements dynamics

To study the dynamics of health and living arrangements I use the continuous-time multistate survival model. The specification and estimation of the model is determined by the panel design of the EU-SILC longitudinal dataset. The event is defined as a change either in a living arrangement state or a health state. In the panel setting the event is interval-censored as it occurred in a time interval with known lower and upper bounds (age at interviews) but at an unknown time within the interval. The model is regarded as a continuous-time model since changes of a state are allowed at any time. Additionally, I model transitions to death which are treated to be known at the exact time. Including transitions to death, an absorbing state, transforms the multistate model into the multistate survival model.

The two main attributes of interest are health and living arrangements. The state space of the multistate model depends on the number of states defined. The model with transition to death only is a two-state model. It is estimated to provide a reference for mortality intensities used in more elaborated models. Models defined with only one attribute, either health or living arrangements, are the three-state models. The final model is defined by a combination of dichotomous health and living arrangements variables, which gives a total of four living states, plus a dead state. Consequently, five states in this model are identified.

The multistate modelling approach allows multiple transitions to be modelled jointly but single transitions can come with different specifications at the same time. The advantage of the approach will be used in this study since both changes in health and changes in living arrangements of the population of older people are modelled together with survival. According to van den Hout (2017): "In many investigations in biostatistics, survival is not of primary interest but it may be that statistical modelling has to take into account dropout due to death because it is associated with the process of interest. For example, dropout due to death cannot be ignored when older people are followed up with respect to a process that is associated with ageing. In such a situation there is a need for a joint model for the process of interest and survival." Both health and living arrangements of older people are associated with ageing as was shown in Chapter 2. Therefore, modelling both processes together with survival is justified.

In the beginning, I concentrate on the simplest two-state model that assumes one living state and a dead state. This model of human mortality is well described with the Gompertz hazard. Once its specification is selected, it is used unchangeably for mortality in all other models. Any modification in the other models concerns only the process of interest, either living arrangement dynamics or health dynamics. The transition to death is kept constant to be able to compare and select the best model solely with regard to the process under study. The effects of additional covariates in the overall model are thus evaluated in isolation from survival.

The three-state health model is a traditional illness-death model in older ages. The states correspond to the current health status and dead state (the absorbing state) (see Figure 23). Health is operationalised with the concept of activity limitations measured via the Global Activity Limitation Indicator (GALI) which captures the presence of long-standing activity limitation due to health problems.[64] The individual's health status is classified into two possible states of being healthy or functionally disabled (unhealthy) based on the GALI question. To be classified into the unhealthy state one has to report severe limitation in

---

64   It is measured with the question: *For at least the past 6 months, to what extent have you been limited because of a health problem in activities people usually do? Would you say you have been ...*

    1. Severely limited 2. Limited but not severely, or 3. Not limited at all?
    More details are presented in Chapter 2 and in the Appendix.

activities. The healthy state is defined as being either not limited at all (no declared limitations) or limited but not severely in activities people usually do. The limitation-based definition of disability is used in the literature and the approach developed can be adjusted to capture other dimensions of health (Hanewald et al., 2017). The deterioration of health in the older population is assumed to be reversible. An individual may experience multiple transitions between living states, that is, one's health may decline but also recover more than once.

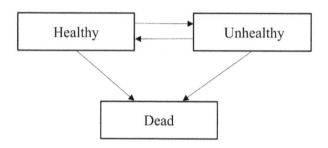

Figure 23. The three-state model of health.
Source: Own elaboration.

Table 11 summarises the multistate data on health. There are 99,182 transitions observed in total out of which 1,667 are transitions to death. The numbers on the diagonal of the table inform how many times each health status was repeated in the next interview. The off-diagonal numbers show how often a change in individual's health status was observed. Changing health status is much less frequent than maintaining the same health status. Health deterioration (transitions from *Healthy* to *Unhealthy*) is observed 4,567 times in the sample which is about 50 % more frequent than health improvement (transitions from *Unhealthy* to *Healthy*).

Table 11. Number of transitions between health states at successive observation times

From	To		
	Healthy	**Unhealthy**	**Dead**
Healthy	81,171	4,567	984
Unhealthy	2,961	8,816	683

Source: Own elaboration based on the EU-SILC data.

Figure 24 depicts possible states and transitions in the three-state model of living arrangements. The living arrangements are operationalised dichotomously and are split into living alone (one-person household) and living with others (not living alone/ two-or-more-persons household). Similar to the health model, return transitions between living states are allowed.

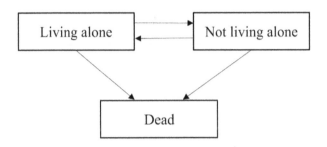

Figure 24. The three-state model of living arrangements.
Source: Own elaboration.

In the dichotomous setting of living alone versus not living alone (i.e. living with others) there are 2,825 transitions that correspond to change in living arrangements states (Table 12), but only 1,158 of them are between living states. The transitions from *Not living alone* to *Living alone* are more than four time more frequent than in the opposite direction. It is also worth noticing that almost no transitions to death from *Living alone* are notified. It presumably results from the fact that there is usually no household to follow once individual living alone dies and no information on death is recorded. As a consequence of small frequencies, transition to death will have to be modelled jointly, without distinction of the state of origin.[65]

Table 12. Number of transitions between living arrangements states (the narrow definition) at successive observation times

From	To		
	Living alone	**Not living alone**	**Dead**
Living alone	14,664	204	2
Not living alone	954	81,693	1,665

Source: Own elaboration based on the EU-SILC data

---

65   It is rather not a serious negligence as living alone is found not to have a detrimental influence on survival (Davis et al., 1997).

It is clear that allowing only two possible states of living arrangements is a strong simplification of the real process. In the research, there are much broader classifications of living arrangements that include not only the size of the household but also the relationship between the household members and/or their household position. It is important in the context of providing care for older people, particularly considering the presence of a partner or child(ren) in the household. The EU-SILC dataset allows identification of a spouse/a partner and a mother/a father relationship directly, but many other relationships cannot be distinguished (more details can be found in Iacovou and Skew (2011)). Estimation of model with a more detailed state space would refine the analysis but is difficult to proceed mainly because of small number of occurrences. For example, in the alternative broader definition of living arrangements four basic categories that represent transient states have been selected: (1) living alone, (2) living with partner/spouse only, (3) living with partner/spouse and others (non-relatives and/or other relative) and (4) living without partner/spouse but with others. The total number of 5,454 between-states transitions in this broader definition of living arrangements are shown in Table 13. In general, mobility between the distinguished states is very low, much lower when compared to changes in health status. In most cases individuals remain in the same household composition from one year to another. There are only several transitions from the living alone state to other states except to living without partner/spouse but with others. The small number of observed transitions between some pairs of states leads to decision to apply the narrower definition of living arrangements in this study.

Table 13. The number of transitions between living arrangements states (the broad definition) at successive observation times

From living	*To living*				
	alone	**with partner/ spouse only**	**with partner/ spouse and others**	**without partner/ spouse but with others**	**Dead**
Alone	14,664	52	6	146	2
with partner/ spouse only	467	31,912	290	225	620
with partner/ spouse and others	16	1,500	32,486	484	461
without partner/ spouse but with others	471	59	71	14,666	584

Source: Own elaboration based on the EU-SILC data.

The possible states and transitions in the final five-state model are shown in Figure 25. The identified living states are *Healthy & Living alone* (State 1), *Unhealthy & Living alone* (State 2), *Healthy & Not living alone* (State 3) and *Unhealthy & Not living alone* (State 4). They are accompanied by the dead state (State 5). One needs to note that not all transitions between transient states are possible. Although direct transition from *Healthy & Living alone* (State 1) to *Unhealthy & Not living alone* (State 4) is possible in practice, the model is restricted by assuming that this transition always goes via other states, either through health decline (State 2) or by change in living arrangements (State 3). State 2 and State 3 are connected in the same manner. Such an assumption makes model more parsimonious and the estimation easier.

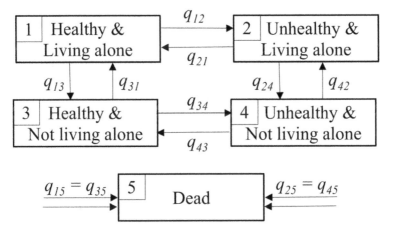

Figure 25. The five-state model of health and living arrangements.
Source: Own elaboration.

In the final state space of the joint model defined by a combination of dichotomous health and living arrangements variables the total number of transitions between different states amounts to 10,235 (compare Table 14). The most moves between different states are recorded for changes in the health states. The least frequent transitions are observed between the *Living alone* to *Not living alone* states.

Table 14. Number of transitions between health & living arrangements states at successive observation times

From	To				
	Healthy & Living alone	Unhealthy & Living alone	Healthy & Not living alone	Unhealthy & Not living alone	Dead
Healthy & Living alone	11,239	995	152	18	1
Unhealthy & Living alone	557	1,873	9	25	1
Healthy & Not living alone	767	49	69,013	3,505	983
Unhealthy & Not living alone	42	96	2,353	6,822	682

Source: Own elaboration based on the EU-SILC data.

The model selection starts from the time-homogeneous exponential hazard model given by formula (4). In the next step, a time dependency is introduced. In order to find the shape of the relationship of transition rates with age I use a piecewise-constant hazard model. It represents a non-parametric approach for which the hazard is constant within specified time intervals but is allowed to change between the intervals. The piecewise-constant hazard model can be used when a hazard cannot be described well by a parametric shape. A disadvantage is that the number of parameters increases quickly with the increase of the number of transition-specific hazards in the multistate model (van den Hout, 2017). In this study, I use this approach to test the parametric model fit to the empirical shape reflected in the piecewise-constant model.

Next, the transitions between living states are added with covariate information using a forward selection. The sex of the respondent is defined as 0 for males and 1 for females. There are three levels of education distinguished based on the ISCED codes: low (ISCED = {1,2}), medium (ISCED = {3,4}) and high (ISCED = {5}). The educational level may be considered as an indicator of a socio-economic status and, therefore, a proxy for income resources. The three-state health model is also checked with living arrangements variable and, likewise, the three-state living arrangements model is extended with health. The dichotomous variable indicating if a person reached the 80+ age group (0 if not, 1 if yes) is also verified for the living arrangements model.

The multistate models are estimated with the R statistical software version 3.6.0 (R Core Team, 2019) using *msm* package (Jackson, 2011) that allows a general multistate model to be fitted to longitudinal data. The time scale is age transformed by subtracting 50 years. Given the youngest individual at baseline is 50 years old, this results in 0 as the minimum age in the data analysis.

3.6 The multistate models: Estimation results

At first, the specification of a transition to death is set up. The baseline model is exponential with no covariates that assumes constant death rate across all age groups. The model has AIC = 16,981.4. In the beginning, it is extended with age dependency parametrised in line with the Gompertz distribution (formula 6). Then, additional covariates are included one by one. Table 15 summarises the comparison of the models. Adding the exponentially increasing age dependency into the model is crucial as it provides the biggest improvement in AIC. Every additional covariate in the model improves it further. The final form of the transition to death model is given by:

$$q_D(age) = \lambda_D \exp(\gamma_D age)\exp(\beta_{D.1}sex + \beta_{D.2}health + \beta_{D.3}edu_{medium} + \beta_{D.4}edu_{high}) \tag{8}$$

where q_D denotes the hazard (intensity) for transition to death, λ_D represents baseline hazards (intercept) for the transition, γ_D stands for the shape of the age effect in Gompertz model, and $\beta_{D.i}$ is the transition-specific effect for covariate i.

Table 15. Akaike's Information Criterion for the transition to death model specification

Model specification	No. of parameters	$-2\log(L_{max})$	AIC
Intercept-only	1	16,979.4	16,981.4
Age	2	15,848.2	15,852.2
age, sex	3	15,589.8	15,595.8
age, sex, health	4	15,133.5	15,141.5
age, sex, health, education	6	15,080.8	15,092.8

Source: Own elaboration based on the EU-SILC data.

The estimated parameters confirm the well-known regularities (see Table 16). Mortality is sex-specific; women experience lower mortality in comparison to men. Adding health dimension (severe limitations *versus* no or not severe limitations) also improves the model. Unhealthy individuals have on average three times higher the odds of transitions to death than healthy individuals.

Education plays the important role as well. The medium and high education levels reduce mortality when compared to the low education. The education gradient is clear as having the higher level of education has more positive effect on risk of death than having the medium level of education only.

Table 16. Parameter estimates for the transition to death model

	Estimate		Odds ratio		95 % confidence interval
Intercept (baseline hazard)	λ_D	0.0022			(0.0018; 0.0026)
Age	γ_D	0.071	$\exp(\gamma_D)$	1.074	(1.068; 1.080)
sex: female	$\beta_{D.1}$	-0.853	$\exp(\beta_{1D})$	0.426	(0.386; 0.471)
health: unhealthy	$\beta_{D.2}$	1.119	$\exp(\beta_{2D})$	3.062	(2.766; 3.389)
education: medium	$\beta_{D.3}$	-0.326	$\exp(\beta_{3D})$	0.722	(0.647; 0.805)
education: high	$\beta_{D.4}$	-0.635	$\exp(\beta_{4D})$	0.530	(0.430; 0.654)

Reference categories: male, healthy, low education. Age variable in years minus 50.
Source: Own elaboration based on the EU-SILC data.

The transition to death model will be further used in other models as the specification for the mortality transition. It will be modelled with age, sex and level of education as covariates since all three were found significant. I will extend the model forward by adding explanatory variables singularly so that the covariate's net effect on transitions between living states is measured. Given the significant health status impact on survival, in a three-state health model the transitions to death from different health states will be modelled separately. It is expected that the transition rates from the unhealthy state will exceed those estimated for the other transition. The three-state living arrangements model will assume the same survival transition specification for both transitions because there are too little observations of transitions to death from living alone to estimate it separately.

The three-state health model

Now, I distinguish two living states, the healthy state and the unhealthy state, from the previously single alive state. Before getting to the results a verification of the relation between the intensities and age (the age-homogeneity assumption) is required. In the first step no parametric form of hazard has been assumed a priori. Instead, in order to approximate the hazard's shape the piecewise-constant hazard approach is used. It keeps the hazard constant within predefined intervals but allows it to differ between them. Intervals of length of 10 years, 5 years and 2.5 years isolating the oldest, open age group are used for comparison. The piecewise-constant hazard with 10 years interval (the solid red line in Figure 26) reflects the increasing intensity for the from *Healthy* to *Unhealthy* transition (left panel) and the decreasing intensity for the reverse transition (right panel). The narrower intervals are more flexible, closer to real pattern but more volatile at the same time. However, both the 5-year (dotted green) and 2.5-year (dot-dashed blue) lines follow the same patterns for respective transitions. The age dependence of health transition is well approximated by the Gompertz model (solid black). The risk of health improvement declines with age while the hazard of health deterioration is growing with age and the change for the considered age span is exponential.

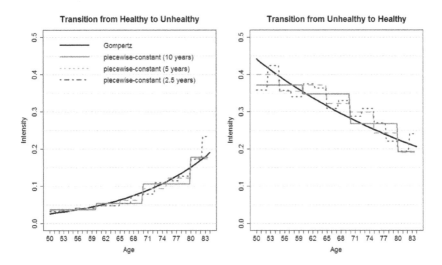

Figure 26. Intensities of health transitions by age with piecewise-constant hazards and in the Gompertz model.

Source: Own elaboration based on EU-SILC data.

Given the exponential shape of the relationship of health dynamics with age, the transitions between living states are modelled with the Gompertz model (formula 6). Taking into account the age dependency in the model improves it a lot which is documented with the change in AIC (Table 17) and highly significant results of the likelihood ratio test (Table 18). Extending the health model with further covariates makes it better as AIC gets lower. The most improvement comes from the extra variable of education. From the point of statistical tests, the relationship between health and education is much stronger than the corresponding health and sex relationship (p-value = 0.0168 in the LR test, the lowest among the covariates tested). Living arrangements defined as *Living alone* versus *Not living alone* is also contributing to the health dynamics representation. The association between health and living arrangements is strong enough to influence the transition intensity between *Healthy* and *Unhealthy* states.

Table 17. Akaike's Information Criterion for the three-state health model specification

Model	Model specification	No. of parameters	$-2\log(L_{max})$	AIC
H0	Intercept-only	12	64,017.9	64,041.9
H1	age	14	62,329.3	62,357.3
H2	age, sex	16	62,321.1	62,353.1
H3	age, sex, liv. arrangements	18	62,306.0	62,342.0
H4	age, sex, liv. arrangements, education	22	62,170.4	62,214.4

Source: Own elaboration based on the EU-SILC data.

Table 18. Results of the likelihood ratio test for each additional covariate in the three-state health model specification

Test	Covariate added	Δ (-2 log LR)	Δdf	P
H1 vs H0	+ age	1,688.6	2	<0.0001
H2 vs H1	+ sex	8.2	2	0.0168
H3 vs H2	+ living arrangements	15.1	2	0.0005
H4 vs H3	+ education	135.6	4	<0.0001

Source: Own elaboration based on the EU-SILC data.

The final three-state health model with age, sex, living arrangements and education as covariates is given by the following formula:

$$q_{rs}(age) = \lambda_{rs}\exp(\gamma_{rs}age)\exp$$
$$(\beta_{rs.1}sex + \beta_{rs.2}liv.arr + \beta_{rs.3}edu_{medium} + \beta_{rs.4}edu_{high})$$

$$\text{for}(r,s) \in \{(Healthy, Unhealthy),(Unhealthy, Healthy)\}$$

$$q_{rs}(age) = \lambda_{rs} \exp(\gamma_{rs} age) \exp(\beta_{rs.1} sex + \beta_{rs.3} edu_{medium} + \beta_{rs.4} edu_{high})$$

$$\text{for}(r,s) \in \{(Healthy, Dead),(Unhealthy, Dead)\}. \qquad (9)$$

The estimated parameters are presented in Table 19. The baseline intensities for the 50-year-olds start with much different values for both transitions, with intensity of health improvement (from *Unhealthy to Healthy*) much exceeding the intensity of health decrement (from *Healthy to Unhealthy*). From age 50 onwards the hazard of becoming severely limited is increasing with age while the hazard of recovery from severe limitations is decreasing with age. The rate of health deterioration is higher than the rate of health improvement. The effect of sex is also transition-specific. The transition from *Healthy to Unhealthy* is on average lower for women than for men. For the transition from *Unhealthy to Healthy* the effect is of the opposite direction. The model estimate suggests the higher intensity to recover from severe limitations for women than for men.[66] The association between health and living arrangements is statistically significant only in case of the *Healthy* to *Unhealthy* transition. Older persons living with others have 15 % lower odds of becoming severely limited when compared to older persons living alone. The effect of education is strong and clearly positive. The higher the education of older adult, the lower the transition rates to become unhealthy (protective effect). On the other end, medium and high education improve the chances to return from severe limitation to better health status when compared to low education.

---

66   Such results are counterintuitive as it could be expected that women have a higher intensity to become unhealthy than men. One potential explanation would be linked to the definition of health status. Currently, *Healthy* means having no or not severe limitations in activities while *Unhealthy* stands for having severe limitations. Hypothetically, women could be more prone to report any limitation (either not severe or severe) versus no limitation than men but this is not captured with the definition used in the study. The fact that the results are sensitive to the health definition would be supported by a higher intensity of becoming unhealthy for women relative to men found for the study based on the same data source but with the different health definition referring to chronic morbidity (Łątkowski, 2015).

Table 19. Parameter estimates for the three-state health model

Transition	Baseline intensities		Hazard ratios for each covariate									
			Age		sex: female		not living alone		education: medium		education: high	
Healthy – Unhealthy	0.047	(0.039; 0.057)	1.053	(1.050; 1.057)	0.927	(0.870; 0.986)	0.849	(0.787; 0.916)	0.822	(0.768; 0.879)	0.596	(0.526; 0.676)
Healthy – Dead	0.006	(0.005; 0.008)	1.077	(1.067; 1.086)	0.336	(0.285; 0.397)	1.000		0.619	(0.521; 0.736)	0.513	(0.380; 0.692)
Unhealthy – Healthy	0.363	(0.289; 0.455)	0.979	(0.975; 0.983)	1.138	(1.054; 1.229)	1.020	(0.926; 1.123)	1.107	(1.019; 1.202)	1.440	(1.248; 1.662)
Unhealthy – Dead	0.027	(0.020; 0.036)	1.057	(1.046; 1.068)	0.568	(0.485; 0.665)	1.000		0.920	(0.774; 1.093)	0.699	(0.486; 1.004)

Reference categories: male, living alone, low education. Age variable in years minus 50. Estimated 95 % confidence intervals in parentheses.
Source: Own calculations based on EU-SILC data.

The three-state living arrangements model

The analysis of the three-state model for living arrangements is performed in the same manner as for health. The results of the age dependency estimation in the three-state living arrangements model can be inspected in Figure 27. When considering the transition from *Living alone* to *Not living alone* the intensities are showing a decreasing trend with age. However, in the ages 80 and over there is a trend reversal suggesting that adults in the oldest age group have slightly higher chances to move from the *Living alone* state to *Not living alone* state than older adults in their seventies. On the contrary, the transition to solitary living is characterised by the increasing hazard with age. A significant increase is observed when seniors reach their seventies. Presumably, it is related to the highest frequency of deaths among men in that ages and women (mostly, but men too) becoming widows. However, in the last age group of 80 years and more the intensities are lower relative to intensities experienced by 70-year-olds. It can be concluded that the transition-specific hazards are time-dependent. The Gompertz parametric model fits relatively well to the shape of hazard with some disturbances in the last age groups. For the oldest individuals transition rates into *Not living alone* are underestimated, while into *Living alone* transition rates are overestimated. To estimate the effects of covariates I will therefore use the parametric Gompertz model with an additional dummy variable for the last age group.

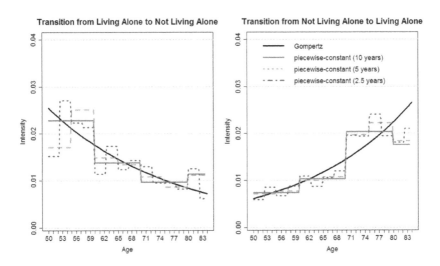

Figure 27. Intensities of living arrangements transitions by age with piecewise-constant hazards and in the Gompertz model.

Source: Own elaboration based on the EU-SILC data.

The evolution of the three-state living arrangements model specification is summarised in Tables 20 and 21. Both criteria, AIC and likelihood ratio test, confirm the significant age dependency of the hazard. Also, there can be identified the impact of sex that differenciates the living arrangement dynamics. However, the next two covariates, health status and level of education, do not provide any improvement into the model (greater AIC than in the reference L2 model; no substantial log-likelihood differential between L2 and the tested L3 and L4 models). Such results suggest that there is no significant effect of either health status or education level on the hazard between *Living alone* and *Not living alone* states. In the last step, the variable indicating the 80+ age group was tested. Its influence on the living arrangements dynamics proved to be meaningful. As a result, the variable was included in the model. The formula for the selected three-state living arrangements model is provided below:

$$q_{rs}(age) = \lambda_{rs}\exp(\gamma_{rs}age)\exp(\beta_{rs.1}sex + \beta_{rs2}age80+)$$

$$for\,(r,s) \in \{(Living\,alone, Not\,living\,alone),$$

$$(Not\,living\,alone, Living\,alone)\} \tag{10}$$

$$q_{rs}(age) = \lambda_D\exp(\gamma_D age)\exp(\beta_{D.1}sex + \beta_{D.2}edu_{medium} + \beta_{D.3}edu_{high})$$

$$for\,(r,s) \in \{(Living\,alone, Dead), (Not\,living\,alone, Dead)\}.$$

As reminder, the transition to death is modelled jointly for both living states. No health covariate is included due to lack of observations from *Living alone* to *Dead*.

Table 20. Akaike's Information Criterion for the three-state living arrangements model specification

Model	Model specification	No. of parameters	$-2\log(L_{max})$	AIC
L0	Intercept-only	7	28,068.0	28,082.0
L1	Age	9	27,873.9	27,891.9
L2	age, sex	11	27,715.3	27,737.3
L3	age, sex, health	13	27,713.6	27,739.6
L4	age, sex, health, education	17	27,712.3	27,746.3
L5	age, sex, health, education, age80+	19	27,700.2	27,738.2
L6	age, sex, age80+	13	27,701.5	27,727.5

Source: Own elaboration based on EU-SILC data.

Table 21. Results of the likelihood ratio test for each additional covariate in the three-state living arrangements model specification

Test	Covariate added	Δ (-2 log LR)	Δdf	P
L1 vs L0	+ age	194.1	2	<0.0001
L2 vs L1	+ sex	158.5	2	<0.0001
L3 vs L2	+ health	1.7	2	0.4256
L4 vs L3	+ education	1.4	4	0.8488
L5 vs L4	+ age80+	12.1	2	0.0024
L6 vs L2	+ age80+	13.9	2	0.0010

Source: Own elaboration based on EU-SILC data.

The estimated parameters show that the intensities between the living arrangements states are much lower when compared to intensities observed in the health model (compare the vertical axis between Figures 26 and 27). The baseline values start from considerably lower levels indicating that the process of changing living arrangements is less dynamic than the health change process. It corresponds to the number of transitions observed in the data (compare the off-diagonals of 2×2 subtables of Tables 11 and 12). The effect of age on the transition hazard depends on the type of transition. The hazard from *Living alone* to *Not living alone* is a decreasing one, while it is increasing for the opposite transition. The effect of sex is systematically indifferent for the *Living alone* to *Not living alone* transition. The move from *Not living alone* to solitary living is more than twice more frequent for females than for males. Again, it is presumably due to excessive mortality pattern among males. The last considered covariate, the 80+ age group indicator, does not impact the intensity to transition from *Living alone* to *Not living alone*. But, it has a statistically significant effect on the transition to *Living alone*. It means that indeed, the transition rates follow the increasing trend, but after the age 80 threshold this trend changes. It is not clear with the data at hand whether it stabilises or reverts to a decrease but the trend is certainly interrupted.

Table 22. Parameter estimates for the three-state living arrangements model

Transition	Baseline intensities		Hazard ratios for each covariate								
			age		sex: female		education: medium		education: high		age: 80 and above
Living alone – Not living alone	0.031	(0.022; 0.043)	0.959	(0.941; 0.977)	0.836	(0.614; 1.139)	1.000		1.000		1.226 (0.696; 2.161)
Living alone – Dead	0.007	(0.006; 0.008)	1.088	(1.082; 1.095)	0.425	(0.385; 0.470)	0.696	(0.624; 0.776)	0.481	(0.390; 0.594)	1.000
Not living alone – Living alone	0.003	(0.003; 0.004)	1.051	(1.043; 1.060)	2.409	(2.085; 2.782)	1.000		1.000		0.647 (0.501; 0.836)
Not living alone – Dead	0.007	(0.006; 0.008)	1.088	(1.082; 1.095)	0.425	(0.385; 0.470)	0.696	(0.624; 0.776)	0.481	(0.390; 0.594)	1.000

Reference categories: male, low education, in 50–79 age group. Age variable in years minus 50. Estimated 95 % confidence intervals in parentheses.
Source: Own calculations based on EU-SILC data.

The five-state joint model of health and living arrangements

In the final model I deliberately do not incorporate additional characteristics besides age and sex. It is explained by the fact that the final population projection extends the traditional projections with two additional attributes of interest: health and living arrangements which are included in the state space. The estimates of parameters of the final model allow the population projection to be produced with the use of microsimulation techniques and the data at hand. They will serve as the input for the preparation of projections in Chapter 4. Extending the model further would require even more information on the population structure, namely its distribution by education, and relative morality risks by education. They are not pursued in the current investigation.

The results of the final five-state model that contains health and living arrangements states are presented in Table 23. The age dependency parametrised as Gompertz is statistically significant for all transitions except for the *Unhealthy & Living alone* to *Unhealthy & Not living alone* (q_{24}) and the *Unhealthy & Not living alone* to *Unhealthy & Living alone* (q_{42}) transitions. The lack of significance is driven by limited occurrences of those transitions in the data. However, the direction of the effects is the same as in the three-state living arrangements model – the transition from *Not living alone* to *Living alone* shows an upward trend and a downward trend for the opposite direction transition is observed. As far as the dynamics of the health process are considered, the risk of becoming unhealthy is increasing with age while the risk of health improvement is declining. It is consistent with the three-state health model findings. The effect of sex is also found important. Women's risk of moving to *Living alone* state is about twice as high as for men. Women have also lower odds of changing their living arrangements to living with others once they report being healthy (significant at p < 0.10).

Table 23. Parameter estimates for the five-state joint model

Transition	Baseline intensities		Hazard ratios for each covariate			
			Age		sex: female	
FROM **Healthy & Living alone** TO:						
Unhealthy & Living alone	0.029	(0.023; 0.036)	1.059	(1.051; 1.068)	1.050	(0.898; 1.228)
Healthy & Not living alone	0.032	(0.022; 0.045)	0.961	(0.944; 0.978)	0.768	(0.545; 1.080)

(Continued)

Table 23. Continued

Dead	0.004	(0.003; 0.005)	1.088	(1.078; 1.097)	0.341	(0.288; 0.403)
FROM Unhealthy & Living alone TO:						
Healthy & Living alone	0.326	(0.254; 0.417)	0.986	(0.976; 0.995)	1.227	(0.988; 1.523)
Unhealthy & Not living alone	0.022	(0.008; 0.065)	0.975	(0.934; 1.019)	1.039	(0.426; 2.533)
Dead	0.026	(0.020; 0.033)	1.057	(1.046; 1.067)	0.576	(0.492; 0.673)
FROM Healthy & Not living alone TO:						
Healthy & Living alone	0.003	(0.003; 0.004)	1.049	(1.042; 1.057)	2.571	(2.186; 3.024)
Unhealthy & Not living alone	0.028	(0.025; 0.030)	1.058	(1.054; 1.062)	0.939	(0.877; 1.005)
Dead	0.004	(0.003; 0.005)	1.088	(1.078; 1.097)	0.341	(0.288; 0.403)
FROM Unhealthy & Not living alone TO:						
Unhealthy & Living alone	0.009	(0.005; 0.014)	1.010	(0.991; 1.030)	1.680	(1.144; 2.468)
Healthy & Not living alone	0.439	(0.403; 0.477)	0.975	(0.971; 0.979)	1.082	(0.997; 1.176)
Dead	0.026	(0.020; 0.033)	1.057	(1.046; 1.067)	0.576	(0.492; 0.673)

Reference category: male. Age variable in years minus 50. Estimated 95 % confidence intervals in parentheses.
Source: Own elaboration based on the EU-SILC data.

The joint model validation

Validation of time-inhomogeneous models based on interval-censored data is not an easy task. It can be done by comparing the expected state prevalence versus the observed one, although it should be treated as a heuristic tool. It does not provide an objective measure of how well or badly the model fits the data (van den Hout, 2017).

The estimated five-state model works pretty well for the prevalence in State 1 (*Healthy & Living alone*) and State 2 (*Unhealthy & Living alone*) through all the ages considered (see Figure 28). The mapping of the expected to the observed prevalence in State 3 (*Healthy & Not living alone*) and State 4 (*Unhealthy & Not living alone*) is not as good. The model underestimates prevalence of *Healthy & Not living alone* systematically for ages 65 and above. For *Unhealthy & Not living alone* the mismatch starts at age 70 and this underestimation increases. The model looks particularly bad at the survival prediction, especially at older ages. The gap between the expected and observed prevalence is increasing with age, highly overestimating the prevalence of deaths among 70-year-olds and older.

If we compared the full (five-state) model with the model without death (four-state) the estimated baseline hazards and covariate effects are very close to each other (compare Figure 29). There is also a difference between the observed and expected counts: the model still underestimates the prevalence for State 3 (*Healthy & Not living alone*) and State 4 (*Unhealthy & Not living alone*), but the difference declines, while the overestimation occurs for State 2 (*Unhealthy & Living alone*). However, the overall mismatch is smaller. It is some reinforcement of the model quality since it is less a concern to model survival precisely. The estimated transition rates to death will not be used directly in the microsimulation model for the population projection. They will be replaced with the parameters fitted to the prospective death rates from the official mortality assumptions.

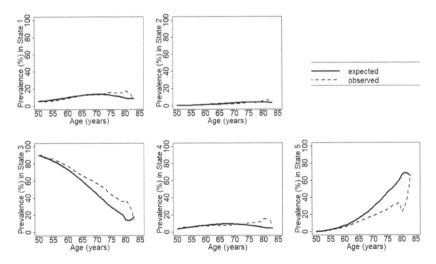

Figure 28. The observed prevalence in the five-state model compared with predicted prevalence.

Source: Own elaboration based on EU-SILC data.

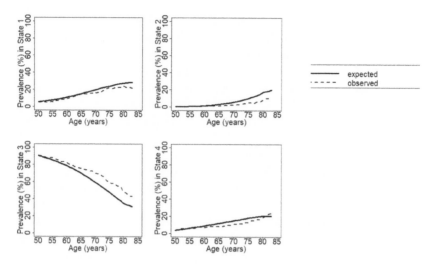

Figure 29. The observed prevalence in the four-state model (without the absorbing state – death) compared with the predicted prevalence.

Source: Own elaboration based on EU-SILC data.

3.7 Discussion

The goal of this chapter was to characterise the dynamics of living arrangements and health status of people aged 50 and over in Poland. The focus was on the transitions and the resulting changes in the health and living arrangements states rather than mechanisms underlying them. Changes in health and living arrangements were modelled as the continuous Markov process with the use of multistate models. Both attributes of interest were measured with dichotomous categories: healthy versus unhealthy for health status (dependent upon whether an individual reported severe limitations in activities) and living alone versus not living alone for living arrangements status. Both health and living arrangements dynamics were at first modelled individually with three-state models (dichotomous categories and death) to verify their association with age, sex and education. Then, both processes were combined into a five-state model to describe interrelationships between both processes. The specification of the final five-state model included age and sex as covariates and was dictated by the subsequent goal of the study, that is, to propel the microsimulation model for population projections by health and living arrangements status, presented in Chapter 4.

The basic finding is the shape of the hazard function itself which is the direct product of dynamic analysis of both health status and living arrangements status (compare Richards et al., 1987). The age-homogeneity assumption was rejected for both investigated processes using the piecewise-constant hazard approach. On the basis of the comparison with the non-parametric modelling results, it can be stated that both health and living arrangements are age-dependent and can be approximated with the Gompertz parametrisation. The intensity of moving to living alone is increasing with age (starting with the age 50 threshold) – with distortions at ages 80 and above, while the intensity of turning to living with others from solitary living is decreasing. It is in line with the U-shaped age pattern found in the rates of movement from most household types to living alone based on the United States historical data (Richards et al., 1987). The reversal of the declining pattern to the increasing one was found relevant to the 50 or over age group which coincides with the age group considered in the present study.

Similar findings pertain to health status. Chances for health improvement among people after age 50 are declining with age as opposed to the risk of health deterioration, which is increasing. It corroborates the conclusions of other studies that also find the increasing likelihood of experiencing disability and decreasing likelihood of recovery with age (e.g. Beckett et al., 1996; Chan et al., 2011 for Japan; Wolf et al., 2007; Wolf & Gill, 2009 for the United States). The same pattern is found in the study by Fong et al. (2015) who drew their analysis on the U.S.-based Health and Retirement Study (HRS) and classified functional disability if difficulty with two or more ADLs was reported. However, they find some distinct age patterns of recovery by sex as males face a decreasing rate of recovery with age, while females experience increasing risk of recovery up to about age 65 before it drops afterwards.

The current study has shown the influence of the covariates on the transition intensities. Females were found to have twice the higher intensity of moving from not living alone to solitary living than males. No gender effect was found for the transition in the opposite direction. The effect of sex on health transitions was found insignificant in the final model; however, the values of the estimated parameters suggested uncommon results of the lower risk of becoming disabled (when living with others) for females than males. The results found in the literature are consistently showing significantly higher rates of becoming disabled for women than men (Beckett et al., 1996; Chan et al., 2011; Fong et al., 2015). These empirical results suggest that the estimates can be sensitive to the definition of disability. In the earlier study also using the EU-SILC data (yet for less years of observation) but with a different definition of disability (based on chronic morbidity as the presence of long-standing health problems) females were experiencing the significantly higher risk of health deterioration than men (Łątkowski, 2015). Another covariate – education – was positively related with health as the better educated had higher intensities to recover and lower risks of becoming severely limited like in the study by Wolf and Gill (2009).[67] The effect of education on health was stronger than the impact of sex.

The results indicate that living arrangements of older adults are much more stable than their health status. According to the EU-SILC data used, a change in living arrangements is much more rare than a change in health status among older individuals. Other studies also show that living arrangements are fairly stable (Börsch-Supan et al., 1988), but it depends on the particular living arrangement under consideration as well as the age of the individual (Wilmoth, 1998).

It has to be mentioned that the analysis performed has some limitations. There are few limitations related directly to the data source used. Firstly, older persons living in institutions are not included in the sample which restricts the analysis to persons living in private households. Secondly, the aggregated information on age for the oldest age group (80 years and above) requires a simplifying assumption to enable estimation of transition rates at that ages. It distorts the illustration of true dynamics among the oldest individuals. Therefore, the results for older adults aged 80 and above, which would be extremely important to examine in the context of the observed trends in population ageing (double ageing), have to be treated as an average. The disaggregated information on one-year age groups would also be particularly useful to verify the age profile of living arrangements, that is, to confirm the increasing intensities to solitary living levelling off around age 80. Thirdly, the study does not allow precise timing of events to be observed and the rotational design of the panel does not allow individuals to be followed for longer than a 4-year period. Longer observation spans would be especially relevant to track living arrangements changes as they are more rare transitions than those related to health states. One-year time intervals are considered narrow in the context of social science studies in general; however, they are still relatively wide in the context of health dynamics. Studies on disability dynamics that use monthly data conclude that changes in health status are much more frequent than studies with wider time intervals (yearly or more) would indicate. Health status changes are volatile and comprise of shorter several months' episodes; therefore, higher frequency data is recommended. Models of transitions over

---

67   Wolf and Gill (2009) report that men and women in the lowest educational group have significantly higher chances of becoming disabled as compared with those better educated.

wide time intervals underestimate the number of brief disability episodes which poses a risk of inaccurate results when the estimated transition probabilities are later used to simulate individual-level disability trajectories (Hardy et al., 2005; Wolf & Gill, 2009).

Another important issue is duration dependence that is not addressed in the study, but might be relevant for both processes under investigation. Duration dependence is found an important predictor of transitions in living arrangements (Dostie & Leger, 2005; Richards et al., 1987) and is also discussed in recovery from disability (Wolf & Gill, 2009). Similar to Fong et al. (2015), it can be pointed at the limited time period of longitudinal data used in the analysis that makes it challenging to detect duration dependence of morbidity, recovery, and transitions in living arrangements.

The estimated transition rates reflect the dynamics of the health status and the living arrangements status of older population of Poland along the age scale. It has to be kept in mind that they represent the collective experience that have been observed in the past, as this study refers to the data from the period of 2005–2015. It can be argued, thus, that using these average results for any purpose of prediction replicates what have already happened rather than describes the future evolution of the process. Indeed, the estimates of transition rates based on the historical data incorporate the factors that have already influenced the process of health and living arrangements changes such us the up-to-date medical progress, health-related behaviours and policy, the economic situation (e.g. housing market, interest rates), etc. It is evident that the same circumstances will not happen ever again, therefore, such critic is valid. However, future is uncertain, and this statement applies to every case. Transition rates from the estimated model are well-suited to be a reference or a starting point for other forecasting exercises, for example, what-if scenarios, or sensitivity analyses. Obviously, there are many variables that influence the examined processes and they are difficult to foresee. The qualitative knowledge that allows formulating descriptive statements about the processes and their possible changes will have to be translated into quantitative assumptions regarding the parameters of the model.

Chapter 4. Projections of demand for care among older people in Poland

This part of the monograph refers to projections of demand for care among people aged 65 or over in Poland. The demand is defined by the number of persons with certain characteristics. Health and living arrangements are assumed to be the main indicative characteristics. Hence, I aim to predict the number of people in the selected health and living arrangements states by age and sex. The projection model proposed combines the population projections by age and sex with estimated transition intensities between health and living arrangements states among older adults as the input to microsimulations. The main output of simulations, that is, the number of people disaggregated into functional states is supplemented with life expectancies and subject to a sensitivity analysis.

The chapter starts with a basic terminology on population projections and explanations about microsimulation used as a method for population projections. Next, the simulation projection model is presented and followed by details about the input data and modelling assumptions. Further, I present and analyse the population projections in comparison with results of sensitivity tests. In conclusion, I summarise the results and discuss the pros and cons of the analytical approach used.

4.1 Population projections

4.1.1 A population projection versus a population forecast

To start with, I introduce terminology related to population projections. The key distinction is between two terms: a projection and a forecast. In demography, both terms refer to estimates published for future reference dates; however, they differ in the level of certainty conveyed (UNECE, 2017).

> *Population projections are calculations which show the future development of a population when certain assumptions are made about the future course of population change, usually with respect to fertility, mortality and migration. They are in general purely formal calculations, developing the implications of the assumptions that are made. A population forecast is a projection in which the assumptions are considered to yield a realistic picture of the probable future development of a population.* (Demopædia, 2010)

According to Wattelar (2006, p. 149), the term 'demographic projection' encompasses both a forecast understood as a short-term prediction of a population's size and its composition based on credible assumptions, and a projection referred more as a longer-term simulation that does not require immediate plausibility. Actually, it is the projection-makers' perception of the capacity to predict that distinguishes both terms – forecasts are more treated as predictions, while projections are not (UNECE, 2017). Historically, the terminology of official population predictions released by the U.S. Census Bureau moved from 'forecasts' in the late 1940s, through 'illustrative projections' in 1950s, to become 'projections' since 1960s. This evolution happened to be the result of "recognition of both the varying forecastability and the historical character of forecasting methodologies" (Alho & Spencer, 2005, p. 226). In the survey on population projections and their communication conducted in 2015 among National Statistical Offices (NSO) from 32 countries, most NSOs reported to use the term 'projection' instead of 'forecast' in their disseminations. Among the reasons stated was the desire to convey less certainty in the results provided by 'projections' (UNECE, 2017). Projections allow for a higher margin of uncertainty which is well summarised by Eurostat:

> The projections should not be considered as forecasts, as they show what would happen to the resulting population structure if the set of assumptions are held constant over the entire time horizon under consideration; in other words, the projections are 'what-if' scenarios that track population developments under a set of assumptions. As these projections are made over a relatively long time horizon, statements about the likely future developments for the EU's population should be taken with caution, and interpreted as only one of a range of possible demographic developments. (Eurostat, 2015, p. 158)

Given that a population projection is a statement about the future of a population it has to be based on a valid description of the various processes that govern the population system, that is, it must be based on a model (van Imhoff & Post, 1998). According to van Imhoff and Post (1998, p. 99): "all demographic projection models are simplified, quantitative descriptions of the processes that determine population structures." The most popular method to project future population developments is the cohort-component method. It is a system of demographic accounting that classifies population by sex and age, at a minimum, and exposes it to the three components of population changes, that is, fertility, mortality and migration, which are expressed by survivorship ratios, fertility rates and migration flows, throughout the projection time (Preston et al., 2001, pp. 119–129). Importantly, the problem of predicting population change is reduced to forecasting the dynamics of vital rates individually (Booth, 2006). Researchers stress importance of the past in predicting future. It is central not only for the extrapolation of the old trends but for the validation of predictions as well. As highlighted by Alho and Spencer (2005, p. 226): "Demographic forecasting is historical activity both in terms of methodology and accuracy: to forecast forward and to predict the accuracy of our forecast, we look backward."

Forecast/projection accuracy is indeed desired. However, studies show that the accuracy of the recent forecasts has not improved, even though the theoretical models used by the forecasters improve over time (Alho & Spencer, 2005; Keyfitz, 1982). Demographers who prepare forecasts are aware that any single prediction of a vital rate over time is probable to be off-target. Therefore, they routinely incorporate uncertainty into forecast by producing more predictions at a time with some indication of their associated probability (Tuljapurkar et al., 2004). Projections can be either deterministic or probabilistic. Recently, many demographers recommend turning to probabilistic projections to incorporate the uncertainty of the future:

> Probabilistic forecasts are necessary because the future is uncertain. There are many different possible futures, and some are more likely to come to pass than others. A probabilistic forecast, as opposed to a deterministic forecast, quantifies the uncertainty about future developments. While a probabilistic forecast is not necessarily more accurate than a deterministic forecast, the former contains more information, which is useful for planning purposes. (Keilman, 2018, p. 1)

The value of population projections is appreciated even though their results are highly uncertain. They fulfil their purpose by "drawing attention to looming public policy issues that would otherwise be neglected" (Alho & Spencer, 2005, p. 227) and nourishing public debate (Malenfant et al., 2012). In this sense Romaniuk (2010) advocates to speak about projections as a tool for managing the future rather than discovering it.

4.1.2 Microsimulation for population projections

Microsimulation modelling dates back to work by Orcutt (1957) who pioneered the use of such a model. The goal of the microsimulation model is to simulate the behaviour of micro-units over time, which often serves for the social and economic policy analysis (Li & O'Donoghue, 2013). In social science applications, the following definition of microsimulation is suggested: "microsimulation consists of drawing a sample of realizations of a prespecified stochastic process" (Wolf, 2001, p. 315). A microsimulation model combines deterministic rules with behavioural assumptions which usually are formulated as stochastic models (Klevmarken, 2008). Models can be formulated as static or dynamic. Static models are using individual's characteristics at one point in time and, therefore, do not incorporate characteristics' changes over time in the analysis. In contrast, dynamic models take the intertemporal perspective and use transition rates or probabilities to update individual characteristics from one period to another

(Zucchelli et al., 2012). In a dynamic model "the processes that underline the changes in the system variables should be explicitly included in the model" indicating how the system will evolve into the projection horizon (van Imhoff & Post, 1998, p. 101).

Microsimulation has the three basic features that distinguish it from a traditional macrosimulation: "the model uses a sample rather than the total population; it works on the level of individual data rather than grouped data; it relies on repeated random experiments rather than on average fractions" (van Imhoff & Post, 1998, p. 98). It must be kept in mind that although the goal of a simulation model is to imitate the real world, it actually cannot be reproduced. Because of the random nature of the process that is modelled in microsimulation, the projections are subject to random fluctuations.[68] Additionally, there are several sources of randomness that are microsimulation specific. Next to general sources of randomness such as variation from statistical inference, there is also: (1) inherent randomness (coming from the nature of simulation itself); (2) starting-population randomness (random variation of the initial sample (of total population) distribution); (3) specification randomness (measurement error + complexity punishment (bias)). It is thus advised to keep the microsimulation model specification as simple as possible (van Imhoff & Post, 1998).

From the point of view of data requirements, microsimulation is a data-intensive undertaking. The necessary data should serve the three different purposes: data for initial values to start individual simulations, data for estimation and data for validation. Ideally, a single longitudinal dataset should provide all the input, however, it is rarely possible (Klevmarken, 2008). The large-scale dynamic models commonly require incorporation of various data sources, both cross-sectional and panel data, which often refer to different samples and different time periods (Wolf, 2001).

Microsimulation modelling is becoming a more popular tool in social sciences that is used in many different applications. O'Donoghue (2001) comes up with a classification between multi-purpose and special-purpose models and provides the survey of dynamic microsimulation models, updated by Li and O'Donoghue (2013). Simulation modelling advancements are presented by Dekkers et al. (2014). The concise summary of the essentials of demographic microsimulation and the

---

68   This is well summarised by van Imhoff and Post (1998, p. 110): "Thus, a perfect conventional microsimulation model does not produce the expected value of the future population: rather, it produces a random number that has the same expected value as the future population."

historical overview of microsimulation models in demography is provided by van Imhoff and Post (1998). The review of existing dynamic microsimulation models that include a component on health is presented by Spielauer (2007) and Zucchelli et al. (2012). And the very recent microsimulation model focusing on health and care needs projections in England can be found in Kingston et al. (2018).

4.2 The simulation model for projections of the persons aged 65 and more by health status and living arrangements status

4.2.1 Overview of the simulation projection model

The simulation projection model exploited in this study is presented in Figure 30.

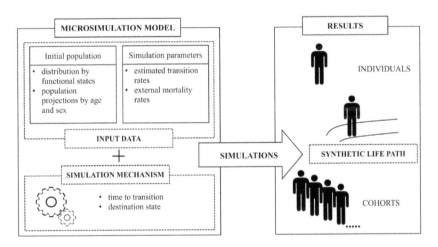

Figure 30. Schematic diagram of the simulation projection model.
Source: Own elaboration.

The microsimulation model consists of two building blocks: input data and simulation mechanism, that together allow simulation of individual synthetic life paths. There are two types of input data required. The first one refers to the initial population. It is a cross-sectional picture of the population of interest – the population composition by age and sex and functional states at the starting time point of the projection period, that is, the health status and the living arrangement status in this case. This type of data, if available, can be obtained from the official population statistics or population projections, prepared by relevant statistical agencies. However, if the population composition by some attributes is not accessible, other data sources are necessary, for example, surveys or administrative data. The second type of data required is the simulation parameters which describe behavioural rules that govern the process under study. They are depicted by parameters of the multistate model, that is, transition rates or transition probabilities. For the description of transitions to death prospective mortality rates from population projections can also be adopted. Simulation parameters are used to simulate synthetic lives over a time period defined for population projections. They constitute a matrix that replicates health and living arrangements changes throughout the simulated life paths accordingly.

Next to the input data, there is a toolkit needed to run microsimulation. It describes the sequence of events that stands behind the simulation procedure, namely how the time to transition and destination states are decided upon. The simulation procedure generates individual life trajectories with respect to health and living arrangements. They incorporate uncertainties stemming from the data used to estimate simulation parameters and uncertainties related to the microsimulation method (Monte Carlo variation).

The generated life histories can be analysed either from the individual perspective or from the aggregated perspective. In this study the latter approach is utilised. The main output of microsimulations is the distribution of selected cohorts among the four living states: *Healthy & Living alone, Unhealthy & Living alone, Healthy & Not living alone* and *Unhealthy & Not living alone* over the projection period. In the next stage, this distribution is used to disaggregate the projected population by age and sex across the functional states. The numbers of persons by age, sex and functional states constitute the final outcome, that is, population projections by the functional states.

As already explained, the structure of the microsimulation model (compare Figure 30) requires two types of input data: information on the age-sex structure of the initial population (stock variable) and the simulation parameters – transition rates that represent the dynamics of moves between the functional states considered (behavioural rules). Both data are necessary to run the microsimulation model, but they can be prepared independently. Such a flexible structure of the model provides an opportunity to prepare multiple alternative scenarios of future population developments. The assumptions on the initial population structure can be analysed independently from changes of the behavioural rules but they also can be implemented jointly.

The next section discusses the input data of the microsimulation model coming from the Eurostat population projections.

4.2.2 Eurostat population projections

The choice of the population projections is fundamental as it determines the size of the population, its composition by age and sex and its development into the future. In the study, I use the 2015-based population projections prepared by Eurostat that cover the 28 EU Member States and Norway (Eurostat, 2017a). The Eurostat population projections are cohort-component deterministic projections for the entire national population. They are prepared by single age up to age 100+ and sex for each single year from 2015 until 2080. No breakdown by other characteristics such as education, health or family status is available.

The assumptions of the population projections are formulated for each of the components of the population change, that is, fertility, mortality and migration. The choice of the models and assumptions for predicting future evolution of each component was made by the Working Group on Population Projections. This Group collects representatives of the national statistical authorities in charge of official projections, under the leadership of Eurostat (European Commission, 2017). Each country projections were supposed to be based on a common methodology and the official statistics available to Eurostat that would ensure the transparency of the process. It has been agreed that population projections are driven by pure demographic mechanisms while non-demographic factors, for example, economic predictors, are not incorporated in the model (European Commission, 2017). Time horizon of the projections has been divided into three periods: 'current' time (2015–2016), short-/medium-term (2017–2050) and long-term (from 2050 onwards). Accordingly, different projection techniques for each period have been used: nowcasting, trends extrapolation and long-term assumptions of partial convergence of the demographic dynamics. Nowcasting uses the provisional observed data on the total numbers of live births, deaths and net migrants to set constraints on the calculations of the first years of projections. The trend extrapolation assumes continuation of the demographic trajectories into the short- and medium-term with a stronger influence for the near future. The extrapolation of parameters for the component-specific models is performed with ARIMA models. The long-term convergence refers to the assumption that in the very long period the socio-economic differentials among EU Member States will slowly disappear which, in turn, will bring national populations closer in demographic terms (European Commission, 2017).

Eurostat published datasets which are composed by the baseline population projections and the following sensitivity tests: Lower fertility, Lower mortality, Higher migration, Lower migration and No migration. For each of them the projected population on 1 January by age and sex, and by single year time interval is provided. Additionally, assumptions on future age-specific fertility, on mortality rates and on international net migration levels is available. Corresponding approximated values of the life expectancy by age and sex are also provided (Eurostat, 2017b).

The Eurostat's baseline population projection is used as the reference population projection for the population projections by functional states. Additionally, the results from the Lower mortality sensitivity test are applied for a what-if scenario analysis. My focus is on population age 50 years and over in 2015 which will turn 65 years and over in 2030; that is, the initial population is defined by people aged 50 years and more in 2015, while the projection horizon is 2030.

According to the baseline projection, the Polish population aged 65 years and over is expected to rise significantly from 5,860 to 8,637 thousand people between 2015 and 2030. It gives a 47 % increase in the next 15 years (an average growth rate of 2.6 % per annum). The strongest increase concerns the 70–74 and 75–79 age groups with 1,128 and 823 thousand more older adults, respectively. The number of the oldest adults aged 90 years or older is to double which is the highest increase in relative terms. More males and females in the 65+ age group will be observed in 2030 with the higher growth for males (57 %) than for females (47 %). Still, in 2030 there will be 1,522 thousand women aged 65+ more than their male counterparts (compare Figure 31). The results of the Eurostat baseline projections are the rudiment for further analysis. In the end of the projection procedure, the same numbers of people, as briefly presented here, will be disaggregated into four states defined by the health and the living arrangements statuses.

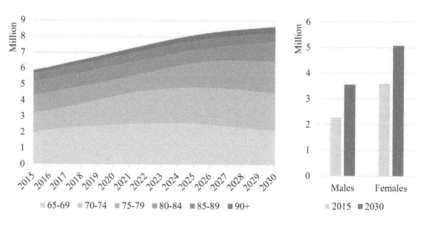

Figure 31. Projected number of people 65 and over for years 2015–2030 by age groups and by sex, baseline projection, Poland.

Source: Eurostat, 2015-based population projections (online data code: proj_15npms).

4.2.3 Initial population assumptions

An important point in microsimulation modelling is a proper assumption on the starting population. A frequent problem met in simulation studies concerns the differences between the structure of the sample used for microsimulation and the structure of the population under focus. One way to address this problem of consistency is to perform the microsimulation on the available sample and then reweighting the results based on external results of relevant macro models. Another method is to use a sample that *ex ante* reflects the population structure under study and can directly match results at the macro level (Strzelecki, 2012). In this study I follow the second approach. Each simulated cohort is redistributed to the four distinguished states according to the initial population state distribution obtained from external data sources.

If the base population is lacking information about the individual health status, it can be imputed using estimates from other studies (e.g. Klevmarken & Lindgren, 2008). Since there are no official statistics on the health status referring to the definition of limitations in basic activities of daily living by sex and age in 2015, the health status composition of the base population had to be imputed from external sources. Figure 32 presents a summary of the prevalence of *Healthy* according to the adopted GALI-related definition of a health status. I considered surveys that included the desired health variable as well as offered a sizeable sample of older adults. This included two waves of SHARE: Wave 6 and Wave 7 conducted in 2015 and 2017, respectively, the EU-SILC cross-sectional data from 2014 and the European Health Interview Survey (EHIS) data collected in 2014. The EU-SILC provides information up to the 80+ age group, while the EHIS last age group available is the 85 years and more. However, the EHIS data is aggregated in 5-year age groups. Both SHARE datasets provided the best data granularity. Given the effective sample size from Wave 7 was more than twice bigger than that of Wave 6, it was decided to move on with SHARE Wave 7. Compared to other studies in the field it can be considered as the extreme assumption as it provides the lowest prevalence of older adults without severe limitations in activities (Figure 32).

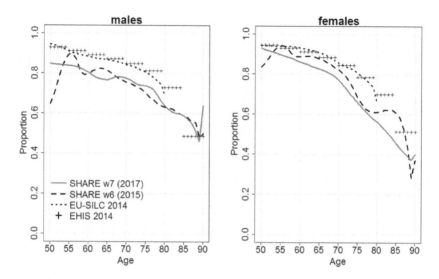

Figure 32. Proportion of *Healthy* in the population by different data sources.
Source: Own elaboration. Results weighted and smoothed.

Similarly, the choice of the initial population distribution by the living arrangements status was deliberated. The data from the most up-to-date Population Census 2011 augmented the previous set of surveys under consideration. The comparison of the results is presented in Figure 33. All the data points unveil the same age pattern of solitary living and the apparent differences between males and females. Given that the census data is surely the most accurate, it was decided to apply it to the initial population in the study. It can be considered as the most conservative approach with respect to the prevalence of *Living alone* among older adults.

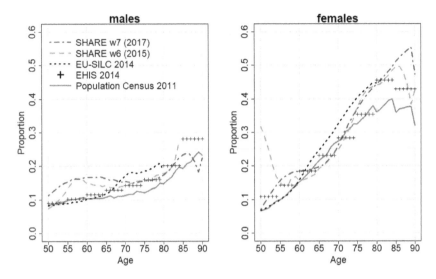

Figure 33. Proportion of *Living alone* in the population by different data sources.

Note: Line for males based on SHARE Wave 6 is shortened to age 84 because of substantial distortions for ages 85 and above due to too few cases observed in the dataset.

Source: Own elaboration. Results weighted and smoothed except for census data.

The distribution of the initial population among functional states is shown in Figure 34. It is a combination of the prevalence of *Healthy* and *Unhealthy* from SHARE Wave 7 with the prevalence of *Living alone* and *Not living alone* from the Population Census 2011. Every synthetic cohort at the beginnig of simulation will be redistributed to the functional states according to the age- and sex-specific distributions estimated in 2015.

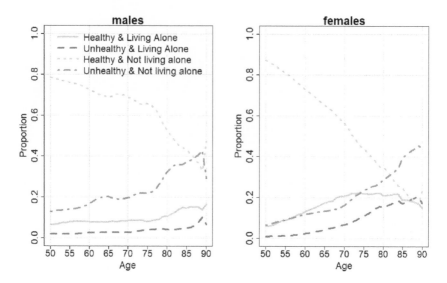

Figure 34. The starting year distribution by functional states.

Source: Own elaboration.

4.2.4 Mortality assumptions

For modelling the transition to death, mortality rates by age and sex are taken from the official Eurostat population projections (Eurostat, 2017a). The Gompertz parametric model is fitted to each cohort's prospective mortality rates separately using *MortalityLaws* R package (Pascariu, 2018). To estimate the relative mortality risk of healthy to unhealthy persons, I run additional models using the EU-SILC data likewise in Chapter 3 but neglecting the education level. The first one is the three-state model of health with two health states and a death state. It is used for calculating the health-specific mortality. The second one is a two-state model with one living state and the death state for the overall mortality. The ratios of baseline mortality and mortality at oldest ages of both models are then used for estimating parameters of the health-specific Gompertz models fitted to the Eurostat data. As a result, the simulation model distinguishes different mortality levels that should be applied to individuals of different health statuses. The estimated mortality rates by age, sex and health status are presented in Figure 35.

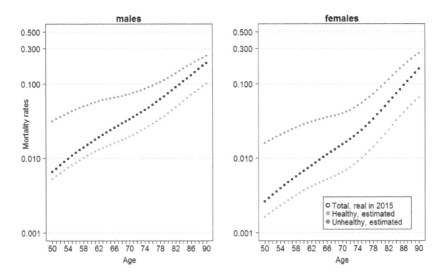

Figure 35. Mortality rates by sex, age and health (estimated).

Source: Own elaboration based on Eurostat, 2015-based population projections (online data code: proj_15naasmr).

There is a clear disproportion in the total mortality between males and females which, however, gets narrower with age. There are also differences in mortality by health status that are more pronounced for younger ages and then shrink when age increases. Still, the heterogeneity of mortality is strongly related to health status.

The use of the same mortality rates as in the official population projections should assure consistency in the number of survivors in each cohort over the projection horizon. This, in turn, allows for applying the obtained state distribution of survivors in each cohort and apply them into official population numbers.

4.2.5 Microsimulation

The simulation of the individual life histories was performed with *simmulti.msm* function in *msm* package (Jackson, 2011) which simulates a number of individual realisations from a continuous-time Markov process up to a given time. Observations of the process were made arbitrarily at every year for each individual. As a result, an annually observed panel data is produced. The *msm* package determines the individual trajectory using transition rates and conditional destination probabilities in a two-step process. In the first step, the time to transition or waiting time in a process with age dependency is related to the age-specific transition rates weighted by exposure time (defined as the time between the starting age and the age at which simulation is discontinued). Then, the weighted age-specific transition rates are summed up to the cumulative transition rates computed at the starting age. Next, the waiting time to the next transition is predestined by a random draw from an exponential waiting time distribution associated with the cumulative transition rate calculated at the starting age. In the second step, the destination state is established, conditional on leaving the current state (Willekens, 2014, Chapter 2).

In the study I simulate life trajectories of individuals who were between 50 and 90 years old in 2015. The simulated individual careers up to 2030 are aggregated into cohorts (compare Figure 36 for illustration). Each cohort consists of 1,000 women and 1,000 men which gives a total sample of 41,000 women and 41,000 men. The life course of each individual is simulated separately. It is exposed to the hazards estimated in the joint model in Chapter 3 and tracked for 15 years. The transition rates are assumed to remain constant during the 15-year simulation period. Uncertainties in the transition rates are assumed to be normally distributed. The aggregate cohort career may differ slightly from the expected cohort career produced by the multistate model because of sample variation (Willekens, 2014). By following the simulated life course of the individuals, I observe different health and living arrangements outcomes of their lives at each year (age) over the projection horizon at the individual level. The outcomes in 2030 are of particular interest in this study.

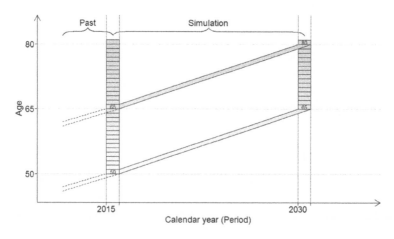

Figure 36. Lexis diagram of microsimulations.
Source: Own elaboration.

Migration is not directly included in the microsimulation model. However, the Eurostat 2015-based population projections include assumptions about changing migration over time which are reflected in the future population estimates. Nevertheless, it is believed that migration will have a greater impact on the younger rather than the older population like in Kingston and Jagger (2017).

To present the capabilities of the microsimulation model I have prepared a number of projections which are called scenarios. These can be interpreted as a sensitivity analysis or what-if scenarios. The baseline projection is the one that is using the baseline population projection by Eurostat and will be referred to as the baseline scenario. The second scenario makes use of the Lower mortality scenario which is based on the lower mortality sensitivity test provided by Eurostat. This scenario foresees the different development of the population due to improvements in survival reflected in lower age-specific mortality rates assumed. Lastly, two additional scenarios on morbidity compression are prepared to depict how potential improvements in health would translate into the number of persons in each of the functional states and the life expectancy composition.[69] They are the baseline scenario duplicates with the exception that the transition rates from *Healthy & Living alone* to *Unhealthy & Living alone* and *Healthy & Not living alone* to *Unhealthy & Not living alone* are reduced by either 10 % or 20 %. The respective scenarios are called *Morbidity compression (10 %)* and *Morbidity compression (20 %)*.

Under each of the formulated scenarios 1,000 simulations have been run. I report median results as well as a 95 % range defined with the 2.5[th] and 97.5[th] percentile simulations for each functional state being individually arranged from the smallest to the greatest projected number of people in the given state in 2030. Additionally, the reference simulation is reported, which is the median simulation for the baseline scenario results being ordered according to the number of older people in *Unhealthy & Living Alone* state. It is a single simulation (random seed 869) that is treated as the reference when discussing results.

---

69   Compression of morbidity is a theoretical concept advocating that the additional life years at older ages are years with less disability due to adoption of healthier lifestyles and postponement or even prevention of chronic diseases Thus, increases in life expectancy are accompanied by decreases in years with morbidity (Nusselder, 2002). More information on morbidity hypotheses can be found in Section 2.2.2.

4.3 Simulation results

This section summarises the ouptut of the simulation exercise aimed to redistribute the official population projections into the predefined functional states. The result of each simulation is a single projection. Performing 1,000 simulations allows an equivalent number of separate projections to be obtained which together can be regarded as their empirical distribution. The projected trajectories by health and living arrangements with the respective confidence intervals and the estimated distributions by functional states in the baseline scenario are presented in Figures 37 and 38, respectively. These distributions reflect uncertainty that is intrinsic to any prediction. Even though the Eurostat projections are deterministic and every projection is set to be equal to the invariant, official total population estimate, there is still uncertainty related to the redistribution. In other words, even if we assume one trajectory of the population development between 2015 and 2030 as projected by Eurostat, there are still many possibilities of the internal composition by health and living arrangements status that can be realised. One needs to keep the above in mind when interpreting results.

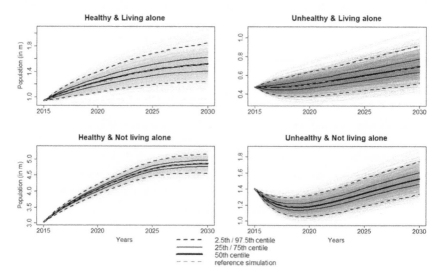

Figure 37. Projected trajectories of the population size by health and living arrangements status, baseline scenario.

Note: Thin coloured lines represent output of each single simulation.

Source: Own elaboration.

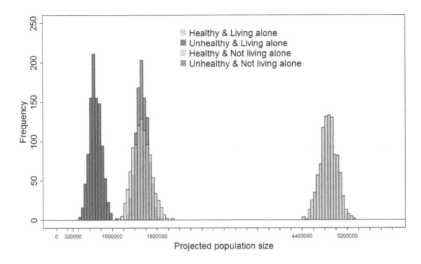

Figure 38. Projected distributions of the population size by health and living arrangements status, baseline scenario.

Source: Own elaboration.

Before getting to the results the simulation output is validated. The only tool available is the comparison of the synthetic cohorts with the ones from the Eurostat population projections. Figure 39 presents the 15-year survival probability of men and women observed in 2030. It compares the expected survival from the official population projections with the survival probability obtained in 10 simulations. The survival from population projections is mostly overlaid with the simulated survival. It can be argued that the transition rates to death by health status used in the simulation model replicate the officially projected mortality rates by sex to a satisfying degree. The simulated survival is overestimated for younger ages up to age 75, especially for males. For older ages the simulated results are more on-the-target for both sexes. For ages above 90 years, the probability to survive is underestimated for females. In general, the simulation's quality of survival representation is assessed as adequate.

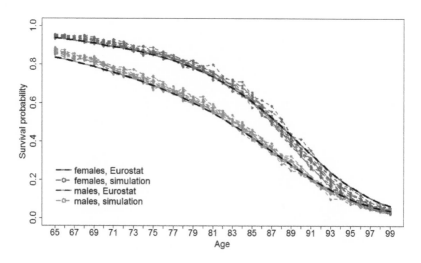

Figure 39. Comparison of the sex-specific 15-year survival probability between Eurostat assumptions and simulation (10 simulations).

Source: Own elaboration.

4.3.1 Baseline scenario projection results

Firstly, the results of the baseline scenario are presented. The absolute numbers of older people by the health and living arrangements status as well as the change between years 2015 and 2030 for the total subpopulation is presented in Table 24. The distribution of the results by five-year age groups (65–69 years, 70–74 years, 75–79 years, 80–84 years, 85–89 years and ≥90 years) can be found in Table 26 while differences by sex are shown in Table 25. Inevitably, the sum across all functional states is consistent with the Eurostat's baseline projection estimates which report that between 2015 and 2030 the absolute numbers of people aged 65 and above in Poland will increase by 47.4 % (from 5.9 to 8.6 million).

The breakdown into health states points at the stronger growth of the number of people in relatively good health as compared to the number people who report severe limitations (60 % *versus* 20 %, see Table 24). This imbalanced growth is mostly driven by about two times higher increase of the *Healthy* than of the *Unhealthy* among people in 70–74 years and 75–79 years age groups (compare Table 26). Both age groups are responsible for biggest increases in absolute terms reaching together almost 2 million people. These are the 1950s post-war baby-boomers who are expected to live their 70s in a relatively good shape.

Still, the overall number of older people reporting severe long-standing activity limitation will expand by 366 thousand people, or by 19.5 %, when comparing to the reference simulation. Most of the new older people in this health status in 2030 are expected to live alone rather that live with others (222 vs 144 thousand people). Even though, among the *Unhealthy*, the majority will constantly share their households with other people.

Looking at living arrangements, the relative increase of the *Living alone* will be stronger than of the *Not living alone*. The expected growth of 57 % in the reference simulation is close to the number published in the official household projections. The Statistics Poland household projections up to 2050 report a 35.1 % growth of the number of households of single-living adults (with no children) between years 2016 and 2030 from 3,605 to 4,871 thousand households (Table 3, Annex 3 in GUS, 2016b). However, this growth can be expected to be higher for the 65+ subpopulation. If the 65 years old and older people were treated as a separate age group, the expected growth in living alone could reach 88 %.[70] The growth rate from the baseline simulation falls into the middle of the range calculated from the household projections.

When further disaggregating the results differences between age groups are visible. The highest increase is observed among the oldest seniors aged 90 and above. The number of *Healthy & Living alone* and *Unhealthy & Living alone* is expected to double and almost reach the size of the population *Not living alone*. On the other side of the age scale one can see the lowest increase among the 65–69 years old. Actually, the number of the *Unhealthy* in this age group will likely shrink by 18 %.

In the next 15 years some common features of change are visible but also differences by sex in the numbers of potentially dependent older adults can be seen (Table 25). The biggest absolute increase for both sexes, and relative for women, is projected for the persons *Healthy & Not living alone*. Their number is projected to rise by as much as 850–950 thousand older adults. It means that in 2030 a half of women at age 65 or older will not report any severe

---

70 The share of 65+ years old people living alone within the overall adults living alone category is based on the Population Census 2011 data on single-living prevalence by age. The growth for the 65+ age group is calculated by keeping the mentioned share constant and by adjusting for the projected change in age composition of the population in 2030.

Table 24. Projected number of people aged 65 and more in Poland by health and living arrangements, baseline scenario

	Projected numbers (thousands)			Change (2015–2030)		
	2015	2030		Relative		Absolute
		Reference	Median (95 % range)	Reference	Median (95 % range)	
	(A)	(B)		(B)/(A) – 1		(B)-(A)
All ≥65 years						
Healthy & Living alone	939	1,527	1,525 (1,246 to 1,852)	62.6 %	62 % (33 to 97)	588
Unhealthy & Living alone	474	696	696 (513 to 918)	46.8 %	47 % (8 to 94)	222
Healthy & Not living alone	3,041	4,865	4,867 (4,566 to 5,157)	60.0 %	60 % (50 to 70)	1,824
Unhealthy & Not living alone	1,405	1,549	1,528 (1,340 to 1,744)	10.2 %	9 % (-5 to 24)	144
Living alone	1,413	2,223	2,230 (1,925 to 2,552)	57.3 %	58 % (36 to 81)	810
Not living alone	4,446	6,414	6,407 (6,085 to 6,713)	44.3 %	44 % (37 to 51)	1,968
Healthy	3,980	6,392	6,392 (6,113 to 6,678)	60.6 %	61 % (54 to 68)	2,412
Unhealthy	1,879	2,245	2,245 (1,959 to 2,524)	19.5 %	19 % (4 to 34)	366
Total	**5,859**	**8,637**		**47.4 %**		**2,778**

Source: Own elaboration.

limitations and will not live alone. The second biggest increase concerns the *Healthy & Living alone* group. The number of men in this group is expected to nearly double; however, their influx to this category will be still almost half as big as the corresponding influx of women. There is also a significant rise in the number of *Unhealthy & Living alone* of 160 thousand females and 63 thousand males until 2030. This group is of special interest because as they are expected to be in bad health and living alone, they are considered as a group of a high demand for support from outside the household and a higher risk of institutionalisation.

Table 25. Projected number of people aged 65 or older in Poland by health and living arrangements, and sex, reference simulation

All ≥65 years	Females						Males					
	2015		2030		Δ		2015		2030		Δ	
Healthy & Living alone	723	20 %	1,109	22 %	+386 53 %		216	10 %	419	12 %	+203 94 %	
Unhealthy & Living alone	392	11 %	552	11 %	+160 41 %		82	4 %	145	4 %	+63 77 %	
Healthy & Not living alone	1,617	45 %	2,582	51 %	+965 60 %		1,424	63 %	2,283	64 %	+859 60 %	
Unhealthy & Not living alone	860	24 %	838	16 %	-22 -3 %		546	24 %	711	20 %	+165 30 %	
Total	3,592	100 %	5,081	100 %	+1,489 41 %		2,268	100 %	3,558	100 %	+ 1,290 57 %	

Source: Own elaboration.

Table 26. Projected number of people aged 65 or older in Poland by health and living arrangements and age groups, baseline scenario

	Projected numbers (thousands)			Change (2015–2030)		
	2015	2030		Relative		Absolute
		Reference	Median (95 % range)	Reference	Median (95 % range)	
	(A)	(B)		(B)/ (A) – 1		(B)-(A)
65–69 years						
Healthy & Living alone	274	296	290 (246 to 342)	8.0 %	6 % (-10 to 25)	22
Unhealthy & Living alone	79	65	66 (46 to 88)	-17.7 %	-16 % (-42 to 11)	-14
Healthy & Not living alone	1,289	1,516	1,519 (1,459 to 1,572)	17.6 %	18 % (13 to 22)	227
Unhealthy & Not living alone	321	262	262 (230 to 295)	-18.4 %	-18 % (-28 to -8)	-59
70–74 years						
Healthy & Living alone	200	403	387 (322 to 463)	101.5 %	94 % (61 to 132)	203
Unhealthy & Living alone	75	119	120 (85 to 160)	58.7 %	60 % (13 to 113)	44
Healthy & Not living alone	705	1,455	1,476 (1,399 to 1,553)	106.4 %	109 % (98 to 120)	750
Unhealthy & Not living alone	245	377	368 (321 to 417)	53.9 %	50 % (31 to 70)	132
75–79 years						
Healthy & Living alone	195	373	374 (304 to 454)	91.3 %	92 % (56 to 133)	178
Unhealthy & Living alone	113	162	160 (116 to 213)	43.4 %	42 % (3 to 88)	49
Healthy & Not living alone	552	1,051	1,048 (972 to 1,125)	90.4 %	90 % (76 to 104)	499
Unhealthy & Not living alone	285	381	380 (330 to 437)	33.7 %	33 % (16 to 53)	96
80–84 years						
Healthy & Living alone	159	249	259 (202 to 322)	56.6 %	63 % (27 to 103)	90

Table 26. Continued

	Projected numbers (thousands)			Change (2015–2030)		
Unhealthy & Living alone	108	161	152 (109 to 202)	49.1 %	41 % (1 to 87)	53
Healthy & Not living alone	315	553	541 (487 to 596)	75.6 %	72 % (55 to 89)	238
Unhealthy & Not living alone	280	273	279 (240 to 323)	-2.5 %	0 % (-14 to 15)	-7
85–89 years						
Healthy & Living alone	83	121	124 (90 to 164)	45.8 %	49 % (8 to 98)	38
Unhealthy & Living alone	72	94	100 (72 to 130)	30.6 %	39 % (0 to 81)	22
Healthy & Not living alone	125	193	188 (160 to 215)	54.4 %	50 % (28 to 72)	68
Unhealthy & Not living alone	196	145	140 (117 to 164)	-26.0 %	-29 % (-40 to -16)	-51
≥90 years						
Healthy & Living alone	29	86	89 (57 to 130)	196.6 %	207 % (97 to 348)	57
Unhealthy & Living alone	28	95	101 (74 to 128)	239.3 %	261 % (164 to 357)	67
Healthy & Not living alone	55	97	94 (73 to 116)	76.4 %	71 % (33 to 111)	42
Unhealthy & Not living alone	77	111	103 (82 to 126)	44.2 %	34 % (6 to 64)	34
All ≥65 years						
Healthy & Living alone	939	1,527	1,525 (1,246 to 1,852)	62.6 %	62 % (33 to 97)	588
Unhealthy & Living alone	474	696	696 (513 to 918)	46.8 %	47 % (8 to 94)	222
Healthy & Not living alone	3,041	4,865	4,867 (4,566 to 5,157)	60.0 %	60 % (50 to 70)	1,824
Unhealthy & Not living alone	1,405	1,549	1,528 (1,340 to 1,744)	10.2 %	9 % (-5 to 24)	144
Total	5,859	8,637		47.4 %		2,778

Source: Own elaboration.

The illustration of changes in the relations between age groups is shown in the population pyramids presented in Figure 40. They depict the projected number of older people by functional states by age and sex for every five years between 2015 and 2030. The increase in absolute terms refers to all ages for both females and males.

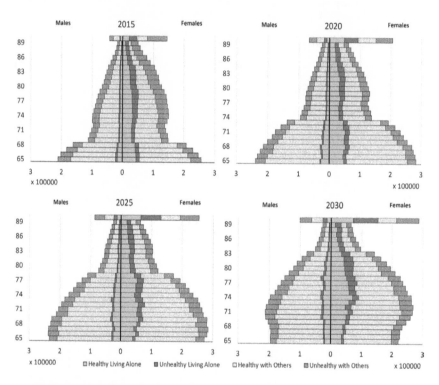

Figure 40. Population by age, sex, health and living arrangements status, year 2015, 2020, 2025 and 2030, reference simulation.

Source: Own elaboration.

Figure 41 shows the projected state distribution by age and sex for years 2015 and 2030. There is an increase in the proportion of unhealthy older adults living alone, especially for males, but also for females in the oldest age group. One can also see relatively less women and men being unhealthy and living with others in 2030 than in 2015. Consequently, the share of *Healthy & Not living alone* is expanding.

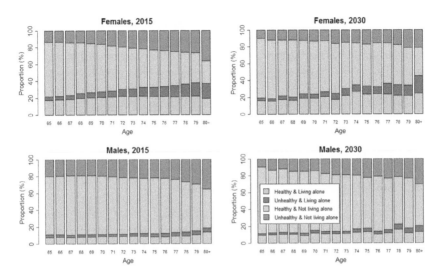

Figure 41. Females' and males' projected distributions by age, health and living arrangements, reference simulation.

Source: Own elaboration.

The projected population distribution over the state space is relatively stable in the projection horizon; however, some deviations, especially in the oldest age group, are also apparent (see Figure 42). In general, the oldest age groups are the most volatile. The proportion of healthy seniors living alone is projected to be constant at around 20 % for females with upturn among the seniors 80 and more years old. For males, the share of *Healthy & Living alone* oscillates around 10 % with slight gains in the 2020s for the 70–79 years old. The projected trend for the proportion of unhealthy older people living alone shows a rather stable pattern. However, there is some divergence between the *Healthy & Not living alone* and the *Unhealthy & Not living alone* in the first years of projections, especially for the 80+ persons and among females. There is observed a growing share of *Healthy & Not living alone* and a contradictory trend for *Unhealthy & Not living alone* at the same time. It might be caused by the data availability problem during the multistate modelling stage, namely a lack of disaggregated data for individuals aged 80 and older (see Section 3.4.2). Rapid changes in the proportions of the *Not living alone* in the first years of the simulation period suggest that the transition rates between those states do not replicate the true process well enough. Given the assumed increasing longevity of both men and women that is incorporated in the original Eurostat population projections, one would rather expect increasing proportions of the *Unhealthy & Not living alone*. The logic would be that the further into the future the more of the old people is assumed to survive, however more of them being unhealthy thus driving changes in relevant proportions. These observations indicate that the share of *Healthy & Not living alone* might be overestimated at the cost of the share of *Unhealthy & Not living alone* which produces the final results to be more optimistic than the reality. This is a potential issue that could be resolved with a better-quality data available at the stage of modelling transition rates.

4.3.2 Model extensions: Sensitivity tests

The presented microsimulation model provides useful information to disaggregate the total population estimated in the official population projections into population by functional states, relevant for predicting demand for care.

In the study two types of scenarios were prepared. In the first one, I keep all the assumptions from the baseline scenario except changes in the simulation parameters which leads us to the *Morbidity compression (10 %)* and *Morbidity compression (20 %)* scenarios. They refer to the behavioural rules. Both scenarios are examples of measuring effects of changes in transition rates on the overall system. In this case I aim to check how alternative assumptions on morbidity affect a redistribution of the population into the functional states. The second type of scenario also implements assumptions on the simulation parameters, but focuses on changes in mortality. It uses the 'lower mortality: sensitivity test' projection by Eurostat which alters the mortality rates assumed and leads to different projected size of the population in 2030. This scenario measures the potential effect of mortality improvements on population composition by functional states given the starting-population assumptions and the other simulation parameters remain unchanged.

Firstly, let's focus on how changes in morbidity affect the population structure by functional states. Figure 43 provides an example of how the projected distributions of population in *Unhealthy & Living alone* state looks like under different morbidity scenarios. Every change in the transition rates concerning morbidity has an effect on the population distribution. The reduction of the intensity from *Healthy* to *Unhealthy* at the individual level provides an aggregated outcome. The expected number of older people in the *Unhealthy & Living alone* state is going down. It is reflected in a horizontal move of the distribution. As the assumption of the uncertainty in transition rates is kept being normal, the shape of the distribution is almost unaffected. It is, however, not clear what

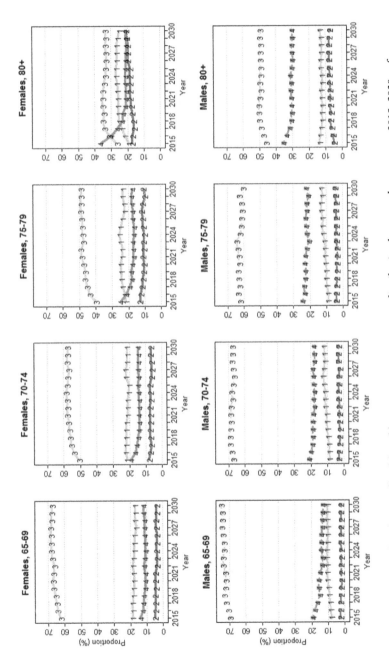

Figure 42. Projected evolution of health and living arrangements status distribution by sex and age groups, 2015–2030, reference simulation.

Source: Own elaboration. State description: 1 *Healthy & Living alone;* 2 *Unhealthy & Living alone;* 3 *Healthy & Not living alone;* 4 *Unhealthy & Not living alone.*

does it mean that a transition rate is reduced to a certain level or by a certain factor as transition rates do not have an easy meaning to understand in reality. But, the output of such a scenario can be translated into healthy life expectancy (limitations-free life expectancy) that would be more accessible to the users of the simulation. It will be shown in the latter part of this section. Before moving to life expectancies, the combined effect on the population structure by functional states is scrutinised.

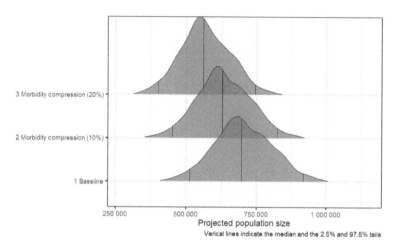

Figure 43. Projected distributions of the population size in *Unhealthy & Living alone* state by morbidity scenarios.

Source: Own elaboration.

Figure 44 presents the comparison of distributions of the projected population in each of the distinguished states according to the morbidity scenarios. In all scenarios, there is a clear dominance of the number of people aged 65 or more who are in the *Healthy & Not living alone* state. On the opposite side, seniors who are projected to be unhealthy and living alone are the fewest in number. In the baseline scenario, the projected median number of healthy older people living alone is very close to the median number of the *Unhealthy & Not living alone* population. The projected distributions of two groups overlap with one another. Considering the other two scenarios, which assume improvement in morbidity by 10 % and 20 %, respectively, one can observe divergent trends for both subpopulations. Along with morbidity compression, the size of *Healthy & Living alone* population is increasing, while the number of *Unhealthy & Not living alone* is decreasing. This is a general regularity that extends to both *Healthy* and both *Unhealthy* states.

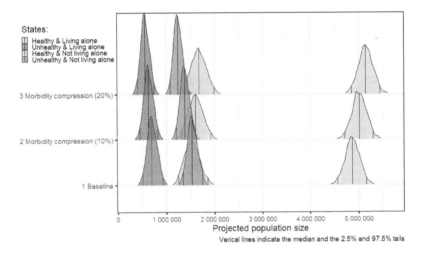

Figure 44. Projected distributions of the population size by health and living arrangements status and morbidity scenarios.

Source: Own elaboration

The situation depicted in Figure 44 is stylised as the size of total population of adults aged 65 and over is forced to be equal to the population size in the official baseline projection. In reality, it would be highly unlikely as the mortality rates differ by health status. Morbidity compression would imply more older persons to be in better health that would lead to the limited number of deaths when compared to the baseline scenario. Additionally, it is unlikely that factors that affect intensities of transitions between health states would not affect transition rates to death. In both scenarios such insensitivity is assumed. Therefore, this analysis of scenarios should be rather considered a sensitivity analysis. This exercise helps to measure impact of potential changes in the assumptions regarding future developments of demographic rates.

For the sake of better understanding of the results of various scenarios it is possible to translate the calculated shares into life expectancies. The life expectancies at the age 65 presented in Table 27 are calculated with the use of Sullivan method (Sullivan, 1971) based on the simulated population structure in 2030. According to Eurostat projection, total increase in male life expectancy at age 65 is expected to grow by 2.3 years in 2030 compared to 2015. The Sullivan method permits to decompose this growth into change in life expectancy by functional states. Most of the increase can be attributed to extra years spent in *Healthy & Not living alone* state (1.3 years). The increase in years spent in *Healthy* state, regardless of living arrangements, amounts to 1.9 years. Additional 0.4 years are projected to be spent in *Unhealthy & Living alone* state. No extra years are expected to be lived in *Unhealthy & Not living alone* state.

The projected increase in extra life years for women will be slightly lower than for men. Life expectancy at age 65 years for women in Poland will increase between 2015 and 2030 by 2.1 years. Women will gain 3.1 years in good health and 0.3 years in *Unhealthy & Living alone* state, but time spent in *Unhealthy & Not living alone* state will decrease by 1.3 years. These changes will affect the proportion of the total life expectancy spent in functional states for both sexes. Relatively more years will be spent living alone (the stronger effect for men) and in good health (the stronger effect for women).

The baseline scenario results can be confronted with alternative visions of the future. The Eurostat sensitivity test assuming lower mortality levels leads to higher increases in the total life expectancy at age 65 years for both men and women. The proportion of the total life expectancy among functional states is relatively stable comparing to the baseline scenario; however, there is a slight increase in proportions of the *Unhealthy* versus *Healthy* (see Table 27). In contrast, the opposite trend in both *Morbidity compression* scenarios is seen. Keeping the survival probability constant and reducing chances to health deterioration have the opposite effect. The proportion of the years lived from age 65 in *Unhealthy* states is diminishing, while the proportion of years spent in good health is increasing. This effect is stronger for the sharper assumption on morbidity compression. For example, in the *Morbidity compression (10 %)* scenario, females gain a total of 0.7 years in *Healthy* state. In the more optimistic scenario, the extra healthy life years amount to 1.3 years. Decomposition of life expectancy gains in 2030 versus 2015 by different scenarios is presented in Figure 45 (men) and Figure 46 (women).

Table 27. Years lived from age 65 years by functional status and sex, and sensitivity scenario, 2015–2030.

	Years lived from age 65					Change over period 2015-2030			
	2015	2030				Baseline	Morbidity compression (10%)	Morbidity compression (20%)	Sensitivity test: lower mortality
		Baseline	Morbidity compression (10%)	Morbidity compression (20%)	Sensitivity test: lower mortality				
Men									
Total life expectancy, years	15.6	17.9	17.9	17.9	18.3	2.3	2.3	2.3	2.7
Healthy & Living alone									
Years	1.5	2.1 (1.8 to 2.6)	2.3 (1.9 to 2.7)	2.4 (2 to 2.8)	2.2 (1.8 to 2.7)	0.6 (0.3 to 1.1)	0.8 (0.4 to 1.2)	0.9 (0.5 to 1.3)	0.7 (0.3 to 1.2)
Proportion of total life expectancy	9.6%	12% (9.8 to 14.6)	12.6% (10.3 to 15.2)	13.1% (10.9 to 15.7)	12% (9.8 to 14.6)	2.3pp. (0.2 to 5)	3pp. (0.7 to 5.6)	3.5pp. (1.3 to 6.1)	2.4pp. (0.2 to 5)
Unhealthy & Living alone									
Years	0.6	1.0 (0.7 to 1.3)	0.9 (0.7 to 1.2)	0.8 (0.6 to 1.1)	1.0 (0.8 to 1.4)	0.4 (0.1 to 0.7)	0.3 (0.1 to 0.6)	0.2 (0 to 0.5)	0.4 (0.2 to 0.8)
Proportion of total life expectancy	3.8%	5.5% (4.1 to 7.4)	5% (3.6 to 6.6)	4.5% (3.2 to 5.9)	5.7% (4.2 to 7.5)	1.7pp. (0.2 to 3.5)	1.1pp. (-0.2 to 2.7)	0.6pp. (-0.6 to 2.1)	1.8pp. (0.4 to 3.7)
Healthy & Not living alone									
Years	9.6	10.9 (10.3 to 11.4)	11.2 (10.7 to 11.8)	11.6 (11.1 to 12.1)	11.0 (10.5 to 11.6)	1.3 (0.7 to 1.8)	1.6 (1.1 to 2.2)	2.0 (1.5 to 2.5)	1.4 (0.9 to 2)
Proportion of total life expectancy	61.5%	60.7% (57.5 to 63.7)	62.8% (59.8 to 65.8)	64.9% (62.1 to 67.8)	60.3% (57.2 to 63.3)	-0.9pp. (-4.1 to 2.1)	1.3pp. (-1.7 to 4.3)	3.3pp. (0.5 to 6.2)	-1.3pp. (-4.3 to 1.8)
Unhealthy & Not living alone									
Years	3.9	3.9 (3.5 to 4.4)	3.5 (3.1 to 3.9)	3.1 (2.8 to 3.5)	4.0 (3.6 to 4.5)	0.0 (-0.4 to 0.5)	-0.4 (-0.8 to 0)	-0.8 (-1.1 to -0.4)	0.1 (-0.3 to 0.6)
Proportion of total life expectancy	25.0%	21.7% (19.3 to 24.4)	19.5% (17.3 to 22)	17.4% (15.5 to 19.7)	21.9% (19.5 to 24.6)	-3.3pp. (-5.7 to -0.6)	-5.5pp. (-7.7 to -3)	-7.6pp. (-9.5 to -5.3)	-3.1pp. (-5.5 to -0.4)
Women									
Total life expectancy, years	19.8	21.9	21.9	21.9	22.3	2.1	2.1	2.1	2.5
Healthy & Living alone									
Years	4.0	4.9 (3.9 to 6.1)	5.2 (4.2 to 6.4)	5.5 (4.5 to 6.6)	5.0 (3.9 to 6.2)	0.9 (-0.1 to 2.1)	1.2 (0.2 to 2.4)	1.5 (0.5 to 2.6)	1.0 (-0.1 to 2.2)
Proportion of total life expectancy	20.2%	22.2% (17.7 to 27.6)	23.7% (19.1 to 29)	25% (20.5 to 30.3)	22.2% (17.7 to 27.7)	2pp. (-2.5 to 7.4)	3.5pp. (-1.1 to 8.8)	4.8pp. (0.3 to 10.1)	2pp. (-2.5 to 7.5)
Unhealthy & Living alone									
Years	2.3	2.6 (1.9 to 3.4)	2.3 (1.7 to 3.1)	2.1 (1.5 to 2.8)	2.7 (2 to 3.6)	0.3 (-0.4 to 1.1)	0.0 (-0.6 to 0.8)	-0.2 (-0.8 to 0.5)	0.4 (-0.3 to 1.3)
Proportion of total life expectancy	11.6%	11.9% (8.6 to 15.7)	10.7% (7.7 to 14.1)	9.5% (6.6 to 12.6)	12.2% (8.7 to 16.1)	0.3pp. (-3 to 4)	-0.9pp. (-3.9 to 2.4)	-2.1pp. (-5 to 1)	0.6pp. (-2.9 to 4.4)
Healthy & Not living alone									
Years	8.5	10.7 (9.8 to 11.6)	11.1 (10.1 to 12)	11.4 (10.4 to 12.3)	10.8 (9.9 to 11.7)	2.2 (1.3 to 3.1)	2.6 (1.6 to 3.5)	2.9 (1.9 to 3.8)	2.3 (1.4 to 3.2)
Proportion of total life expectancy	42.9%	49% (44.6 to 52.9)	50.5% (46.2 to 54.6)	52.1% (47.5 to 56.1)	48.6% (44.3 to 52.5)	6.1pp. (1.6 to 10)	7.6pp. (3.2 to 11.7)	9.1pp. (4.6 to 13.1)	5.7pp. (1.4 to 9.6)
Unhealthy & Not living alone									
Years	5.0	3.7 (3.1 to 4.3)	3.3 (2.7 to 3.8)	2.9 (2.4 to 3.4)	3.7 (3.2 to 4.4)	-1.3 (-1.9 to -0.7)	-1.7 (-2.3 to -1.2)	-2.1 (-2.6 to -1.6)	-1.3 (-1.8 to -0.6)
Proportion of total life expectancy	25.3%	16.7% (14.1 to 19.5)	14.9% (12.4 to 17.4)	13.2% (11.1 to 15.5)	16.8% (14.2 to 19.7)	-8.6pp. (-11.1 to -5.7)	-10.4pp. (-12.8 to -7.9)	-12pp. (-14.1 to -9.7)	-8.5pp. (-11.1 to -5.5)

Source: Own elaboration. The reported value is median; data in parentheses are 95 % range.

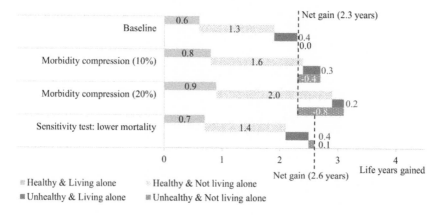

Figure 45. Decomposition of life expectancy gains in 2030 vs 2015 by scenario, men.
Source: Own elaboration

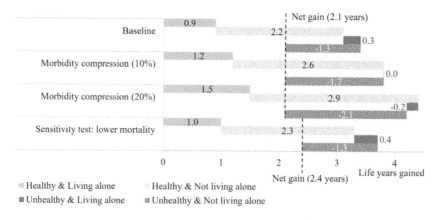

Figure 46. Decomposition of life expectancy gains in 2030 vs 2015 by scenario, women.
Source: Own elaboration

4.4 Summary and discussion

In this chapter, the microsimulation model was used to generate individual health and living arrangements life histories of older adults aged 65 or more over the 15 years projection period. The cohorts of simulated 1,000 individuals were used to redistribute the traditional population projections by age and sex into additional categories of the health and living arrangements statuses. The foundation of the simulation exercise was the transition rates derived from the previously estimated multistate models (see Chapter 3). Transition rates represented expected values derived from the continuous-time Markov process model that describes experience of a synthetic cohort. Microsimulation allows calculation of individual values' distribution around the expected values needed to provide confidence intervals.

The consistency between simulations at the micro-level and population projections at the macro level was achieved by imposing important restrictions. Firstly, the real population structure by functional states was reflected in the initial simulation sample. Secondly, mortality rates used in the model followed directly mortality assumptions of the official projections. As a result, the official population projections up to 2030 were disaggregated into mutually exclusive groups of *Healthy & Living alone*, *Unhealthy & Living alone*, *Healthy & Not living alone* and *Unhealthy & Not living alone*.

Population projections of adults aged 65 and more by functional states fulfil the cognitive aspect of the monograph. The reported results indicate that among the growing population of both men and women aged 65 and more in Poland the proportion of functionally independent older people will increase between 2015 and 2030. The total senior population will increase by 2,778 thousand people, of which 366 thousand will be *Unhealthy* and 810 thousand will be living alone, affecting its composition by health status and by living arrangements status. In 2030 one can expect 74 % of seniors to be functionally independent (73 % of females and 76 % of males), while the respective proportion in 2015 amounted to 68 % (65 % of females and 72 % of males). The growth in the projection horizon among the *Healthy* (by 61 %) is expected to exceed that of the *Unhealthy* (by 19 %). Similarly, older people living alone will increase faster (by 57 %) than those not living alone (by 44 %). The disaggregation of the *Unhealthy & Living alone* shows that this (theoretically) the most vulnerable group will increase from 1,405 thousand people in 2015 to 1,549 thousand in 2030 (reference scenario), even though its share in the total senior population will drop by 6 percentage points to 18 %. The overall findings also reveal some differences in the projected population changes between males and females (e.g. the projected decrease in the number of *Unhealthy & Not living alone* among females with accompanying considerable growth among males) as well as age groups (e.g. the extraordinary increase in the number and the share of *Living alone* among seniors aged 90 and above).

The population of people aged 65 and over projected to be dependent (i.e. in the *Unhealthy* state) in Poland in 2030 amounts to 2,245 thousand (reference simulation) and 2,224 thousand (median). The comparison of the results with other, independent studies is rather limited, but quite promising.

According to the AWG reference scenario[71] the number of dependent people aged 65 and above is to reach 2,287 thousand in 2030 (European Commission, 2018). In the previous analyses by Abramowska-Kmon (2011) the total number of dependent, that is, being completely or seriously limited in activities of daily living, adults aged 65 and more in 2035 was projected to almost 3,040 thousand in the 'pessimistic' scenario and 2,840 thousand in the 'optimistic' scenario (the projected number of seriously, but not completely limited reached 2,270 thousand in 2035 for both scenarios). It has to be kept in mind, however, that study by Abramowska-Kmon was based on the population projection for 2008–2035 provided by Statistics Poland and the reported projection horizon as well as the definition of dependency differed from those used in this study.[72]

There are several features of the data and methods used that can be argued as strengths of this projection approach. From the data point of view, the microsimulation model relies on the transition rates based on yearly intervals between the waves of EU-SILC. Given the yearly interviews, the dynamic estimations based on this study relate to annual changes. It should be considered as a strength of the model as it is a relatively short interval for a longitudinal study; for example, when compared to the UK's largest household longitudinal study *Understanding Society* (the former *British Household Panel Survey*), the US *Health and Retirement Study* (HRS) or the *Survey of Health, Ageing and Retirement in Europe* (SHARE) which all are biannual surveys. As mentioned in Chapter 3, the intervals between survey measurements highly affect the precision of transition rates, especially for health transitions which are easily to be underestimated when spacing increases (Wolf & Gill, 2009). Shorter intervals between observations make the modelling of the transitions to better capture and reflect the dynamics of the underlying process. Taking yearly

---

71 The AWG reference scenario uses the same definition of dependency as well as version of the Eurostat's population projection as in this study, but prevalence rates of dependency and macrosimulation rather than incidence rates and microsimulation.

72 Other results that could be potentially referenced with this study come from (Szweda-Lewandowska, 2016). According to this study the number of dependent people aged 65 years and more in 2030 is expected to reach 735 thousand. However, the study used the Statistics Poland population projection in order to estimate the need for care among seniors. The prevalence indicators of dependency differed as well as they were based on a combination of: (i) having decision of being unable to an independent existence used for people aged 65–74, and (ii) being dependent according to a scale of ADL limitations for people aged 75 and more.

observed data can already be considered as an improvement, but it can be taken even further to reduce spacing and increase the volatility of the process (and interaction) by translating yearly rates into monthly rates using mathematical transformations (e.g. Kingston & Jagger 2017). Secondly, differential effects of health status (severe limitations versus not severe or no limitations in activities of daily living) on mortality are included in the model. Therefore, transition to mortality depends not only on the age and sex of the person but also on his/her health status.

From the point of view of the modelling techniques used, the microsimulation model gives possibilities to test and verify various scenarios of future evolution of mortality, morbidity and changes in living arrangements. It can be viewed as a flexible tool to analyse both the initial population assumptions as well as the claims about the parameters governing the processes of interest, that is, behaviours of individuals, either independently or jointly. Specified scenarios aimed to illustrate these possibilities. Additionally, the presentation of results is not restricted only to the stock of predefined categories. It can also be translated into life expectancies which can be more informative in some applications and help to communicate projections results more effectively.

There is, however, some room for extensions of the models used. The results of the model are primarily expressed in the number of people in a certain state. Such information is valuable *per se* because it may be treated as an indication of demand for some services, for example, demand for care. However, it can easily be extended into financial dimensions/categories by applying cost measures related to individuals. Such approach might be useful and attractive for financial planning of the care services supply allowing accommodation of multiple variants of future. Siegel (2012b) highlights analytical utility of forecasts and projections, and places it above their accuracy. Their use in the sensitivity analysis that provides more insight into the effects of changes of single component of the population system is of particular importance.

The study's goal was to prepare a dynamic microsimulation projection model based on a multistate model including health status and living arrangements status of older people. The conducted analysis shows that microsimulation is a useful tool for making population projections that go beyond the conventional age and sex distribution. The projected changes in the number of people in the selected health and living arrangements states may be an useful estimate of future demand for care. The model used for population projection may be treated as purely demographic model, that is, the future changes are explained from characteristics of the current population only, that is, from the current population classified by age, sex, health status and living arrangements status (Van Imhoff et al., 1995, p. 12). Other non-demographic variables that might play a role, for example, housing market that informs on the availability of housing as a limiting or enabling factor for household characteristics, are not taken into account. Still, the projection results are believed to be informative for developing reforms in social policy.

Conclusions

Population ageing is a global and universal phenomenon that provides context for the near, mid-term and long-term future with regard to populations, economies and societies. It implies a growth in the number of older people as well as their proportion in the total population that have already been observed for a number of decades now, especially in developed countries. Since over four decades the consequences of population ageing have been central in the debate about the economic and social challenges that emerge with more and more older people living longer than ever. However, age alone has been proven not to be a good enough indicator to precisely measure the advancement of population ageing and the magnitude of the related economic and societal pressures. Scientific community advocates to account for additional dimensions of life that are crucial to its quality, health in particular, in order to enhance more comprehensive and accurate studies on population ageing and its consequences.

One of the important aspects strongly related to population ageing and population health is demand for care services among older people. The age-related health deterioration together with the rising number of older people raises questions about growing future care needs and their fulfilment. Along with quantitative changes on the care demand side (e.g. more people with serious health limitations), there are parallel and equally important developments – both quantitative and qualitative – on the care supply side. Changes in the family model, shrinking kinship networks as well as different modes of care provision with a dominance of informal supply of care by family members determine how the care needs of seniors are being met today and will be fulfilled tomorrow. Family relations and living arrangements of older individuals play a central role in the intergenerational care exchange as well. A discussion of the future needs of older people with respect to care provision is relevant not only to contemporary demographic research but also to policy planning and economics. It should be based however on an adequate assessment of demand for care that accounts for both the care needs of older people as well as the care provision potential.

Hence, this monograph aims to estimate future demand for care among people aged 65 years and over in Poland by preparing appropriate population projections. The demand for care has been defined as the number of people with declared severe limitations in activities of daily living. The main thesis states that to estimate the future demand for care among older people advances in population ageing should be matched with individual-level changes in health and living arrangements of older people. Consequently, a projection model needs to account for relevant individual behaviours as well as changes in the population dynamics. The analytical tool which incorporates microsimulation modelling of people's behaviours into the population projection model offers more adequate predictions of future care demands. In supporting this book, three basic research tasks have been formulated and elaborated in subsequent chapters.

The first, introductory chapter sets the frame for research. It presents briefly the current knowledge about population ageing and its measurement along with the description of changes in the family model to understand their influence on the care arrangements for older people in developed countries. The key takeaway is that in the future the expected growing demand for care among subpopulation of older people is likely to meet with declining supply of family care and unsatisfactory provision of institutional care that remains underdeveloped. Inevitable increase in the number of older people will exert pressure on care arrangements, even if one accounts for prospective measures of ageing that call for reassessment of the challenges related to population ageing. On the supply side, which has been historically dominated by care from family networks, one needs to acknowledge changes in the family-related behaviours and organisation of family life. Demographic changes in fertility, longevity and family formation and dissolution patterns lead to shrinking kinship networks, more complex families and lower rates of intergenerational co-residence. Value reorientation associated with the Second Demographic Transition and the spread of gender-egalitarian norms affect interrelations between and within generations. The interaction of both processes gives reasons to expect a reduction in the reservoir of family care resources that will probably need to be substituted either with state-funded or privately funded replacements.

In the second chapter I explored trends, determinants and interrelations between living arrangements and health status of older people, with special attention paid to Poland, that was realisation of the first research task. The examination of living arrangements of older people shows an increasing importance of living alone accompanied by a downward trend in co-residence between parents aged 65 and older and their adult children. Comparative data demonstrate a clear positive connection between the prevalence of solitary living and age which is relevant in the context of higher support needs at older ages and the lack of care transfers within one-person households. Living alone can be also characterised by a clear gender gap associated with differences in life expectancy and spousal age gaps as well as prevalence of widowhood and re-partnering rates at older ages. While living with a partner at old age is a dominant form of living for men, women's living arrangements show much more diversity as there are countries (Poland included) in which there are more older women running one-person households than living with a partner. Poland is also characterised with a higher prevalence of women aged 80 and more living in institutional households in comparison to men, which, however, is consistently very low for both males and females. It is clear that health deteriorates with age; that is, older people are prone to be less independent with age. This leads to the conclusion that with more seniors surviving to older ages, more care towards older people will be required. However, according to the different concepts of the future of morbidity, the change in care demand may not be proportional because, for example, the continuing improvement in healthy life expectancy may prolong the period of older peoples' self-reliance and consequently reduce the scale of care requirements. Even though this hypothesis is debatable, empirical data have been supporting it for the past years in Poland. It is, therefore, particularly important to pay attention to the oldest-old seniors that live alone as this group emerges as the most exposed to requesting care (due to advanced age) and at the same time lacking the possibility to be cared for from household members (because of living alone).

The first two chapters, based on the rich literature review, were aimed at setting the stage for the next part of the book dealing with analytical approaches to estimate demand of care among older people. The second research task was to model the dynamics of health and living arrangements. The multistate representation of both processes in terms of transition intensities between defined health states and living arrangements states has been chosen. The analysis for Poland was underpinned by the panel component of the EU-SILC dataset. The results confirm that the shape of the hazard function of both health and living arrangements at ages above 50 is age-dependent. Moreover, they show that with age intensities of health deterioration are increasing, while chances for health improvement are decreasing. Similarly, the probability of moving to living alone is rising with age, whilst turning to living with others is declining. The intensities to change health status at older ages are exceeding those of living arrangement status which reflects more frequent health transitions than living arrangements transitions. The intensity of moving from not living alone to solitary living was found significantly higher for women that for men, but no gender difference was found for the transition in the opposite direction. Unexpectedly, the health transitions in the final joint model did not differ significantly by gender. Education was found positively related with health as the better educated had higher intensities to recover and lower risks of becoming severely limited than the lower educated.

The construction of a population projection model, which includes the health status and the living arrangements of older people, served the last research task. The fourth chapter presents an implementation of a dynamic projection model of health status and living arrangements status of older people to estimate demand for care among population aged 65 and more. The previously estimated parameters of the multistate models constituted the input information to the microsimulation model which was used to generate individual health and living arrangements life histories of older adults over the projection horizon. The proposed microsimulation projection model reflected the assumed survival in the official population projections to produce coherent results and ensure comparability. The output of the microsimulation exercise allowed the official projections of population of people aged 65 and above to be disaggregated by health and living arrangements statuses. The growth of population aged 65 and above in Poland between 2015 and 2030 is expected to be mostly driven by the subpopulation of functionally independent older adults that will lead to an increase in the proportion of healthy in the total population of interest. However, the subpopulation of unhealthy older adults is predicted to grow as well. The number of older people requiring care who live with others in 2030 is projected to be in the 95 % confidence range from 1,335 to 1,744 thousand people (compared with 1,405 thousand in 2015 – that is, the starting year of the projection interval). The number of older people requiring care and living alone – potentially the group with the greatest demand for institutional care – falls in 2030 into the 512 to 918 thousand range (versus 474 thousand in the starting year 2015). This considerable increase in the number of older people requiring care in a relatively short time interval indicates a real challenge for care provision in Poland. It refers mainly to families, which are main suppliers of informal care, but also to the state that is the main care provider of formal care, in particular the institutional one. In addition, market services complemented with care provided by immigrants in the grey market will be reducing the potential remaining gap between the care supply and care demand.

Moreover, the use of microsimulation model allowed checking the effect of alternative assumptions on morbidity as well as the potential effect of mortality improvements on the redistribution of the older subpopulation into the functional states. The performed sensitivity analyses showed that – conditional on keeping the predicted survival probability constant – lowering chances of health deterioration would reduce the proportion of the years lived in bad health from age 65, while the proportion of years spent in good health would be increasing. At the same time relatively more years would be spent living alone. Microsimulation proved to be an effective tool for combing the results of modelling of individual behaviours that generate demographic processes with a detailed disaggregation of population projections.

Ambition of this monograph was to contribute to the scientific discussion regarding the future demand for care among older people and to methods of its assessment. The current knowledge regarding the effects of demographic developments defines the background for my discussion on care needs of older people in Poland and their appropriate assessment. Demographic developments are expressed mainly in terms of the evolving age structure of the population and changes in the family model generated by transformations of fertility and family formation and dissolution. The study is not restricted to debating population ageing and its consequences only with traditional measures of ageing, but it also includes more comprehensive measures (prospective and adjusted for the economic life cycle) that broaden the scope of the discussion. It gathers facts and figures about the population of older people in Poland, especially with respect to health, living arrangements and organisation of care toward older adults, and puts them in a comparative, international perspective.

My exploration of health and living arrangements of seniors in Poland is based on multiple data sources that describe and confront a variety of aspects related to both analysed categories. I critically evaluate datasets that could be potentially useful for modelling purposes. The results of the multistate model used to estimate transition rates between health and living arrangements states among people aged 50 years and more contribute to existing literature on the dynamics of health and living arrangements of older people in Poland. In particular, they extend our understanding of the age dependency as well as potential effects of sex and education for health and living arrangements. The dynamic approach used to include additional measures of health and living arrangements is novel in Polish studies on projecting care needs among older persons.

The microsimulation projection model proposed makes it possible to obtain results consistent with the official population projections (at the macro level, here the Eurostat's EUROPOP2015 figures) and to account directly for the micro-level analyses relevant for the projection purpose. Using multistate models in projections is advantageous: "Because of the pivotal role of transitions, multistate models picture more closely the mechanism of demographic change taking place in the real world. As a result, they are better suited for integrated population projections in which functional states and interactions between functional states play a crucial role. In addition, the transitions provide a way to assess the impact on population dynamics of behavioural changes brought about by technological, economic or cultural change, or policies. The transitions are age-specific. As a result the multistate model gives at each age the distribution of cohort members among functional states" (Willekens, 2007, p. 11). The agility of microsimulation due to relative easiness of representation of the current knowledge about demographic processes shaping human life course may contribute to the improved accuracy of population projections. Adding extra variables into projections provides more information valuable for all the stakeholders. The flexibility of both tools, that is, the multistate model and the microsimulation model, does not restrict the state space to the one used in that particular application. The states of interest can be easily replaced or extended with other attributes. More categories can be specified within the selected attributes depending on research questions and data availability, too. The results of the study are primarily expressed in the number of people in a certain state being an indication of demand for some services, for example, demand for care. Even though not a part of the study, it can easily be extended into the financial dimension by applying cost measures related to individuals.

This study is consistent with the paradigm shift in demography, and social sciences in general, that brings the adoption of the life-course perspective to the forefront of the research (Willekens, 1999). Firstly, it tries to explain (and eventually predict) population changes as outcomes of individual agents' actions and interactions. Here, I represent the individual-level survey data on changes in health status and living arrangements status in terms of transition rates that are later used in microsimulations to generate cohorts' trajectories. As a result, the population composition by variables of interest is simulated. This way I follow the advocated moves from macro to micro and from micro to macro via integration of the observation of processes at the micro-level with the macro-level outcomes. It is in line with the so-called *methodological individualism* that views population dynamics as the composite effect of individual life courses (Willekens, 1999). Next, thanks to microsimulations I was able to link multiple processes that are intertwined at the micro-level level, that is, individual ageing and evolution of individuals' health and living arrangements transitions, to generate trajectories that built up to a comprehensive picture of the projected population of older people by health and living arrangements over the appointed time horizon. Additionally, the methods used in the study, especially estimation of transition rates that reflect the risk of moving between the predefined statuses, allow the effects of chance (uncertainty) on change to be captured. Next to the estimated transition rates used for simulations, the uncertainty was incorporated into the study by comparing different mortality scenarios prepared by Eurostat and by offering own scenarios on morbidity compression. Incorporating uncertainty into the model generates results that reflect it directly. It is important to demonstrate the necessity to associate the results with some variation to the projection users. Placing the output in adequate confidence intervals helps to grasp its magnitude.

The choice of the topic of this monograph as well as the approach to address the research tasks can be valued as a contribution to the development of the discipline. The identification and formulation of the research problem is definitely embedded in the mainstream of research and is addressing the actual research needs and challenges in Poland. It presents a novel analytical tool to meet some of them. However, the extended analytical approach requires appropriate data. Their lack is the main source of some limitations of this study, already mentioned in the previous chapters. Here, they are also reiterated and summarised. Conceptually, the dichotomous operationalisation of living arrangements in the model and its interpretation in the study could be extended and more comprehensive in the context of the potential of family care supply. It can be easily imagined that in case older person living alone becomes dependent, he or she could count on support from outside the household (family, friends, neighbours), especially when potential caregivers live in close proximity to the senior in need (residential patterns appear to be important for exchange relationships between older people and their kin – compare, for example, Glaser (1997) or Iacovou (2000)). Assuming that living alone and reporting severe limitations in ADL automatically triggers a need for formal care leads to overestimation of demand for formal care. Simultaneously, co-residing with other persons does not necessarily mean opportunity of getting sufficient support from inside the household. The other household members may be dependent persons themselves who cannot transfer care to others or may be reluctant to support others, for example, because of bad family relations. Then, the potential of informal support is overestimated as well. Similar reasoning refers to the operationalisation of health – reporting severe limitations in ADL does not always translate one-to-one into a loss of independence of an older person. Including more categories of living arrangements in the model based on a richer dataset could alleviate these shortcomings, but only to a limited extent. A more comprehensive approach would apply agent-based models that simultaneously simulate the operations and interactions of multiple agents who could be described with either dependency status or 'caring potential' in this case. Such approach would, on the one hand, help to account for social interactions that would have meaning in terms of potential care transfers and, on the other hand, address the problem of internal consistency that is not covered in the current study. The consistency problem refers to change in the living arrangements that are the result of interactions between two or more individuals (Van Imhoff & Keilman, 1991). Because transition rates are sex-specific, there is no mechanism currently in the model that would adjust living arrangements status by sex. For example, when partners live together as a couple there is no direct move from living with others to living alone for one partner when the other partner dies. In this sense changes in the living arrangements status by sex are independent and, therefore, inconsistent, even though they are relatively reliable estimate at the population level. The above issues are subject to justified criticism, but are strongly related to data limitations. As already mentioned, the information on age in the EU-SILC is restricted to the last open age group of 80 years and above which hinders learnings from the dynamic individual-level analysis. It also has to be kept in mind that the study's results refer only to persons living in private households. Also, duration dependence, which is a relevant predictor of health and living arrangements transitions, is not addressed in the study because of the limited time period of longitudinal data used in the analysis.

In light of the findings of this monograph some policy implications can be formulated. The study is innovative as it fills in the gap in the studies dedicated to demographic changes in Poland and their implications for the functioning of the services sector or shaping social policy. Ideational changes propelling evolution of the family model and intergenerational relations – also regarding care obligations – are out of control of policymakers who, however, can influence the potential care supply. The review of the ongoing changes in the family model and care provision, presented in Chapter 1, suggests that the availability of children and siblings – typical care providers in the absence of a spouse or partner – is going to continue to diminish. Facing shortages in other care resources will push for better co-operation and substitution of informal and formal care services dedicated to older adults (Henz, 2009). Many previous studies have formulated recommendations to address upcoming challenges in care provision. This study provides new data points to allow formulating a more informed policy that would accord with commonly accepted direction; for example, "countries of the European Union should not be complacent in their responses, and health care, long-term care, and welfare systems need to adapt to respond to population ageing; Health systems should become more age-friendly through active health promotion and disease prevention (for older people and across the life course), enabling better self-care, ensuring capacities of health services, improving coordination of care and management of hospital admissions and discharges, and addressing the ageing of the health workforce" (Rechel et al., 2013, p. 1312).

The projected increase in demand for care among older people is affecting not only care recipients but also care providers. Providing care to older adults has effects on care providers that can be considered either a gain or loss on their well-being (Kramer, 1997). Even though there are benefits from giving care to older people, for example, companionship, feeling of usefulness and sense of duty and obligation (Cohen et al., 2002), much more attention is put on the adverse effects of caregiving, such as restricted time for professional (employment), personal and social (leisure) life as well as psychological distress imposed by worsening health of care receivers and growing care needs (Pinquart & Sörensen, 2003). On average the negative consequences outweigh the positive ones (Verbakel et al., 2017). In the context of labour market, unpaid caregiving activities have an impact on labour force participation. Caregivers work fewer hours and are more likely to withdraw from employment in comparison to non-caregivers when the caring commitments become heavy and more time-consuming, which puts them at a higher risk of poverty, women especially (Ciccarelli & Van Soest, 2018; Lilly et al., 2007). Intensive caregiving is also negatively associated with everyday leisure (Stanfors et al., 2019). Findings for Poland are in line with the results described in the literature. Providing regular care to dependent adults is detrimental to the subjective quality of life of caregivers and longer periods of care provision are associated with increased levels of loneliness (Abramowska-Kmon & Maciejasz, 2018). Providing unpaid care is one of the reasons for staying out of employment and taking early retirement, too (Sowa-Kofta, 2018). Addressing this aspect should also be found on the priority list. In order to support the challenging roles of informal cares flexible working arrangements should be widely implemented. They allow workers with care responsibilities to alter their working time to flexibly adjust work duties to their caring roles and personal lives (UNECE, 2019). It is also pointed out that the existing entitlements such as flexible working hours or family-caregiver leave should be available for a wider spectrum of caregiving situations and at short notice to meet the often unpredictable caring needs (OECD, 2017). The findings of this book could also be used to stimulate discussions about inequalities in health and inequality in access to care services. It is important to think about social inequalities as categories that influence demographic processes with a reciprocal effect – to understand what is the impact of demographic processes, such as ageing and living arrangement patterns, on those inequalities.

Another aspect that calls for closer attention is the subpopulation of older persons living alone. The preference of living alone coupled with (financial) resources (now available more broadly from private pensions and social security) and increasing absence of kin is reflected in the growing percentage of seniors living alone. Distinction between living arrangements in population projections – even the very basic between living alone and not living alone – provides important insight as the receipt of formal care services in later life have been shown to be disproportionately concentrated on those older people living alone (Evandrou & Falkingham, 2004). Additionally, poverty rates among older people (especially among the over-80s) are much higher for those living alone (OECD, 2017). The groups that are identified to be more prone to various risks may by targeted with policies more effectively (Dostie & Leger, 2005).

Despite the limitations mentioned, the study provides relevant insights into the discussion about the future demand for care among older people in Poland. It offers an extension of traditional population projections which provides added value for both researchers and policymakers, but also may perform an important educational function for other non-specialised audience. The dynamic approach used in the study contributes to better understanding of interrelations between individual-level health and living arrangements trajectories and the macro-level outcomes related to care demand and care supply. The study also adds to the field by investigating the dynamics of health and living arrangements of people aged 50 and more and their relationship with selected demographic variables. The microsimulation model is relatively easy to be updated with the most recent findings on the relevant micro-level dynamics after translating them into parameters of the model. Additionally, the model offers flexibility in formulating assumptions and, therefore, is an efficient tool for conducting sensitivity analyses which is clearly advantageous in the context of possible (abrupt) changes in demographic and social processes over time. Importantly, it provides results that are consistent with the population projections published officially by the authorised agencies which is an important argument for their accessibility and usability. Various types of population ageing measures shed different light on the consequences of population ageing, but changes in the demographic structures undoubtedly translate into the increasing size of the older population which is the most affected by the loss of independence. Repeating the analysis with the most recent data, both from the perspectives of population projections and the individual-level parameters' estimates, would provide actual projections that would foster both scientific discussions and policy decision-making processes. If the projection model were to be applied more widely, much more attention and time should be paid to the assumptions of the model in sensitivity analyses. Understanding how the changes in the parameters of the model translate into interpretable output categories (e.g. healthy life years) would provide results that would better reflect reality.

Epilogue

When I finally submitted my PhD dissertation, which essentially forms the basis of this monograph, in early May 2020, it was already clear that the outbreak of the pandemic had irrevocably changed the face of the world as we had known it so far. The SARS-CoV-2 virus that spreads coronavirus disease (Covid-19) had been compared to the Spanish flu virus that took its heavy death toll nearly a century earlier. The new highly infectious virus has significantly affected the global economy, and basically the lives of everyone in the world. The introduction of far-reaching restrictions on everyday economic and social life to limit the transmission of the virus, including lockdowns that pertained to general population in many countries around the world, was unprecedented. Almost overnight, most everyday social interactions have gone from face-to-face to online. Consumer spending slumped, global supply chains were disrupted and unemployment was on the rise. Sharp declines in economic activity followed by periods of economic recovery resembled a kind of recurring cycle, dependent on the rise in infections and tightening of sanitary restrictions. Despite unprecedented support provided by governments and interventions by financial institutions, uncertainty was high. Inevitably, the pandemic also influenced all the processes described in this book, from mortality and population health to the supply of care for older people. The highly recommended social distancing as well as health care oriented towards Covid-19 patients made access to care more difficult, reduced the quality of life of individuals and significantly affected their chances of receiving other health services. At the level of scientific considerations, population projections based on assumptions about the evolution of human mortality and health before Covid-19 have rapidly become outdated. Instantaneously, short-term mortality risks, especially in the older population, hiked, while medium- and long-term uncertainties increased. The heavy burden on health care providers, which limited access to health care for non-covid patients, raised questions about the impact of the backlog on future population health.

In these closing remarks I would like to comment on the aforementioned phenomena, which have not been touched upon in the main parts of the book because they have not yet appeared at the time of its writing. It is a kind of postscript that, on the one hand, is necessary to include as a matter of chronicle duty and, on the other hand, advances additional arguments for incorporating uncertainty in scientific attempts to predict social processes.

The unanticipated Covid-19 pandemic induced severe mortality and macroeconomic shocks. They were costly, both economically and, more importantly, in terms of human lives. Over time, the ability to understand the underlying mechanisms and consequences – both at the individual and macro levels, and how to address them – has increased. From the *ex post* perspective, the longer after the outbreak of the pandemic, the more it was possible to quantify its diverse effects and to recognise the degree of uncertainty that should be associated with assumptions for future forecasting efforts.

The death toll of the pandemic was substantial. It is estimated that in 2020 and 2021 together, 18.2 million people died from Covid-19 globally, three times more than suggested by official statistics (Wang et al., 2022). Over the first year of the pandemic, prior to widespread vaccine-acquired immunity, Poland experienced at least 20 % higher mortality than it would have had the pandemic not occurred (Kontis et al., 2022). Early cross-national studies showed strong relationship between age and the infection fatality rate for Covid-19, and had already underlined how hazardous it can be not only for older people but also for middle-aged adults (Levin et al., 2020). Still, persons aged 60 or more years accounted for more than 80 % of the overall Covid-19 mortality across all income groups (Wong et al., 2023). Some later studies focused more on the impacts of the pandemic on life expectancy. The study by Aburto et al. (2022) showed that drop in life expectancy at birth due to Covid-19 was universal as 27 out of group of 29 studied high-income countries have encountered a decline from 2019 to 2020. Moreover, in majority of countries life expectancy losses in 2020 were more pronounced for men (contributing to a widening of the gap in life expectancy between the two sexes) and their magnitude offset most gains in life expectancy in the five years prior to the pandemic. As noted in that paper, in recent history such magnitudes of losses were comparable only to those seen during World War II in many countries of Western Europe and in the beginning of 1990s in Central and Eastern European countries around the breakup of the Soviet Union. In terms of the age pattern of mortality, elevated mortality rates among the older age groups had the highest contribution to sharp declines in life expectancy.[73]

---

73   For females, the drop in life expectancy was driven mostly by increased death rates at ages ≥80 years, while for males by elevated death rates at ages 60–79 years. In some countries, the contribution of increased mortality below age 60 years was sizeable, too (Aburto et al., 2022).

The later study by Schöley et al. (2022) extended the summary of the impact of pandemic on mortality to 2021. It showed divergent trends in mortality as countries in Western Europe experienced significant life expectancy bounce backs from 2020 losses, while countries in Central and Eastern Europe and the United States continued to drop further throughout 2021. In the latter countries the pandemic had induced a protracted mortality shock, however, in all countries life expectancy in 2021 was lower than expected if the pre-pandemic trends were continued. Consistent with previous research, in majority of countries males were more affected by excess deaths which contributed to widening the life expectancy sex gap.[74] The most recent communication on life expectancy in Poland[75] informs about the rebound in life expectancy in 2022. According to the official statistics, life expectancy for both sexes combined at age 60 went up from 19.9 years in 2021 to 21.2 years in 2022. However, it has not yet returned to its pre-pandemic levels (21.8 years in 2019). Interestingly, the most current Eurostat population projections EUROPOP2023, which already incorporated the Covid-19 outbreak, assume that in 2022 and 2023 the mortality rates have not completely aligned with levels observed before the pandemic, but that they will fully return to that level by 2024 (Eurostat, 2023). The population projections for years 2023–2060 by Statistics Poland also consider the drop in mortality due to Covid-19 as a temporary deviation from the long-term trend of increasing life expectancy. All three mortality scenarios proposed assume continued advances in longevity but at different rates (Potyra et al., 2023).

The introduction of SARS-CoV-2 vaccines during the first months of 2021 shifted the landscape again, because they have considerably lowered mortality rates among people who contract the virus and among the general population (Wang et al., 2022). Still, the highest Covid-19 mortality rates continued to be observed in the oldest age groups, despite those ages specifically were targeted with vaccinations in the first place (Torres et al., 2023). Severe Covid-19 continued to disproportionately affect older adults and individuals with underlying comorbidities as every new wave of infection indicated the largest

---

74 In Poland, males were more affected in the first year of the pandemic (life expectancy in 2020 reduced by 1.46 years) than in the second (a further drop of 0.86 years in 2021), while females were similarly affected in both years (life expectancy decline by 1.04 and 1.03 years respectively) (Wojtyniak et al., 2022).

75 Communication of the President of Statistics Poland of 27 March 2023 on life expectancy for both sexes combined, https://stat.gov.pl/en/latest-statistical-news/communications-and-announcements/list-of-communiques-and-announcements/life-expectancy-for-both-sexes-combined,295,11.html.

increases in hospital admissions and increasing length of hospital stay among individuals aged 65 and above (ECDC, 2023).

The impact of the pandemic on mortality was obvious as deaths reported as Covid-19 explained most life-expectancy losses[76] (Aburto et al., 2022), but it had side effects on several aspects related to health, too. These effects were directly related to the Covid-19 morbidity as well as to disruptions in accessing health services for the non-Covid patients. For example, in the Netherlands higher exposure to the Covid-19 pandemic[77] among older adults was associated with worse functioning across various domains, including physical, mental and social domains (Hoogendijk et al., 2022). It became quickly evident that the disadvantageous effect of deficit in access to health services will be protracted. Scientific community pointed out its prolonged negative effects on mortality (e.g. Wang et al. (2022) emphasised that "the effect of changes in health-care use on excess mortality might also be greater in later years, rather than in 2020 or 2021"), but also on population health (e.g. Aburto et al. (2022, p. 72) underlined the long-lasting effects of the pandemic on health: "Although COVID-19 might be seen as a transient shock to life expectancy, the evidence of potential long-term morbidity due to long COVID and impacts of delayed care for other illnesses as well as health effects and widening inequalities stemming from the social and economic disruption of the pandemic suggest that the scars of the COVID-19 pandemic on population health may be longer-lasting"). Indeed, the analysis of excess mortality in Poland for the 1 January 2020 to 15 October 2022 period showed a persistent level of excess deaths, but only a part of them could be attributed to Covid-19 mortality. In most recent months (from March to mid-October 2022), although no longer very high, the excess of deaths was basically identified only among people aged 65 and over. It is treated as an argument for the so-called health debt, that is, the long-term impact of the pandemic on the health of the population (Wojtyniak et al., 2022). Moreover, the measures

---

76 Importantly, Aburto et al. (2022, p. 66) highlight that "in most countries, the contribution of official COVID-19 deaths to changes in life expectancy can be interpreted as a lower bound due to limited testing and the potential misclassification of COVID-19 deaths".

77 The Covid-19 exposure index introduced by Hoogendijk et al. (2022) included variables that measured older adults' direct and indirect exposure to the Covid-19 pandemic resulting in a 35-item index. It included, among others, information on Covid-19 infection of respondents and their close relatives, assessment of the healthcare use and access, personal care provision and receipt as well as changes in income, lifestyle and social behaviour during pandemic.

implemented to contain the pandemic have had wide-reaching implications on daily living and behaviour of individuals. The imposed restrictions had highly reduced the level of physical activity in the population of older people worldwide. As a consequence, physical fitness of older people declined and sedentary lifestyle increased. In the context of preserving autonomy among older people, the emergence of both factors is highly disadvantageous as they are related to increased frailty in this population (Oliveira et al., 2022).

Disruptions in access to health services for the non-Covid patients due to the pandemic were significant. Consequently, unmet health care needs have remained high during the first two years of the pandemic. Across the EU countries, nearly one in five people reported that they were still having current unmet medical care needs in spring 2021 (17.4 %) and spring 2022 (17.8 %). The rate of unmet medical care needs in Poland was much higher, by 13.3 and 12.2 percentage points than the EU average respectively (OECD, 2022). According to the OECD report, overall problems with access to hospital or specialist care were reported by 47 % of the EU population in 2021 (43 % in 2022). The number of surgical procedures across the EU countries was 16 % lower in 2020 than a year before; that is, one out of six people did not get surgery. These missing interventions have contributed to longer waiting times (OECD, 2022). The study by Mularczyk-Tomczewska et al. (2022) confirmed that the Covid-19 pandemic has worsened access to health services in Poland. In this research almost half of adults in Poland reported barriers to access health services in the past 12 months, which even included temporary closures of healthcare facilities for non-Covid patients. According to Wróblewska et al. (2022), almost one in ten people aged 50 and over in Poland experienced a deterioration in health in during the first year of the pandemic, with a greater risk of health deterioration associated with lower self-rated health before the outbreak. In terms of healthcare use, due to a fear of coronavirus infection about 9 % of population aged 50 years and over in Poland has withdrawn from treatment, especially from visits to a specialist. Additionally, 27 % of respondents declared they had their medical appointment postponed due to coronavirus.

In addition to respondents' declarations from the survey data, the analysis of changes in the structure of health care spending and the structure of service provision by the publicly funded National Health Fund allows similar observations to be made. In Poland, the pandemic led to a significant reduction in planned hospitalisations and outpatient advice in favour of the creation of temporary hospitals dedicated to the treatment of Covid-19 patients (Dudek-Godeau et al., 2022). A drop in the number of services was largely due to a reduction in some procedures (mainly elective procedures) in hospitals, halted diagnostic tests as well as a reduction in the performance of life-saving procedures. Between 2021 and 2022, the budget for hospital care has decreased by around 10 %. In particular, the decrease in funding could be seen in the areas of geriatrics, palliative, hospice and long-term care (Dudek-Godeau et al., 2022). It is worth noting that the reduced access to health services was unequal, especially for people on a lower income. Eurofound (2023) reported that in 2020, the risk of having an unmet medical need for people in the lowest income quintile was 5.4 times that of those in the highest quintile (up from 4.6 in 2019). Findings from the study by Dudek-Godeau et al. (2022) showed that women in Poland were more likely than men to report barriers to access healthcare during pandemic, even though they were more likely to visit a doctor. However, in the first two years of the pandemic the Healthy Life Years at age 65 indicator for Poland was relatively stable for females (8.7 years in 2020 and 8.9 years in 2021 from 9.0 years in 2019) and somewhat lower for males (7.6 and 7.7 years in 2020 and 2021 respectively versus 8.1 years in 2019)[78] indicating that in absolute terms males were worse off.

Population health in the future may be further undermined by loneliness and social isolation among older adults, which increased substantially compared to pre-pandemic levels. Loneliness and social isolation was on the rise over time as the pandemic progressed, and their detrimental effects on health may lead to rising needs for psychological aid among older adults and create additional demand that will have to be addressed (Su et al., 2023). The pressure for isolation and social distancing as well as the fear of developing the disease had also a negative impact on mental health among older population in Poland. According to survey by Dziedzic et al. (2021) conducted in October 2020, when a sudden increase in the number of coronavirus infections was observed in Poland, almost 20 % of older people aged 60 year and over reported anxiety and depressive symptoms. To larger extent it pertained to older women, persons living alone and those with a lower subjective health rating. However, it is younger age that is primarily correlated with a higher anxiety, depression and loneliness rather than older age (Kobos et al., 2022).

There is no question that the Covid-19 pandemic has presented a significant obstacle to intergenerational interactions. Yet, in the European context, the intergenerational contact (without the distinction whether it was in-person contact or contact by electronic means) between older parents aged 65 years and

---

78   Eurostat, *Healthy life years by sex (from 2004 onwards)*, online data code: HLTH_ HLYE.

over and their non-coresident adult children did not reduce after the outbreak of the pandemic, but rather remained stable or even increased[79] (Vergauwen et al., 2022). However, the authors identified some socio-demographic groups, especially older men, less educated older adults and adults living in nursing homes that were more likely to report decreased parent-child interactions than their counterparts. In the study about France, Italy and Spain that distinguished between physical and non-physical contact, Arpino et al. (2020) found out that during the pandemic about 40 % of people aged 65 and over reduced their physical contact with children, but more than 50 % increased their non-physical intergenerational interactions. These findings indicate a trade-off between the two forms of contact – social interactions that take place remotely (via digital communication) compensated for decreased physical interactions. In this context, it is noteworthy that in some EU countries, there has been an upward trend in the share of young adults aged 25–34 living with their parents. This trend has been particularly noticeable in Poland, where this proportion grew up by 3.6 percentage points between 2019 and 2020 (reaching 47.5 % in 2020) and in the subsequent years increased further to 48.8 % in 2021 and 51.0 % in 2022. By contrast, the proportion remained constant at approximately 30.4 % throughout the EU.[80] Presumably, economic reasons related to the wider adoption of remote working (e.g. reducing rental costs) and financial hardship (e.g. due to job loss or losing financial liquidity) were probably the main reason for the increase in the co-residence rates. It, however, cannot be ruled out that part of the decision to cohabit was based on the need to provide care for elderly family members.

The consequences of the Covid-19 outbreak were particularly affecting people in need of care as well as care providers. Epidemiological control measures such as physical distancing or recommendations to stay at home increased barriers to receive personal care from outside the household (e.g. due to reduced availability of paid services) and put an additional pressure to both family caregivers and care receivers. In the early phase of the pandemic the provision of personal care towards older family members outside one's own household strongly increased across Europe. The elevated parental caregiving led to greater anxiety and feelings of depression among care providers, though (Bergmann & Wagner, 2021).

---

79 Vergauwen et al. (2022) hypothesised that the reduction in physical interactions might have been substituted with more frequent digital communication or the contact has been intensified via downwards support patterns, such as grandparental care.

80 Eurostat, *Share of young adults aged 18–34 living with their parents by age and sex – EU-SILC survey*, online data code: ILC_LVPS08.

Similarly, in the US informal caregivers reported higher caregiving intensity that translated into increased caregiving burden (Beach et al., 2021; S. A. Cohen et al., 2021). Other research on care provision for older people also showed increased caring engagement during the pandemic. The average number of weekly hours of informal care provided in European countries has grew up by almost 8 hours (+17 %) compared to before the pandemic, with women experiencing a greater increase than men (Eurocarers/IRCCS-INRCA, 2021). The intensified activity of family carers in Poland during the pandemic was accompanied a by decline in access to external formal and informal support. In turn, family carers reported being overloaded with caring activities and experiencing greater loneliness (Bakalarczyk, 2021). The situation of care receivers has deteriorated as well. According to Bergmann and Wagner (2021), about 21 % of all care recipients reported difficulties in receiving home care. The highest share of respondents with difficulties obtaining adequate care from outside the household during the pandemic was reported in Southern European countries (about 33 %) and the lowest in Eastern European countries (less than 10 %). The study also showed that the longer the period of the stay-at-home orders implemented at the country level, the higher the probability of perceiving difficulties in receiving care by care recipients. On a more positive note, the study revealed that those care recipients who strongly rely on personal care, that is, oldest-old, living alone, still received the care they needed during the first phase of the pandemic (Bergmann & Wagner, 2021).

Finally, a brief comment on an event as unexpected as the outbreak of the pandemic, but potentially significant for the domestic supply of care. The armed aggression of Russia against Ukraine on 24 February 2022 resulted in an unprecedented influx of Ukrainian refugees into Poland. Labour market in Poland has already been strongly influenced by the presence of immigrant workers – in this respect, Poland has gone a substantial qualitative change in recent years, transitioning from a country with a high level of economic emigration to one with a surplus of immigrants. Even though large-scale immigration of Ukrainian citizens to Poland has already been observed since 2013 and had important contribution to Poland's economic growth (Strzelecki et al., 2022), yet the scale of the inflow of Ukrainian war refugees (estimated at between 1 to 1.5 million persons residing in Poland at different points in time) and its demographic structure (mostly children and women, with low numbers and proportions of men and older people) were atypical (Kaczmarczyk, 2023). Thanks to rapid introduction of a special law granting Ukrainians legal status and access to public education, health care, social services as well as the labour market, the relatively large number of refugees quickly found jobs, however, a lot of them being employed below their qualifications (skill mismatch) (Gromadzki & Lewandowski, 2023). At the same time, despite the ongoing war, almost 20 % of Ukrainian refugees indicated they would stay in Poland permanently (Chmielewska-Kalińska et al., 2023). In this context, although it is unclear how many refugees will stay and for how long, the influx of forced migration from Ukraine could help alleviate the unfulfilled care needs of older individuals because (non-medical) care provision typically does not require qualifications and often can be provided informally.

The overall cost of the Covid-19 pandemic is not known and probably will never to be found. Scientific community alerts that long Covid, a long-term complex system profile resulting from a positive infection with SARS-CoV-2 (also known as post-Covid condition/syndrome), will undoubtedly have a lasting impact on social and economic activities and should be considered as the next global health crisis (Faghy et al., 2022). The persistence of excess mortality in Poland indicates the presence of an extended pandemic effect which will contribute to increasing 'health debt'. Given that those in lower income groups were affected most by the disruption to healthcare services (Eurofound, 2023), health inequalities could be even greater among older population. Additionally, challenges of providing care to older people were exacerbated by the Covid-19 pandemic. Accumulation of health deficits (failure to undertake medical procedures and diagnostics for new cases, delay in receiving them or abandonment of treatment for those being treated) may consequently lead to an increase in demand for care among older population. The extra strain on family caregivers through reportedly increased duties resulted in worse mental health outcomes and well-being. In longer perspective, it may negatively affect the supply side of caregivers in the future. Migrant care may partially fill this gap in the future but the prospects are not too optimistic.

Last but not least, another aspect of the book that was highlighted by the coronavirus pandemic was the use of the stochastic approach and simulation in modelling the spread of Covid-19. Various institutions and research centres[81] were modelling and forecasting the spread of the coronavirus using a wide range of approaches including the stochastic approach. One of its advantages was that it allowed for the variability of unknown parameters according to their

---

81 For example, the European Covid-19 Forecast Hub which produced short-term forecasts of Covid-19 cases and deaths across Europe, created by a multitude of infectious disease modelling teams, coordinated by the European Centre for Disease Prevention and Control (https://covid19forecasthub.eu).

distributions, and then assigning confidence intervals to the outcomes of relevant pre-assumed scenarios. Indeed, the experience of the pandemic strengthened the argument for scenario-based predictions. During subsequent waves of infections epidemiological modelling centres produced projections that took into account different variants of the virus and their virulence, as well as considered different levels of severity of potential social and economic restrictions and their impact on the number and distribution of deaths. These data-driven forecasting models were essential tools for policymakers to allocate scarce medical and economic resources in order to minimise the negative effects of the pandemic. They also helped decision makers fine tune various epidemiological measures. In this book I employ similar tools, but for a less short-term and rather more forward-looking purpose. Population ageing and the evolution of care needs are a much less dynamic process to foresee than the transmission of a virus, yet they can be conceptualised in a similar way. My approach also relies on modelling that combines simulation techniques with demographic parameters characterised by stochasticity which, in turn, generate results that can be described by confidence intervals. It also aims to be a useful tool for decision-makers to help them design public policies that serve society.

The ideas and research conclusions summarised here are just a brief indication of the many questions that need to be considered when trying to project complex processes in the future. The turbulent times of the Covid-19 pandemic have only reinforced the perception of how strong the effects of external conditions are on the actual course of social processes. Past and present experience show that the future is increasingly difficult to predict. But models that simplify reality can provide us with projections that may be helpful in measuring the scale of potential effects of changes in quantifiable assumptions. However, the attempt to imagine the future course of a complex reality requires nuanced scenarios to be considered. Projections based on a set of scenarios depicting different trajectories of social processes in the future seem an appropriate tool to be better prepared for uncertainty. It can provide public policy with insights that may be utilised for informed decision-making.

Appendix

A.1 Data sources

The European Health Interview Survey (EHIS) offers comprehensive data on the health status of the population and health-related topics based on answers by respondents of a representative sample of a population. The EHIS consists of four modules: health status, health care utilisation, determinants of health and general socio-economic variables. It targets the population aged at least 15 years and living in private households. It is run every five years. The first wave of the European Health Interview Survey (EHIS 1) was conducted between years 2006 and 2009. The second wave (EHIS 2) took place between 2013 and 2015. The third wave (EHIS 3) was planned for 2019. In Poland, the first wave of the survey was conducted in 2009 and the second one in 2014 (the fieldwork for the third wave was scheduled for September–December 2019; however, the results were not available at the time of the study). There are two questionnaires dedicated to adults (15 years old and more) and to children (below age 15) separately. The adult's sample size was 35,100 individuals in 2009 and 24,156 individuals in 2014. The effective sample sizes when restricting only for adults aged 60 and more were 9,317 and 7,874 individuals in 2009 and 2014, respectively. Information on age is grouped into 5-year age intervals with age 85 and more being the last (open) age interval.

The European Union Statistics on Income and Living Conditions (EU-SILC) provides comparable cross-sectional and longitudinal multidimensional microdata on income, poverty, social exclusion and living conditions in the European Union Member States. The EU-SILC has replaced the European Communities Household Panel (ECHP) carried out from 1994 to 2001. The EU-SILC provides two types of annual data:

- cross-sectional data pertaining to a given time or a certain time period with variables on income, poverty, social exclusion and other living conditions, and
- longitudinal data pertaining to individual-level changes over time, observed periodically over a four-year period.

Data are collected on a yearly basis, in Poland since year 2005. The average cross sectional sample size of adults aged 15 years and more exceeds 30,000 individuals. The effective sample sizes when restricting only for adults aged 60 and more were 8,196 and 9,255 individuals in 2009 and 2014, respectively. The dataset allows analysing age with 1-year age groups with age 80 and more being the last (open) age group. The reference population of the EU-SILC is all private households and their current members residing in the territory of the Member States at the time of the data collection. Persons living in collective households and in institutions are excluded from the target population (European Commission, 2016). It should be therefore kept in mind that all results refer to the non-institutionalised population. One of the biggest advantages of this data source is the fact that both the cross-sectional and the longitudinal data are produced annually. It also provides the individual-level characteristics such as age, sex, health status or level of education together with the household-level data, for example, household size. However, it is not well designed to identify relationships between household members since no traditional full household grip is provided. The EU-SILC allows identification of a spouse/partner and a mother/father relationship directly but many other relationships cannot be distinguished (more details can be found in Iacovou and Skew 2011). Due to those limitations, the cross-sectional analysis distinguishes four basic categories of living arrangements: living alone, living with partner/spouse only, living with partner/spouse and others (non-relatives and/or other relative) and living without partner/spouse but with others.

In the analysis, I examined living arrangement patterns in Poland using the EU-SILC data and the 2011 Census database available at Eurostat's Census Hub portal as well as the 2011 Census elaborations by the Statistics Poland. I also compared the health questions distribution between the corresponding years of the EU-SILC and EHIS surveys (2009 and 2014). The results from both datasets presented here are weighted and representative for the 60+ population.

Health

According to Eurostat, the Minimum European Health Module (MEHM) is a set of three general questions characterising three different concepts of health:

1. *Self-perceived health* as the self-assessment of a person's own health in general,
2. *Chronic morbidity* as the presence of long-standing health problems,
3. *Activity limitations* as the presence of long-standing activity limitation due to health problems measured via the Global Activity Limitation Indicator (GALI).[82]

The module was developed to be used in all social surveys. At present, it is implemented in the EHIS and the EU-SILC. The EU-SILC questionnaire in each

---

82 https://ec.europa.eu/eurostat/statistics-explained/index.php?title=Glossary: Minimum_European_Health_Module_(MEHM)

country contains the MEHM in the successive years since 2004. A module on health status in the EHIS conducted every five years includes the MEHM either. The standard English version of the module includes the following three questions:

1. **How is your health in general?**
   1. Very Good 2. Good 3. Fair 4. Bad 5. Very Bad
2. **Do you suffer from/have any chronic (long-standing) illness or condition (health problem)?** INTERVIEWER: Problems that are seasonal or recurring should be included.
   1. Yes 2. No
3. **For at least the past 6 months, to what extent have you been limited because of a health problem in activities people usually do?** Would you say you have been …
   1. Severely limited 2. Limited but not severely, or 3. Not limited at all?

The MEHM reliability proved to be acceptable in a sample of individuals in Belgium (Cox et al., 2009). A self-rated health (SRH) is a measure of health that is considered as a reliable predictor of morbidity, health utilisation and mortality (Verropoulou, 2012). Some other studies validated the relevance of GALI as a single measure of a general activity limitation in European populations (Berger et al., 2015; Jagger et al., 2010; van Oyen et al., 2006).

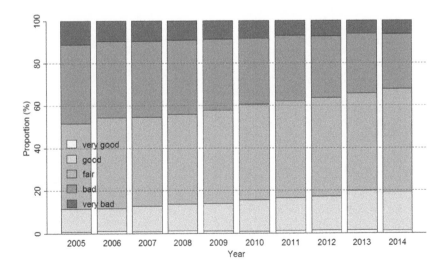

Figure 47. Self-perceived health by years 2005–2014, Poland.

Source: Own elaboration based on the EU-SILC cross-sectional data, weighted.

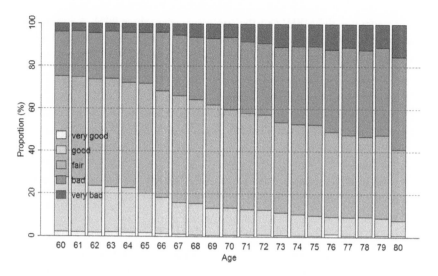

Figure 48. Self-perceived health by age, average for years 2005–2014, Poland.
Source: Own elaboration based on EU-SILC cross-sectional data, weighted.

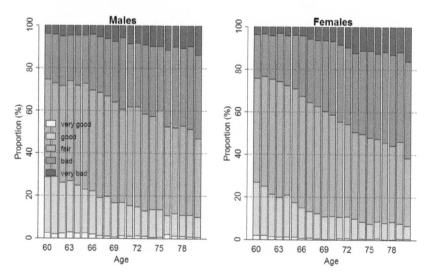

Figure 49. Self-perceived health by age and sex, average for years 2005–2014, Poland.
Source: Own elaboration based on EU-SILC cross-sectional data, weighted.

Table 28. Household status by age and sex (%), 2011 Census data.

Household status	60 to 64 years			65 to 69 years			70 to 74 years			75 to 79 years			80 year and over		
	Total	Male	Female	Total	Male	Female	Total	Male	Female	Total	Male	Female	Total	Male	Female
Persons living in a private household	99.4	99.2	99.6	99.4	99.2	99.5	99.2	99.2	99.3	99.1	99.1	99.0	98.1	98.9	97.8
Persons in a family nucleus	79.2	85.0	74.2	73.0	84.3	64.3	65.4	82.4	53.8	56.4	79.2	43.1	40.9	67.1	29.5
Persons in a married couple	69.1	79.0	60.6	64.4	80.1	52.3	56.2	78.6	41.1	45.8	74.6	28.8	27.0	60.5	12.5
Partners in a consensual union	1.2	1,5	0,9	0.8	1,1	0,6	0,5	0.8	0.4	0.4	0,6	0.2	0.2	0.4	0,1
Other	8.9	4,6	12.6	7,8	3,1	11.4	8.6	3,1	12.3	10.3	4.0	14.0	13.7	6,2	16.9
Persons not in a family nucleus	20.8	15.0	25.8	27.0	15.7	35.7	34.6	17.6	46.2	43.6	20.8	56.9	59.1	32.9	70.5
Living alone	14.3	10.5	17.6	18.3	11.0	24.0	22.7	11.9	30.1	27.2	13.3	35.3	32.0	18.6	37.8
Not living alone	6.5	4.5	8.2	8.7	4.8	11.7	11.9	5.6	16.1	16.4	7,5	21.6	27.1	14.3	32.7
Persons not living in a private household	0,6	0.8	0.4	0,6	0.8	0,5	0.8	0.8	0.7	0,9	0,9	1,0	1,9	1,1	2.2

Source: Own elaboration based on 2011 Census data, https://ec.europa.eu/CensusHub2.

A.2 The calculation of age in the EU-SILC dataset

Age of the respondent is used as the time scale in the study. The EU-SILC questionnaire collects information on month and year of birth of the respondent as well as on day, month and year of the personal/household interview. In case of death of respondent, month and year of death is also recorded. However, in order to ensure disclosure control and confidentiality of the User Database,[83] some variables collected are removed or modified. The information on the day of interview is unavailable and both month of respondent's birth and month of the personal/household interview (or death) have been grouped into quarters. In order to facilitate research some new variables were also supplied. One of the added variables is *Age at the time of interview* (RX010), and it serves as the reference age indicator in the study. It gives age in full years and is calculated by subtracting date of birth (in year and month) from date of interview (in year and month). RX010 may vary by one digit compared to real age at the exact day of interview, as the day of birth is not known, yet in most cases it provides precise information on age in completed years. Importantly, a household member coded '80' is 80 years old or over.

The use of multistate modelling techniques requires having two different age values in two points in time. The age of respondents expressed in years that is available in the EU-SILC database causes some technical problems. The *EU-SILC Methodological Guidelines* documentation recommends the collection of data for the longitudinal component, for a given unit (household or person), between successive waves to be kept as close as possible to 12 months (European Commission, 2016). Still, a respondent may have the same age value for two subsequent interviews. It might be the case if the month of interview is close to respondent's month of birth and the spacing between two interviews is less than full year. For example, if a person born on 11 July 1956 had been interviewed on 1 August 2016, his or her calculated age (RX010) would be 60 years. If the next interview was conducted on 30 June 2017, the calculated age would be 60 years again. The same situation is apparent to age at death which cannot rise given death of the respondent happens within one-year period from the last interview.

To overcome this deficiency it is possible to extended the age in years into age in quarters. For that purpose one needs to use information on year and quarter of birth and year and quarter of personal interview or year and quarter when the

---

83   User Database (UDB) is the EU-SILC database shared for research. It is based on the original database but it is anonymised which means that some variables are removed or changed. In order to ease the use of the data, some calculated variables are added.

person died. The assumptions used in the calculations are as follows. The basic information on the quarter of interview is taken from the quarter of personal interview (PB100). If it is missing, the quarter of household interview (HB050) is used. All quarters and years of death are available. If quarter of birth is missing, it is assumed the respondent was born in the second quarter.

For the oldest respondents who reached 80 years it is unknown exactly how old they are. For all interviews their age value is set to 80, so in reality they could be younger than 84 years but might be well over 100 as well. However, for some of them it is possible to find true year of birth and, consequently, age provided they turned 80 during the study period. Inspection of the year of birth across all waves that respondents took part in allows a proper assignment of age value for them. For respondents who are 80 years or over across all interviews, age is manually increased by one year for each year so that they can age with time, yet their true age is unknown.[84] Therefore, estimations for the oldest age groups have to be interpreted cautiously as averages.

Respondents who died and have the same age between the last interview and time of death even after recalculating age in years into age in quarters are having increased their age at death by one-quarter.

---

84 The approach used is one possibility only. The other would be to use external data sources, for example, to randomly attach an age value of 80 or more to respondents so that their age distribution reflects the observed one in the population of olders.

List of figures

List of tables

References

Abeliansky, A. L., & Strulik, H. (2019). Long-run improvements in human health: Steady but unequal. *The Journal of the Economics of Ageing, 14,* 100189. https://doi.org/10.1016/j.jeoa.2019.01.003

Abramowska, A. (2006). Sytuacja rodzinna osób starszych w Polsce w świetle wyników NSP 2002. *Zeszyty Sekcji Analiz Demograficznych KND PAN, 14.*

Abramowska-Kmon, A. (2011). *Zmiany modelu rodziny a zapotrzebowanie na usługi opiekuńcze dla osób starszych* [Praca doktorska]. praca doktorska, Kolegium Analiz Ekonomicznych, Szkoła Główna Handlowa w Warszawie.

Abramowska-Kmon, A. (2014). Przemiany struktur rodzin i gospodarstw domowych. In I. E. Kotowska (Ed.), *Niska dzietność w Polsce w kontekście percepcji Polaków – Diagnoza Społeczna 2013. Raport tematyczny* (pp. 25–31). Ministerstwo Pracy i Polityki Społecznej i Centrum Rozwoju Zasobów Ludzkich.

Abramowska-Kmon, A. (2015). Determinanty sprawowania opieki nad starszymi rodzicami w Polsce w świetle danych badania GGS-PL. *Studia Demograficzne, 168*(2), 39–60.

Abramowska-Kmon, A., Antczak, R., Kubicki, P., Perek-Białas, J., & Szweda-Lewandowska, Z. (2020). Srebrna gospodarka szansą rozwoju krajów Europy Środkowo-Wschodniej. In M. Strojny (Ed.), *Raport SGH i Forum Ekonomicznego 2020* (pp. 347–383). Oficyna Wydawnicza SGH – Szkoła Główna Handlowa w Warszawie.

Abramowska-Kmon, A., Kalbarczyk-Stęclik, M., Kotowska, I. E., & Nicińska, A. (2014). Finansowe i pozafinansowe transfery w SHARE. In A. Chłoń-Domińczak (Ed.), *Portret generacji 50+ w Polsce i w Europie. Wyniki badania zdrowia, starzenia się i przechodzenia na emeryturę (SHARE)* (pp. 47–54). Instytut Badań Edukacyjnych.

Abramowska-Kmon, A., Kotowska, I. E., & Łątkowski, W. (2015). *The organization of caring responsibilities both 'up' and 'down' family lines* (Working paper series 61). FamiliesAndSocieties.

Abramowska-Kmon, A., & Maciejasz, M. (2018). Subjective quality of life of informal caregivers aged 50–69 in Poland. *Studia Demograficzne, 2*(174), 37–65.

Abramowska-Kmon, A., & Mynarska, M. (2020). Opieka nad bezdzietnymi osobami starszymi w Polsce: opinie, doświadczenia, potrzeby. *Ubezpieczenia Społeczne. Teoria i Praktyka, 3*(146), 97–117. https://doi.org/10.32088/0000_35

Aburto, J. M., Schöley, J., Kashnitsky, I., Zhang, L., Rahal, C., Missov, T. I., Mills, M. C., Dowd, J. B., & Kashyap, R. (2022). Quantifying impacts of the COVID-19 pandemic through life-expectancy losses: A population-level study of 29 countries. *International Journal of Epidemiology, 51*(1), 63–74. https://doi.org/10.1093/ije/dyab207

Agree, E. M., & Glaser, K. (2009). Demography of Informal Caregiving. In P. Uhlenberg (Ed.), *International handbook of population aging* (pp. 647–668). Springer Science+Business Media B.V.

Albertini, M., Kohli, M., & Vogel, C. (2007). Intergenerational transfers of time and money in European families: Common patterns – different regimes? *Journal of European Social Policy, 17*(4), 319–334. https://doi.org/10.1177/0958928707081068

Albertini, M., & Mencarini, L. (2014). Childlessness and support networks in later life: New pressures on familistic welfare states? *Journal of Family Issues, 35*(3), 331–357. https://doi.org/10.1177/0192513X12462537

Alho, J. M., & Spencer, B. D. (2005). Uncertainty in demographic forecasts: Concepts, issues, and evidence. In J. M. Alho & B. D. Spencer (Eds.), *Statistical demography and forecasting* (pp. 226–268). Springer. https://doi.org/10.1007/0-387-28392-7_8

Andersen, P. K., & Keiding, N. (2002). Multi-state models for event history analysis. *Statistical Methods in Medical Research, 11*(2), 91–115. https://doi.org/10.1191/0962280202SM276ra

Andersen-Randberg, K., Christensen, K., Jeune, B., Skytthe, A., Vasegaard, L., & Vaupel, J. W. (1999). Declining physical abilities with age: A cross-sectional study of older twins and centenarians in Denmark. *Age and Ageing, 28*(4), 373–377.

Antonowicz, D. (2012). External influences and local responses. Changes in Polish Higher Education 1990–2005. In M. Kwiek & P. Maassen (Eds.), *National higher education reforms in a European context comparative reflections on Poland and Norway* (pp. 87–110). Peter Lang.

Anttonen, A., & Sipilä, J. (1996). European social care services: Is it possible to identify models? *Journal of European Social Policy, 6*(2), 87–100. https://doi.org/10.1177/095892879600600201

Anttonen, A., & Sipilä, J. (2005). Comparative approaches to social care: Diversity in care production modes. In B. Pfau-Effinger & B. Geissler (Eds.), *Care and social integration in European societies* (pp. 115–134). The Policy Press University of Bristol. https://doi.org/10.1332/policypress/9781861346049.003.0006

Anttonen, A., & Zechner, M. (2011). Theorizing care and care work. In B. Pfau-Effinger & T. Rostgaard (Eds.), *Care between work and welfare in European societies* (pp. 15–34). Palgrave Macmillan UK. https://doi.org/10.1057/978023 0307612

Arpino, B., Pasqualini, M., Bordone, V., & Sole-Auro, A. (2020). Indirect consequences of COVID-19 on people's lives. Findings from an on-line survey in France, Italy and Spain. *SocArXiv.* https://doi.org/10.31235/osf.io/4sfv9

Bakalarczyk, R. (2021). Aktywność opiekunów rodzinnych osób starszych w czasie pandemii Covid-19. *Polityka Społeczna, 571*(10), 28–36. https://doi. org/10.5604/01.3001.0015.5574

Balachandran, A., & James, K. S. (2019). A multi-dimensional measure of population ageing accounting for Quantum and Quality in life years: An application of selected countries in Europe and Asia. *SSM – Population Health, 7,* Art. 100330. https://doi.org/10.1016/j.ssmph.2018.100330

Barnett, K., Mercer, S. W., Norbury, M., Watt, G., Wyke, S., & Guthrie, B. (2012). Epidemiology of multimorbidity and implications for health care, research, and medical education: A cross-sectional study. *The Lancet, 380*(9836), 37–43. https://doi.org/10.1016/S0140-6736(12)60240-2

Beach, S. R., Schulz, R., Donovan, H., & Rosland, A.-M. (2021). Family caregiving during the COVID-19 pandemic. *The Gerontologist, 61*(5), 650–660. https://doi.org/10.1093/geront/gnab049

Beckett, L. A., Brock, D. B., Lemke, J. H., Mendes de Leon, C., Guralnik, J. M., Fillenbaum, G. G., Branch, L. G., Wetle, T. T., & Evans, D. A. (1996). Analysis of change in self-reported physical function among older persons in four population studies. *American Journal of Epidemiology, 143*(8), 766–778. https://doi.org/10.1093/oxfordjournals.aje.a008814

Belanger, A. (1989). Multistate life table with duration dependence: An application to Hungarian female marital history. *European Journal of Population / Revue Européenne de Démographie, 5*(4), 347–372. https://doi.org/10.1007/BF0 1796792

Berger, N., Van Oyen, H., Cambois, E., Fouweather, T., Jagger, C., Nusselder, W., & Robine, J.-M. (2015). Assessing the validity of the Global Activity Limitation Indicator in fourteen European countries. *BMC Medical Research Methodology, 15*(1), 1. https://doi.org/10.1186/1471-2288-15-1

Bergmann, M., Kneip, T., De Luca, G., & Scherpenzeel, A. (2019). *Survey participation in the Survey of Health, Ageing and Retirement in Europe (SHARE), Wave 1–7. Based on Release 7.0.0.* (SHARE Working Paper Series 41-2019). SHARE-ERIC.

Bergmann, M., & Wagner, M. (2021). The impact of COVID-19 on informal caregiving and care receiving across Europe during the first phase of the pandemic. *Frontiers in Public Health, 9.* https://doi.org/10.3389/fpubh.2021.673874

Bijak, J., Kupiszewska, D., Kupiszewski, M., & Saczuk, K. (2013). Population Ageing, Population Decline and Replacement Migration in Europe. In M. Kupiszewski (Ed.), *International Migration and the Future of Populations and Labour in Europe* (pp. 243–265). Springer Netherlands. https://doi.org/10.1007/978-90-481-8948-9_14

Bijak, J., Kupiszewska, D., Kupiszewski, M., Saczuk, K., & Kicinger, A. (2007). Population and labour force projections for 27 European countries, 2002-052: Impact of international migration on population ageing. *European Journal of Population / Revue Européenne de Démographie, 23*(1), 1. https://doi.org/10.1007/s10680-006-9110-6

Billari, F. C., & Liefbroer, A. C. (2010). Towards a new pattern of transition to adulthood? *Advances in Life Course Research, 15*(2), 59–75. https://doi.org/10.1016/j.alcr.2010.10.003

Błędowski, P. (2012). Potrzeby opiekuńcze osób starszych. In M. Mossakowska, A. Więcek, & P. Błędowski (Eds.), *Aspekty medyczne, psychologiczne, socjologiczne i ekonomiczne starzenia się ludzi w Polsce* (pp. 449–466). Termedia Wydawnictwa Medyczne.

Błędowski, P., & Maciejasz, M. (2013). Rozwój opieki długoterminowej w Polsce – stan i rekomendacje. *Nowiny Lekarskie, 82*(1), 61–69.

Błędowski, P., Mossakowska, M., Chudek, J., Grodzicki, T., Milewicz, A., Szybalska, A., Wieczorowska-Tobis, K., Wiecek, A., Bartoszek, A., Dabrowski, A., & Zdrojewski, T. (2011). Medical, psychological and socioeconomic aspects of aging in Poland: Assumptions and objectives of the PolSenior project. *Experimental Gerontology, 46*(12), 1003–1009. https://doi.org/10.1016/j.exger.2011.09.006

Błędowski, P., Szatur-Jaworska, B., Szweda-Lewandowska, Z., & Kubicki, P. (2012). *Raport na temat sytuacji osób starszych w Polsce.* Instytut Pracy i Spraw Socjalnych.

Bloom, D. E., Canning, D., & Fink, G. (2010). Implications of population ageing for economic growth. *Oxford Review of Economic Policy, 26*(4), 583–612. https://doi.org/10.1093/oxrep/grq038

Bloom, D. E., Canning, D., & Sevilla, J. (2003). *The demographic dividend: A new perspective on the economic consequences of population change.* RAND.

Bogaert, P., Van Oyen, H., Beluche, I., Cambois, E., & Robine, J.-M. (2018). The use of the global activity limitation indicator and healthy life years by member states and the European Commission. *Archives of Public Health, 76*(1), 30. https://doi.org/10.1186/s13690-018-0279-z

Bojanowska, E. (2009). Opieka nad ludźmi starszymi. In P. Szukalski (Ed.), *Przygotowanie do starości. Polacy wobec starzenia się* (pp. 207–230). Fundacja Instytut Spraw Publicznych.

Bolin, K., Lindgren, B., & Lundborg, P. (2008). Informal and formal care among single-living elderly in Europe. *Health Economics, 17*(3), 393–409. https://doi.org/10.1002/hec.1275

Bongaarts, J. (2002). The end of the fertility transition in the developed world. *Population and Development Review, 28*(3), 419–443. https://doi.org/10.1111/j.1728-4457.2002.00419.x

Bongaarts, J., & Sobotka, T. (2012). A demographic explanation for the recent rise in European fertility. *Population and Development Review, 38*(1), 83–120. https://doi.org/10.1111/j.1728-4457.2012.00473.x

Bonneux, L., & van der Gaag, N. (2012). The future of disability in Poland. *Polityka Społeczna,* 20–25.

Booth, H. (2006). Demographic forecasting: 1980 to 2005 in review. *International Journal of Forecasting, 22*(3), 547–581. https://doi.org/10.1016/j.ijforec ast.2006.04.001

Börsch-Supan, A. (2003). Labor market effects of population aging. *LABOUR, 17*(s1), 5–44. https://doi.org/10.1111/1467-9914.17.specialissue.2

Börsch-Supan, A., Brandt, M., Hunkler, C., Kneip, T., Korbmacher, J., Malter, F., Schaan, B., Stuck, S., & Zuber, S. (2013). Data resource profile: The survey of health, ageing and retirement in Europe (SHARE). *International Journal of Epidemiology, 42*(4), 992–1001. https://doi.org/10.1093/ije/dyt088

Börsch-Supan, A., Kotlikoff, L. J., & Morris, J. N. (1988). The dynamics of living arrangements of the elderly. *NBER Working Paper Series, 2787,* 1–28.

Bowling, A. (2005). *Measuring health: A review of quality of life measurement scales* (3rd ed.). Open University Press.

Brandt, M., Haberkern, K., & Szydlik, M. (2009). Intergenerational help and care in Europe. *European Sociological Review, 25*(5), 585–601. https://doi.org/10.1093/esr/jcn076

Breeze, E., Sloggett, A., & Fletcher, A. (1999). Socioeconomic and demographic predictors of mortality and institutional residence among middle aged and older people: Results from the longitudinal study. *Journal of Epidemiology and Community Health, 53*(12), 765–774. https://doi.org/10.1136/jech.53.12.765

Broese van Groenou, M. I., Glaser, K., Tomassini, C., & Jacobs, T. (2006). Socio-economic status differences in older people's use of informal and formal help: A comparison of four European countries. *Ageing and Society, 26*(5), 745–766. https://doi.org/10.1017/S0144686X06005241

Brown, S. L., & Lin, I.-F. (2012). The Gray divorce revolution: Rising divorce among middle-aged and older adults, 1990–2010. *The Journals of Gerontology: Series B, 67*(6), 731–741.

Brown, S. L., Lin, I.-F., Hammersmith, A. M., & Wright, M. R. (2018). Later life marital dissolution and repartnership status: A national portrait. *The Journals of Gerontology: Series B, 73*(6), 1032–1042. https://doi.org/10.1093/geronb/gbw051

Cambois, E., Solé-Auró, A., Brønnum-Hansen, H., Egidi, V., Jagger, C., Jeune, B., Nusselder, W. J., Van Oyen, H., White, C., & Robine, J.-M. (2016). Educational differentials in disability vary across and within welfare regimes: A comparison of 26 European countries in 2009. *Journal of Epidemiology and Community Health, 70*(4), 331–338. https://doi.org/10.1136/jech-2015-205978

Chan, A., Zimmer, Z., & Saito, Y. (2011). Gender differentials in disability and mortality transitions: The case of older adults in Japan. *Journal of Aging and Health, 23*(8), 1285–1308. https://doi.org/10.1177/0898264311408417

Chatterji, S., Byles, J., Cutler, D., Seeman, T., & Verdes, E. (2015). Health, functioning, and disability in older adults – present status and future implications. *The Lancet, 385*(9967), 563–575. https://doi.org/10.1016/S0140-6736(14)61462-8

Cherlin, A. J. (2004). The deinstitutionalization of American marriage. *Journal of Marriage and Family, 66*(4), 848–861. http://www.jstor.org/stable/3600162

Chłoń-Domińczak, A. (2016). Reversing the 2013 retirement age reform in Poland. *ESPN Flash Report, 7*, 2013–2014.

Chłoń-Domińczak, A. (2019). Impact of retirement age changes on the old-age pension take up in Poland after 1990. *Ubezpieczenia Społeczne. Teoria i Praktyka, 3*, 41–65. https://doi.org/10.32088/0000_10

Chłoń-Domińczak, A., & Łątkowski, W. (2019). *Estimation of national transfer accounts for Poland in 2016 and comparison to the results from 2012* (p. 23). Report prepared for the Statutory Research No KAE/S18/37/18, Warsaw School of Economics.

Chmielewska-Kalińska, I., Dudek, B., & Strzelecki, P. (2023). *The living and economic situation of Ukrainian migrants in Poland – the impact of the pandemic and the war on the nature of migration in Poland. Report of the questionnaire survey*. Department of Statistics, National Bank of Poland.

Christensen, K., Doblhammer, G., Rau, R., & Vaupel, J. W. (2009). Ageing populations: The challenges ahead. *The Lancet, 374*(9696), 1196–1208. https://doi.org/10.1016/S0140-6736(09)61460-4

Ciccarelli, N., & Van Soest, A. (2018). Informal caregiving, employment status and work hours of the 50+ population in Europe. *De Economist, 166*(3), 363–396. https://doi.org/10.1007/s10645-018-9323-1

Cohen, C. A., Colantonio, A., & Vernich, L. (2002). Positive aspects of caregiving: Rounding out the caregiver experience. *International Journal of Geriatric Psychiatry, 17*(2), 184–188. https://doi.org/10.1002/gps.561

Cohen, S. A., Kunicki, Z. J., Drohan, M. M., & Greaney, M. L. (2021). Exploring changes in caregiver burden and caregiving intensity due to COVID-19. *Gerontology and Geriatric Medicine, 7*, Art. 2333721421999279. https://doi.org/10.1177/2333721421999279

Coleman, D. (2008). The demographic effects of international migration in Europe. *Oxford Review of Economic Policy, 24*(3), 452–476.

Colombo, F., Llena-Nozal, A., Mercier, J., & Tjadens, F. (2011). *Help wanted?: Providing and paying for long-term care* (p. 328). OECD Publishing. https://doi.org/10.1787/9789264097759-en

Comas-Herrera, A., Wittenberg, R., Costa-Font, J., & Gori, C. (2006). Future long-term care expenditure in Germany, Spain, Italy and the United Kingdom. *Ageing and Society, 26*(2), 285–302. https://doi.org/10.1017/S0144686X05004289

Commenges, D. (1999). Multi-state models in epidemiology. *Lifetime Data Analysis, 5*(4), 315–327. https://doi.org/10.1023/A:1009636125294

Commenges, D. (2003). Likelihood for interval-censored observations from multi-state models. *SORT-Statistics and Operations Research Transactions, 27*(1), 1–12.

Cox, B., Oyen, H. Van, Cambois, E., Jagger, C., Roy, S. le, Robine, J.-M., & Romieu, I. (2009). The reliability of the minimum European health module. *International Journal of Public Health, 54*(2), 55–60. https://doi.org/10.1007/s00038-009-7104-y

Crimmins, E. M., Hayward, M. D., & Saito, Y. (1994). Changing mortality and morbidity rates and the health-status and life expectancy of the older population. *Demography, 31*(1), 159–175. https://doi.org/10.2307/2061913

Crimmins, E. M., Zhang, Y., & Saito, Y. (2016). Trends over 4 decades in disability-free life expectancy in the United States. *American Journal of Public Health, 106*(7), 1287–1293. https://doi.org/10.2105/AJPH.2016.303120

Czapiński, J. (2015). Indywidualna jakość i styl życia. Diagnoza Społeczna 2015, Warunki i Jakość Życia Polaków – Raport. *Contemporary Economics, 9*(4), 200–372. https://ce.vizja.pl/en/download-pdf/volume/9/issue/4/id/419

Czapiński, J., & Panek, T. (Eds.). (2015). Social diagnosis 2015. Objective and subjective quality of life in Poland. In *Contemporary economics* (Vol. 9, Issue 4).

Czekanowski, P., & Bień, B. (2006). Older people and their needs for care. In B. Bień (Ed.), *Family caregiving for the elderly in Poland* (pp. 66–84). Wydawnictwo Uniwersyteckie Trans Humana.

Czepulis-Rutkowska, Z. (2016). Long term care for the elderly in Poland. In B. Greve (Ed.), *Long term care for the elderly in Europe. Development and prospects* (pp. 38–58). Routledge.

Davis, M. A., Moritz, D. J., Neuhaus, J. M., Barclay, J. D., & Gee, L. (1997). Living arrangements, changes in living arrangements, and survival among community dwelling older adults. *American Journal of Public Health, 87*(3), 371–377. https://doi.org/10.2105/ajph.87.3.371

de Jong Gierveld, J. (2004). Remarriage, unmarried cohabitation, living apart together: Partner relationships following bereavement or divorce. *Journal of Marriage and Family, 66*(1), 236–243. https://doi.org/10.1111/j.0022-2445.2004.00015.x

de Jong Gierveld, J., de Valk, H., & Blommesteijn, M. (2001). Living arrangements of older persons and family support in more developed countries. *Population Bulletin of the United Nations, Special Issue 42–43*, 193–217.

Deeg, D. J. H., Verbrugge, L. M., & Jagger, C. (2003). Disability measurement. In J.-M. Robine, C. Jagger, J. C. Mathers, E. M. Crimmins, & R. M. Suzman (Eds.), *Determining health expectancies* (pp. 203–219). https://doi.org/10.1002/0470858885.ch10

Dekkers, G., Keegan, M., & O'Donoghue, C. (Eds.). (2014). *New pathways in microsimulation*. Ashgate Publishing.

Demeny, P. (2007). A clouded view of Europe's demographic future. *Vienna yearbook of population research*, 27–35. https://doi.org/10.1553/populationyearbook2007s27

Demopædia. (2010). *Multilingual demographic dictionary* (2nd unified ed.). http://en-ii.demopaedia.org/wiki/Population_forecast

Doblhammer, G., Ziegler, U., Martikainen, P., Nihtilä, E., & Apt, W. (2008). Health and its effect on the future demand for care. In J. Gaymu, P. Festy, M. Poulain, & G. Beets (Eds.), *Future Elderly Living Conditions in Europe* (pp. 141–163). Les Cahiers de l'Ined, INED.

Dostie, B., & Leger, P. T. (2005). The living arrangement dynamics of sick, elderly individuals. *Journal of Human Resources, 40*(4), 989–1014.

Dudek-Godeau, D., Partyka, O., Pajewska, M., & Czerw, A. (2022). Impact of the Covid-19 pandemic on health financing mechanisms in the context of changes in the structure of health needs. In B. Wojtyniak & P. Goryński (Eds.), *Health status of Polish population and its determinants 2022*. National Institute of Public Health NIH – National Research Institute.

Dykstra, P. A. (2018). Cross-national differences in intergenerational family relations: The influence of public policy arrangements. *Innovation in Aging, 2*(1), igx032. https://doi.org/10.1093/geroni/igx032

Dykstra, P. A., & Fokkema, T. (2011). Relationships between parents and their adult children: A West European typology of late-life families. *Ageing and Society, 31*(4), 545–569. https://doi.org/10.1017/S0144686X10001108

Dykstra, P. A., & Hagestad, G. O. (2007). Childlessness and parenthood in two centuries: Different roads – different maps? *Journal of Family Issues, 28*(11), 1518–1532. https://doi.org/10.1177/0192513X07303881

Dziedzic, B., Idzik, A., Kobos, E., Sienkiewicz, Z., Kryczka, T., Fidecki, W., & Wysokiński, M. (2021). Loneliness and mental health among the elderly in Poland during the COVID-19 pandemic. *BMC Public Health, 21*(1), 1976. https://doi.org/10.1186/s12889-021-12029-4

Eggink, E., Woittiez, I., & Ras, M. (2016). Forecasting the use of elderly care: A static micro-simulation model. *The European Journal of Health Economics, 17*(6), 681–691. https://doi.org/10.1007/s10198-015-0714-9

Esping-Andersen, G. (1990). *The three worlds of welfare capitalism*. Polity Press.

Esping-Andersen, G. (1999). *Social foundations of postindustrial economies*. Oxford University Press.

Esping-Andersen, G., & Billari, F. C. (2015). Re-theorizing family demographics. *Population and Development Review, 41*(1), 1–31. https://doi.org/10.1111/j.1728-4457.2015.00024.x

Eurocarers/IRCCS-INRCA. (2021). *Impact of the Covid-19 outbreak on informal carers across Europe – final report.* https://eurocarers.org/wp-content/uplo ads/2021/05/EUC-Covid-study-report-2021.pdf

Eurofound. (2023). *Economic and social inequalities in Europe in the aftermath of the COVID-19 pandemic.* Publications Office of the European Union. https://doi.org/10.2806/439913

European Centre for Disease Prevention and Control. (2023). *Interim public health considerations for COVID-19 vaccination roll-out during 2023.* ECDC.

European Commission. (2014). *Population ageing in Europe: Facts, implications and policies.* Publications Office of the European Union. https://doi.org/10.2777/60452

European Commission. (2016). *Methodological guidelines and description of EU-SILC target variables, 2015 operation (Version August 2016).*

European Commission. (2017). *Summary methodology of the 2015-based population projections* (p. 13).

European Commission. (2018). *The 2018 Ageing Report: Economic and budgetary projections for the EU member states (2016–2070).* Publications Office of the European Union. https://doi.org/10.2765/615631

Eurostat. (2015). *People in the EU: Who are we and how do we live?* (M. Kotzeva, Ed.). Publications Office of the European Union. https://doi.org/10.2785/406462

Eurostat. (2017a). *EUROPOP2015 – Population projections at national level (2015–2080)*. European Commission.

Eurostat. (2017b). *EUROPOP2015 – Population projections at national level. Reference metadata*.

Eurostat. (2019). *EUROPOP2018 – Population projections at national level (2018–2100)*. European Commission.

Eurostat. (2023). *Population projections in the EU – methodology*. https://ec.eur opa.eu/eurostat/statistics-explained/index.php?title=Population_projections _in_the_EU_-_methodology

Evandrou, M., & Falkingham, J. (2004). Demographic change in Europe: Implications for future family support of older people. In P. Kreager & E. Schroder-Butterfill (Eds.), *Ageing without children* (pp. 175–197). Berghahn Books.

Faghy, M. A., Owen, R., Thomas, C., Yates, J., Ferraro, F. V, Skipper, L., Barley-McMullen, S., Brown, D. A., Arena, R., & Ashton, R. E. (2022). Is long COVID the next global health crisis? *Journal of Global Health, 12*, Art. 03067. https:// doi.org/10.7189/jogh.12.03067

Fenger, H. (2007). Welfare regimes in Central and Eastern Europe: Incorporating post-communist countries in a welfare regime typology. *Contemporary Issues and Ideas in Social Sciences, 3*(2).

Ferrera, M. (1996). The 'southern model' of welfare in social Europe. *Journal of European Social Policy, 6*(1), 17–37. https://doi.org/10.1177/09589287960 0600102

Fihel, A. (2005). Consensual unions in Poland: An analysis of the 2002 Population Census. *Studia Demograficzne, 1*(147), 104–120.

Fihel, A., Janicka, A., & Kloc-Nowak, W. (2018). The direct and indirect impact of international migration on the population ageing process: A formal analysis and its application to Poland. *Demographic Research, 38*(43), 1303–1338. https://doi.org/10.4054/DemRes.2018.38.43

Fihel, A., Kiełkowska, M., Kordasiewicz, A., & Radziwinowiczówna, A. (2017). Determinanty spadku płodności w Polsce. Próba syntezy. *Studia Demograficzne, 2*(172), 35–69. https://doi.org/10.33119/SD.2017.2.1

Fihel, A., & Okólski, M. (2017). Starzenie się ludności Polski w warunkach intesywnej migracji międzynarodowej. In P. Lewandowski & J. Rutkowski (Eds.), *Starzenie się ludności, rynek pracy i finanse publiczne w Polsce* (pp. 35–40). Przedstawicielstwo Komisji Europejskiej w Polsce. https://doi. org/10.2775/210871

Flandorfer, P., & Fliegenschnee, K. (2010). Education and health: Theoretical considerations based on a qualitative grounded theory. *Vienna Yearbook of*

Population Research, 8, 237–259. https://doi.org/10.1553/populationyearbook2010s237

Fokkema, T., & Liefbroer, A. P. (2008). Trends in living arrangements in Europe: Convergence or divergence? *Demographic Research*, 19(36), 1351–1418. https://doi.org/10.4054/DemRes.2008.19.36

Fong, J. H., Shao, A. W., & Sherris, M. (2015). Multistate actuarial models of functional disability. *North American Actuarial Journal*, 19(1), 41–59. https://doi.org/10.1080/10920277.2014.978025

Francavilla, F., & Giannelli, G. C. (2019). Dressing a ghost: Size and value of unpaid family care. *Applied Economics*, 51(28), 3015–3030. https://doi.org/10.1080/00036846.2018.1564116

Freedman, V. A. (1996). Family structure and the risk of nursing home admission. *The Journals of Gerontology Series B: Psychological Sciences and Social Sciences*, 51B(2), S61–S69. https://doi.org/10.1093/geronb/51B.2.S61

Frejka, T., & Sobotka, T. (2008). Fertility in Europe: Diverse, delayed and below replacement. *Demographic Research*, S7(3), 15–46. https://doi.org/10.4054/DemRes.2008.19.3

Fries, J. F. (1980). Aging, natural death, and the compression of morbidity. *New England Journal of Medicine*, 303(3), 130–135. https://doi.org/10.1056/NEJM198007173030304

Fuentes-García, A. (2014). Katz activities of daily living scale. In A. C. Michalos (Ed.), *Encyclopedia of quality of life and well-being research* (pp. 3465–3468). Springer. https://doi.org/10.1007/978-94-007-0753-5_1572

Gałęzewska, P., Perelli-Harris, B., & Berrington, A. (2017). Cross-national differences in women's repartnering behaviour in Europe: The role of individual demographic characteristics. *Demographic Research*, S21(8), 189–228. https://doi.org/10.4054/DemRes.2017.37.8

Gaugler, J. E., Duval, S., Anderson, K. A., & Kane, R. L. (2007). Predicting nursing home admission in the U.S: A meta-analysis. *BMC Geriatrics*, 7. https://doi.org/10.1186/1471-2318-7-13

Gaymu, J., Delbès, C., Springer, S., Binet, A., Désesquelles, A., Kalogirou, S., & Ziegler, U. (2006). Determinants of the living arrangements of older people in Europe. *European Journal of Population*, 22(3), 241–262. https://doi.org/10.1007/s10680-006-9004-7

Gaymu, J., Ekamper, P., & Beets, G. (2007). Who will be caring for Europe's dependent elders in 2030? *Population (English Edition, 2002–)*, 62(4), 675–706. https://doi.org/10.3917/pope.704.0675

Gaymu, J., Ekamper, P., & Beets, G. (2008). Future trends in health and marital status: Effects on the structure of living arrangements of older Europeans in 2030. *European Journal of Ageing*, *5*(1), 5–17. https://doi.org/10.1007/s10 433-008-0072-x

Geerlings, S. W., Margriet Pot, A., Twisk, J. W. R., & Deeg, D. J. H. (2005). Predicting transitions in the use of informal and professional care by older adults. *Ageing and Society*, *25*(1), 111–130. https://doi.org/10.1017/S01446 86X04002740

Geerts, J., Willeme, P., & Mot, E. (2012). *Long-term care use and supply in Europe: Projections for Germany, the Netherlands, Spain and Poland* (ENEPRI Research Report No. 116).

Geissler, B., & Pfau-Effinger, B. (2005). Change in European care arrangements. In B. Pfau-Effinger & B. Geissler (Eds.), *Care and Social Integration in European Societies* (pp. 3–20). Policy Press.

Gierveld, J., Dykstra, P. A., & Schenk, N. (2012). Living arrangements, intergenerational support types and older adult loneliness in Eastern and Western Europe. *Demographic Research*, *S11*(7), 167–200. https://doi.org/ 10.4054/DemRes.2012.27.7

Gil Alonso, F. (2009). Can the rising pension burden in Europe be mitigated by immigration? Modelling the effects of selected demographic and socioeconomic factors on ageing in the European Union, 2008–2050. *Vienna Yearbook of Population Research*, 123–147. https://doi.org/10.1553/populat ionyearbook2009s123

Gill, T. M., Allore, H., Hardy, S. E., Holford, T. R., & Han, L. (2005). Estimates of active and disabled life expectancy based on different assessment intervals. *The Journals of Gerontology: Series A*, *60*(8), 1013–1016. https://doi.org/ 10.1093/gerona/60.8.1013

Giudici, C., Arezzo, M. F., & Brouard, N. (2013). Estimating health expectancy in presence of missing data: An application using HID survey. *Statistical Methods & Applications*, *22*(4), 517–534. https://doi.org/10.1007/s10260-013-0233-8

Glaser, K. (1997). The living arrangements of elderly people. *Reviews in Clinical Gerontology*, *7*(1), 63–72. https://doi.org/10.1017/S0959259897000075

Glaser, K., Tomassini, C., & Grundy, E. (2004). Revisiting convergence and divergence: Support for older people in Europe. *European Journal of Ageing*, *1*(1), 64–72. https://doi.org/10.1007/s10433-004-0006-1

Glauber, R. (2017). Gender differences in spousal care across the later life course. *Research on Aging*, *39*(8), 934–959. https://doi.org/10.1177/01640 27516644503

Glynn, L. G., Valderas, J. M., Healy, P., Burke, E., Newell, J., Gillespie, P., & Murphy, A. W. (2011). The prevalence of multimorbidity in primary care and its effect on health care utilization and cost. *Family Practice*, *28*(5), 516–523. https://doi.org/10.1093/fampra/cmr013

Goldscheider, F., Bernhardt, E., & Lappegård, T. (2015). The gender revolution: A framework for understanding changing family and demographic behavior. *Population and Development Review, 41*(2), 207–239. https://doi.org/10.1111/j.1728-4457.2015.00045.x

Goldstein, J. R. (2009). How populations age. In P. Uhlenberg (Ed.), *International handbook of population aging* (pp. 7–18). Springer. https://doi.org/10.1007/978-1-4020-8356-3_1

Goldstein, J. R., & Kluge, F. (2016). Demographic pressures on European unity. *Population and Development Review, 42*(2), 299–304. https://doi.org/10.1111/j.1728-4457.2016.00137.x

Goldstein, J. R., & Lee, R. D. (2014). How large are the effects of population aging on economic inequality? *Vienna Yearbook of Population Research, 12*, 193–209. https://doi.org/10.1553/populationyearbook2014s193

Golinowska, S., & Sowa-Kofta, A. (2018). Imbalance between demand and supply of long-term care. The case of post-communist Poland. In K. Christensen & D. Pilling (Eds.), *The Routledge handbook of social care work around the world* (pp. 172–186). Routledge. https://doi.org/10.4324/9781315612805-13

Gore, P. G., Kingston, A., Johnson, G. R., Kirkwood, T. B. L., & Jagger, C. (2018). New horizons in the compression of functional decline. *Age and Ageing, 47*(6), 764–768. https://doi.org/10.1093/ageing/afy145

Gourbin, C., & Wunsch, G. (2006). Health, illness, and death. In G. Caselli, J. Vallin, & G. Wunsch (Eds.), *Demography: Analysis and synthesis* (Vol. 3, pp. 5–12). Academic Press.

Gratton, B., & Gutmann, M. P. (2010). Emptying the nest: Older men in the United States, 1880–2000. *Population and Development Review, 36*(2), 331–356. https://doi.org/10.1111/j.1728-4457.2010.00332.x

Grigoryeva, A. (2017). Own gender, sibling's gender, parent's gender: The division of elderly parent care among adult children. *American Sociological Review, 82*(1), 116–146. https://doi.org/10.1177/0003122416686521

Gromadzki, J., & Lewandowski, P. (2023). Refugees from Ukraine on the Polish labour market. *Ubezpieczenia Społeczne. Teoria i Praktyka, 154*(3), 1–13. https://doi.org/10.5604/01.3001.0016.2353

Gruenberg, E. M. (1977). The failures of success. *The Milbank Memorial Fund Quarterly. Health and Society, 55*, 3–24.

Grundy, E. (1992). The living arrangements of elderly people. *Reviews in Clinical Gerontology, 2*(4), 353–361. https://doi.org/10.1017/S0959259800003191

Grundy, E. (2001). Living arrangements and the health of older persons in developed countries [Special Issue]. *United Nations Population Bulletin, 42/43*.

Grundy, E., & Murphy, M. (2007). Marital status and family support for the oldest-old in Great Britain. In J.-M. Robine, E. M. Crimmins, S. Horiuchi, & Z. Yi (Eds.), *Human longevity, individual life duration, and the growth of the oldest-old population* (pp. 415–436). Springer. https://doi.org/10.1007/978-1-4020-4848-7_18

Grundy, E., van den Broek, T., & Keenan, K. (2017). Number of children, partnership status, and later-life depression in Eastern and Western Europe. *The Journals of Gerontology: Series B*, gbx050–gbx050.

GUS. (2012). *Rocznik demograficzny 2012*. Zakład Wydawnictw Statystycznych.

GUS. (2013a). *Gospodarstwa domowe w 2011 roku – wyniki spisu ludności i mieszkań 2011*. Zakład Wydawnictw Statystycznych.

GUS. (2013b). *Ludność. Stan i struktura demograficzno-społeczna. Narodowy Spis Powszechny Ludności i Mieszkań 2011*. Zakład Wydawnictw Statystycznych.

GUS. (2014a). *Gospodarstwa domowe i rodziny. Charakterystyka demograficzna. Narodowy Spis Powszechny Ludności i Mieszkań 2011*. Zakład Wydawnictw Statystycznych.

GUS. (2014b). *Sytuacja demograficzna osób starszych i konsekwencje starzenia się ludności Polski w świetle prognozy na lata 2014–2050*.

GUS. (2016a). *Ludność w wieku 60 lat i więcej*. Notatka przygotowana na posiedzenie Sejmowej Komisji Polityki Senioralnej dotyczące 'Informacji Ministra Zdrowia na temat wpływu zmian demograficznych i starzenia się społeczeństwa na organizację systemu ochrony zdrowia i Narodowy Program Zdrowia'.

GUS. (2016b). *Prognoza gospodarstw domowych na lata 2016–2050*.

GUS. (2016c). *Stan zdrowia ludności Polski w 2014 r.* Zakład Wydawnictw Statystycznych.

GUS. (2018). *Informacja o sytuacji osób starszych na podstawie badań Głównego Urzędu Statystycznego*.

GUS. (2019). *Informacja o rozmiarach i kierunkach czasowej emigracji z Polski w latach 2004–2018 [Information on the scale and directions of temporary emigration from Poland in the years 2004–2018]*. Główny Urząd Statystyczny.

GUS. (2020a). *Rocznik demograficzny 2020*.

GUS. (2020b). *The situation of older people in Poland in 2018* (p. 74).

GUS. (2020c). Trwanie życia w zdrowiu w Polsce w latach 2009–2019. *Analizy Statystyczne*.

GUS. (2020d). *Glossary. Terms used in official statistics*. https://stat.gov.pl/en/metainformation/glossary/terms-used-in-official-statistics/list.html

Haberkern, K., Schmid, T., & Szydlik, M. (2015). Gender differences in intergenerational care in European welfare states. *Ageing & Society, 35*(2), 298–320. https://doi.org/10.1017/S0144686X13000639

Haberkern, K., & Szydlik, M. (2010). State care provision, societal opinion and children's care of older parents in 11 European countries. *Ageing and Society, 30*(2), 299–323. https://doi.org/10.1017/S0144686X09990316

Hakim, C. (2003). A new approach to explaining fertility patterns: Preference theory. *Population and Development Review, 29*(3), 349–374. https://doi.org/10.1111/j.1728-4457.2003.00349.x

Hanewald, K., Li, H., & Shao, A. W. (2017). *Modeling multi-state health transitions in China: A generalized linear model with time trends* (2017/10; ARC Centre of Excellence in Population Ageing Research Working Paper Series).

Hardy, S. E., Dubin, J. A., Holford, T. R., & Gill, T. M. (2005). Transitions between states of disability and independence among older persons. *American Journal of Epidemiology, 161*(6), 575–584. https://doi.org/10.1093/aje/kwi083

Hays, J. C. (2002). Living arrangements and health status in later life: A review of recent literature. *Public Health Nursing, 19*(2), 136–151. https://doi.org/10.1046/j.1525-1446.2002.00209.x

Hayward, M. D., Crimmins, E. M., & Zhang, Z. (2006). Consequences of educational change for the burden of chronic health problems in the population. In A. H. Gauthier, C. Y. C. Chu, & S. Tuljapurkar (Eds.), *Allocating public and private resources across generations. Riding the age waves* (Vol. 2, pp. 227–242). Springer Netherlands.

Henz, U. (2009). Couples' provision of informal care for parents and parents-in-law: Far from sharing equally? *Ageing and Society, 29*(3), 369–395. https://doi.org/10.1017/S0144686X08008155

Herlofson, K., & Brandt, M. (2019). Helping older parents in Europe: The importance of grandparenthood, gender and care regime. *European Societies*, 1–21. https://doi.org/10.1080/14616696.2019.1694163

Hoogendijk, E. O., Schuster, N. A., Tilburg, T. G. van, Schaap, L. A., Suanet, B., Breij, S. De, Kok, A. A. L., Schoor, N. M. Van, Timmermans, E. J., Jongh, R. T. de, Visser, M., & Huisman, M. (2022). Longitudinal aging study Amsterdam COVID-19 exposure index: A cross-sectional analysis of the impact of the pandemic on daily functioning of older adults. *BMJ Open, 12*(11), Art. e061745. https://doi.org/10.1136/bmjopen-2022-061745

Hoogendijk, E. O., van der Noordt, M., Onwuteaka-Philipsen, B. D., Deeg, D. J. H., Huisman, M., Enroth, L., & Jylhä, M. (2019). Sex differences in healthy life expectancy among nonagenarians: A multistate survival model using data from the Vitality 90+ study. *Experimental Gerontology, 116*, 80–85. https://doi.org/10.1016/j.exger.2018.12.015

Hougaard, P. (1999). Multi-state models: A review. *Lifetime Data Analysis, 5*(3), 239–264. https://doi.org/10.1023/A:1009672031531

Iacovou, M., & Skew, A. J. (2011). Household composition across the new Europe: Where do the new Member States fit in? *Demographic Research, 25*, 465–490. https://doi.org/10.4054/DemRes.2011.25.14

Iparraguirre, J. L. (2018a). Caregiving need. In J. L. Iparraguirre (Ed.), *Economics and ageing. Volume II: Policy and applied* (pp. 205–227). Springer International Publishing. https://doi.org/10.1007/978-3-319-93357-3_6

Iparraguirre, J. L. (2018b). Demand for and supply of LTC services. In J. L. Iparraguirre (Ed.), *Economics and ageing. Volume II: Policy and applied* (pp. 229–316). Springer International Publishing. https://doi.org/10.1007/978-3-319-93357-3_7

Jackson, C. H. (2011). Multi-state models for panel data: The msm package for R. *Journal of Statistical Software, 38*(8), 1–29.

Jacobs, M. T., Broese van Groenou, M. I., Aartsen, M. J., & Deeg, D. J. H. (2018). Diversity in older adults' care networks: The added value of individual beliefs and social network proximity. *The Journals of Gerontology: Series B, 73*(2), 326–336.

Jacobzone, S., Cambois, E., Chaplain, E., & Robine, J.-M. (1998). *The health of older persons in OECD countries: Is it improving fast enough to compensate for population ageing?* (Ageing Working Papers 4.2).

Jagger, C., Gillies, C., Cambois, E., Van Oyen, H., Nusselder, W., & Robine, J. M. (2010). The Global Activity Limitation Index measured function and disability similarly across European countries. *Journal of Clinical Epidemiology, 63*(8), 892–899. https://doi.org/10.1016/j.jclinepi.2009.11.002

Jakubowski, M., Patrinos, H. A., Porta, E. E., & Wiśniewski, J. (2010). The impact of the 1999 education reform in Poland. *Policy Research Working Paper, 5263*, Art. 5263. https://doi.org/10.1787/5kmbjgkm1m9x-en

Janssen, F., & de Beer, J. (2019). The timing of the transition from mortality compression to mortality delay in Europe, Japan and the United States. *Genus, 75*(1), 10. https://doi.org/10.1186/s41118-019-0057-y

Jette, A. M., Tennstedt, S. L., & Branch, L. G. (1992). Stability of informal long-term care. *Journal of Aging and Health, 4*(2), 193–211. https://doi.org/10.1177/089826439200400203

Kaczmarczyk, P. (2023). Ukraińscy migranci w Polsce w czasie wojny: stan wiedzy i kluczowe wyzwania. *Ubezpieczenia Społeczne. Teoria i Praktyka, 154*(3), 1–22. https://doi.org/10.5604/01.3001.0016.2359

Kalbarczyk, M., & Mackiewicz-Łyziak, J. (2019). Physical activity and healthcare costs: Projections for Poland in the context of an ageing population. *Applied Health Economics and Health Policy, 17*(4), 523–532. https://doi.org/10.1007/s40258-019-00472-9

Kalbfleisch, J. D., & Lawless, J. F. (1985). The analysis of panel data under a Markov assumption. *Journal of the American Statistical Association, 80*(392), 863–871.

Kałuża-Kopias, D. (2018). Imigranci w systemie opieki nad osobami starszymi. *Rynek Pracy, 3*(166), 36–45.

Kałuża-Kopias, D., & Szweda-Lewandowska, Z. (2018). Potencjalny popyt na opiekunów osób starszych. Spojrzenie z perspektywy dwóch pokoleń – wspierającego i wspieranego. *Polityka Społeczna, 3*, 28–34.

Kannisto, V., Lauritsen, J., Thatcher, A. R., & Vaupel, J. W. (1994). Reductions in mortality at advanced ages: Several decades of evidence from 27 countries. *Population and Development Review, 20*(4), 793–810. https://doi.org/10.2307/2137662

Karpinska, K., & Dykstra, P. A. (2019). Intergenerational ties across borders: A typology of the relationships between Polish migrants in the Netherlands and their ageing parents. *Journal of Ethnic and Migration Studies, 45*(10), 1728–1745. https://doi.org/10.1080/1369183X.2018.1485204

Kashnitsky, I., & Schöley, J. (2018). Regional population structures at a glance. *The Lancet, 392*(10143), 209–210. https://doi.org/10.1016/S0140-6736(18)31194-2

Kassebaum, N. J., Arora, M., Barber, R. M., Bhutta, Z. A., Brown, J., Carter, A., Casey, D. C., Charlson, F. J., Coates, M. M., Coggeshall, M., Cornaby, L., Dandona, L., Dicker, D. J., Erskine, H. E., Ferrari, A. J., Fitzmaurice, C., Foreman, K., Forouzanfar, M. H., Fullman, N., ... Murray, C. J. L. (2016). Global, regional, and national disability-adjusted life-years (DALYs) for 315 diseases and injuries and healthy life expectancy (HALE), 1990–2015: A systematic analysis for the Global Burden of Disease Study 2015. *The Lancet, 388*(10053), 1603–1658. https://doi.org/10.1016/S0140-6736(16)31460-X

Katz, S., Branch, L. G., Branson, M. H., Papsidero, J. A., Beck, J. C., & Greer, D. S. (1983). Active life expectancy. *The New England Journal of Medicine, 309*(20), 1218–1224.

Katz, S., Ford, A. B., Moskowitz, R. W., Jackson, B. A., & Jaffe, M. W. (1963). Studies of illness in the aged. The Index of ADL: A standardized measure of biological and psychosocial function. *JAMA, 185*(12), 914–919. https://doi.org/10.1001/jama.1963.03060120024016

Keilman, N. (2006). Households and families. In G. Caselli, J. Vallin, & G. Wunsch (Eds.), *Demography: Analysis and synthesis* (Vol. 3, pp. 457–476). Academic Press.

Keilman, N. (2018). Probabilistic demographic forecasts. *Vienna Yearbook of Population Research, 16*, 25–35. https://doi.org/10.1553/populationyearbook2018s025

Keilman, N. (2019). Family projection methods: A review. In R. Schoen (Ed.), *Analytical family demography* (pp. 277–301). Springer International Publishing. https://doi.org/10.1007/978-3-319-93227-9_12

Kemper, P. (1992). The use of formal and informal home care by the disabled elderly. *Health Services Research, 27*(4), 421–451.

Keyfitz, N. (1982). Can knowledge improve forecasts? *Population and Development Review, 8*(4), 729–751. https://doi.org/10.2307/1972470

Kingston, A., Comas-Herrera, A., & Jagger, C. (2018). Forecasting the care needs of the older population in England over the next 20 years: Estimates from the Population Ageing and Care Simulation (PACSim) modelling study. *The Lancet Public Health, 3*(9), e447–e455. https://doi.org/10.1016/S2468-2667(18)30118-X

Kingston, A., & Jagger, C. (2017). *Population Ageing and Care Simulation model (PACSim). Baseline dataset and model construction (version: 241017).*

Kinsella, K., & Phillips, D. R. (2005). Global aging: The challenge of success. In *Population bulletin* (Vol. 50, Issue 1, pp. 5–42). Population Reference Bureau.

Kirk, D. (1996). Demographic transition theory. *Population Studies, 50*(3), 361–387. https://doi.org/10.1080/0032472031000149536

Klevmarken, A. (2008). Chapter 2. Dynamic microsimulation for policy analysis: Problems and solutions. In A. Klevmarken & B. Lindgren (Eds.), *Simulating an ageing population: A microsimulation approach applied to Sweden* (Vol. 285, pp. 31–53). Elsevier. https://doi.org/10.1016/S0573-8555(07)00002-8

Klevmarken, A., & Lindgren, B. (Eds.). (2008). *Simulating an ageing population: A microsimulation approach applied to Sweden* (Vol. 285). Emerald Group Publishing Limited. https://doi.org/10.1016/S0573-8555(07)00020-X

Knijn, T., & Kremer, M. (1997). Gender and the caring dimension of welfare states: Toward inclusive citizenship. *Social Politics: International Studies in Gender, State & Society, 4*(3), 328–361. https://doi.org/10.1093/oxfordjournals.sp.a034270

Kobos, E., Knoff, B., Dziedzic, B., Maciąg, R., & Idzik, A. (2022). Loneliness and mental well-being in the Polish population during the COVID-19 pandemic: A cross-sectional study. *BMJ Open, 12*(2), Art. e056368. https://doi.org/10.1136/bmjopen-2021-056368

Kohler, H.-P., Billari, F. C., & Ortega, J. A. (2002). The emergence of lowest-low fertility in Europe during the 1990s. *Population and Development Review*, 28(4), 641–680. https://doi.org/10.1111/j.1728-4457.2002.00641.x

Kohli, M., Künemund, H., & Lüdicke, J. (2005). Family structure, proximity and contact. In A. Börsch-Supan, A. Brugiviani, H. Jürges, J. Mackenbach, J. Siegrist, & G. Weber (Eds.), *Health, ageing and retirement in Europe. First results from the Survey of Health, Ageing and Retirement in Europe* (pp. 164–170). Research Institute for the Economics of Aging.

Kontis, V., Bennett, J. E., Parks, R. M., Rashid, T., Pearson-Stuttard, J., Asaria, P., Zhou, B., Guillot, M., Mathers, C. D., Khang, Y.-H., McKee, M., & Ezzati, M. (2022). Lessons learned and lessons missed: Impact of the coronavirus disease 2019 (COVID-19) pandemic on all-cause mortality in 40 industrialised countries and US states prior to mass vaccination. *Wellcome Open Research*, 6, 279. https://doi.org/10.12688/wellcomeopenres.17253.2

Kotowska, I. E. (1994). *Population dynamics in Poland 1950–2050. Internal migration and marital changes*. International Institute for Applied Systems Analysis.

Kotowska, I. E. (2009). Zmiany modelu rodziny a zmiany aktywności zawodowej kobiet w Europie. In I. E. Kotowska (Ed.), *Strukturalne i kulturowe uwarunkowania aktywności zawodowej kobiet w Polsce* (pp. 15–56). Wydawnictwo Naukowe SCHOLAR.

Kotowska, I. E. (2010). Prognozowanie gospodarstw domowych. In J. Kurkiewicz (Ed.), *Procesy demograficzne i metody ich analizy* (pp. 298–325). Wydawnictwo Uniwersytetu Ekonomicznego w Krakowie.

Kotowska, I. E. (2017). Panelowe badanie przemian relacji między pokoleniami, w rodzinie oraz między kobietami i mężczyznami jako podstawa diagnozowania zmian demograficznych w Polsce. *Studia Demograficzne*, 2(172), 23–34.

Kotowska, I. E. (2018). Zmiany zachowań dotyczących rodziny w Polsce po 1989 roku – zakładanie rodziny i rodzicielstwo. In J. Hrynkiewicz, J. Witkowski, & A. Potrykowska (Eds.), *Fazy rozwoju rodziny a polityka społeczna* (pp. 90–102). Rządowa Rada Ludnościowa.

Kotowska, I. E. (2019a). Ewolucja badań nad procesami ludnościowymi i relacji między demografią a naukami ekonomicznymi – zarys problematyki. In M. Gorynia (Ed.), *Ewolucja nauk ekonomicznych. Jedność a różnorodność, relacje do innych nauk, problemy klasyfikacyjne* (pp. 153–172). Polska Akademia Nauk.

Kotowska, I. E. (2019b). Uwagi o urodzeniach i niskiej dzietności w Polsce oraz polityce rodzinnej wspierającej prokreację. *Studia Demograficzne*, 2(176), 11–29. https://doi.org/10.33119/SD.2019.2.1

Kotowska, I. E., & Jóźwiak, J. (2012). Nowa demografia Europy a rodzina. *Roczniki Kolegium Analiz Ekonomicznych, 26,* 1–25.

Kotowska, I. E., Jóźwiak, J., Matysiak, A., & Baranowska-Rataj, A. (2008). Poland: Fertility decline as a response to profound societal and labour market changes? *Demographic Research, S7*(22), 795–854. https://doi.org/10.4054/DemRes.2008.19.22

Kotowska, I. E., Matysiak, A., & Mynarska, M. (2016). *Od opuszczenia domu rodzinnego do przejścia na emeryturę. Życie Polaków w świetle danych z badania ankietowego 'Generacje i Rodziny'* (I. E. Kotowska, A. Matysiak, & M. Mynarska, Eds.). Instytut Statystyki i Demografii, Kolegium Analiz Ekonomicznych, Szkoła Główna Handlowa w Warszawie.

Kotowska, I. E., & Wóycicka, I. (2008). *Sprawowanie opieki oraz inne uwarunkowania podnoszenia aktywności zawodowej osób w starszym wieku produkcyjnym. Raport z badań.*

Kramer, B. J. (1997). Gain in the caregiving experience: Where are we? What next? *The Gerontologist, 37*(2), 218–232. https://doi.org/10.1093/geront/37.2.218

Kuijsten, A. (1999). Households, families and kin networks. In L. J. G. van Wissen & P. A. Dykstra (Eds.), *Population issues. An interdisciplinary focus* (pp. 87–122). Springer.

Kulkarni, V. G. (2011). *Introduction to modeling and analysis of stochastic systems.* Springer. https://doi.org/10.1007/978-1-4419-1772-0

Kurkiewicz, J. (2007). Struktura gospodarstw domowych ludzi starszych jako odzwierciedlenie przepływu wsparcia między generacjami. In J. Kurkiewicz (Ed.), *Ludzie starsi w rodzinie i społeczeństwie* (pp. 54–85). Wydawnictwo Uniwersytetu Ekonomicznego w Krakowie.

Kurkiewicz, J., & Soja, E. (2015). Informal support for the elderly in the context of their living arrangements in selected European countries. *Studia Demograficzne, 1*(167), 61–81.

Kwiek, M. (2013). From system expansion to system contraction. Access to higher education in Poland. *Comparative Education Review, 57*(3), 553–576. https://doi.org/10.1086/670662

Lamb, V. L., & Siegel, J. S. (2004). Health demography. In J. S. Siegel & D. A. Swanson (Eds.), *Methods and materials of demography* (pp. 341–370). Elsevier Academic Press.

Łątkowski, W. (2015). Estymacja prawdopodobieństw przejścia między stanami zdrowia osób w wieku 50 lat i więcej w Polsce w modelu wielostanowym. *Studia Demograficzne, 2*(168), 25–37. https://doi.org/10.33119/SD.2015.2.2

Lawless, J. F., & Nazeri Rad, N. (2015). Estimation and assessment of Markov multistate models with intermittent observations on individuals. *Lifetime Data Analysis, 21*(2), 160–179. https://doi.org/10.1007/s10985-014-9310-z

Lawton, M. P., & Brody, E. M. (1969). Assessment of older people: Self-maintaining and instrumental activities of daily living. *The Gerontologist, 9*(3_Part_1), 179–186. https://doi.org/10.1093/geront/9.3_Part_1.179

Lee, R. D. (2011). The outlook for population growth. *Science, 333*(569), 569–573. https://doi.org/10.1126/science.1208859

Lee, R. D., & Mason, A. (Eds.). (2011). *Population aging and the generational economy: A global perspective.* Edward Elgar.

Lee, R. D., & Mason, A. (2014). Is low fertility really a problem? Population aging, dependency, and consumption. *Science, 346*(6206), 229–234. https://doi.org/10.1126/science.1250542

Leopold, T., Raab, M., & Engelhardt, H. (2014). The transition to parent care: Costs, commitments, and caregiver selection among children. *Journal of Marriage and Family, 76*(2), 300–318. https://doi.org/10.1111/jomf.12099

Lesthaeghe, R. (2010). The unfolding story of the second demographic transition. *Population and Development Review, 36*(2), 211–251.

Lesthaeghe, R. (2014). The second demographic transition: A concise overview of its development. *Proceedings of the National Academy of Sciences of the United States of America, 111*(51), 18112–18115. http://www.jstor.org/stable/43279106

Levin, A. T., Hanage, W. P., Owusu-Boaitey, N., Cochran, K. B., Walsh, S. P., & Meyerowitz-Katz, G. (2020). Assessing the age specificity of infection fatality rates for COVID-19: Systematic review, meta-analysis, and public policy implications. *European Journal of Epidemiology, 35*(12), 1123–1138. https://doi.org/10.1007/s10654-020-00698-1

Li, J., & O'Donoghue, C. (2013). A survey of dynamic microsimulation models: Uses, model structure and methodology. *International Journal of Microsimulation, 6*(2), 3–55.

Lilly, M. B., Laporte, A., & Coyte, P. C. (2007). Labor market work and home care's unpaid caregivers: A systematic review of labor force participation rates, predictors of labor market withdrawal, and hours of work. *The Milbank Quarterly, 85*(4), 641–690.

Liu, C., & Esteve, A. (2020). *Living arrangements across households in Europe* (MPIDR Working Paper WP-2020-002). https://doi.org/10.4054/MPIDR-WP-2020-002

Loichinger, E., Hammer, B., Prskawetz, A., Freiberger, M., & Sambt, J. (2017). Quantifying economic dependency. *European Journal of Population*, *33*(3), 351–380. https://doi.org/10.1007/s10680-016-9405-1

Luppa, M., Luck, T., Weyerer, S., König, H.-H., Brähler, E., & Riedel-Heller, S. G. (2010). Prediction of institutionalization in the elderly. A systematic review. *Age and Ageing*, *39*(1), 31–38. https://doi.org/10.1093/ageing/afp202

Luppi, M., & Nazio, T. (2019). Does gender top family ties? Within-couple and between-sibling sharing of elderly care. *European Sociological Review*, *35*(6), 772–789. https://doi.org/10.1093/esr/jcz035

Lutz, W., & Scherbov, S. (2005). Will population ageing necessarily lead to an increase in the number of persons with disabilities? Alternative scenarios for the European Union. *Vienna Yearbook of Population Research*, 219–234. https://doi.org/10.1553/populationyearbook2005s219

Mackenbach, J. P., Valverde, J. R., Artnik, B., Bopp, M., Brønnum-Hansen, H., Deboosere, P., Kalediene, R., Kovács, K., Leinsalu, M., Martikainen, P., Menvielle, G., Regidor, E., Rychtaříková, J., Rodriguez-Sanz, M., Vineis, P., White, C., Wojtyniak, B., Hu, Y., & Nusselder, W. J. (2018). Trends in health inequalities in 27 European countries. *Proceedings of the National Academy of Sciences*, *115*(25), 6440 LP – 6445. https://doi.org/10.1073/pnas.1800028115

Majer, I. M., Nusselder, W. J., Mackenbach, J. P., & Kunst, A. E. (2011). Life expectancy and life expectancy with disability of normal weight, overweight, and obese smokers and nonsmokers in Europe. *Obesity*, *19*(7), 1451–1459. https://doi.org/10.1038/oby.2011.46

Malenfant, É. C., Lebel, A., & Martel, L. (2012). Demosim, Statistics Canada's microsimulation model for projecting population diversity. In N. Hoque & D. A. Swanson (Eds.), *Opportunities and challenges for applied demography in the 21st century* (pp. 371–383). Springer. https://doi.org/10.1007/978-94-007-2297-2_20

Mamun, A. A. (2003). *Life history of cardiovascular disease and its risk factors: Multistate life table approach and application to the Framingham Heart Study*. Rozenberg Publishers.

Manton, K. G. (1982). Changing concepts of morbidity and mortality in the elderly population. *The Milbank Memorial Fund Quarterly. Health and Society*, *60*(2), 183–244. https://doi.org/10.2307/3349767

Manton, K. G., Stallard, E., & Tolley, H. D. (1991). Limits to human life expectancy: Evidence, prospects, and implications. *Population and Development Review*, *17*(4), 603–637. https://doi.org/10.2307/1973599

Marois, G., Bélanger, A., & Lutz, W. (2020). Population aging, migration, and productivity in Europe. *Proceedings of the National Academy of Sciences*, *117*(14), 7690–7695. https://doi.org/10.1073/pnas.1918988117

Martin, L. G., & Schoeni, R. F. (2014). Trends in disability and related chronic conditions among the forty-and-over population: 1997–2010. *Disability and Health Journal, 7*(1, Supplement), S4–S14. https://doi.org/10.1016/j.dhjo.2013.06.007

Mathers, C. D., Sadana, R., Salomon, J. A., Murray, C. J. L., & Lopez, A. D. (2001). Healthy life expectancy in 191 countries, 1999. *The Lancet, 357*(9269), 1685–1691. https://doi.org/10.1016/S0140-6736(00)04824-8

Matysiak, A. (2009). Is Poland really 'immune' to the spread of cohabitation? *Demographic Research, 21*(8), 215–234. https://doi.org/10.4054/DemRes.2009.21.8

Matysiak, A., Sobotka, T., & Vignoli, D. (2020). The great recession and fertility in Europe: A sub-national analysis. *European Journal of Population.* https://doi.org/10.1007/s10680-020-09556-y

McDonald, P. (2000). Gender equity, social institutions and the future of fertility. *Journal of the Australian Population Association, 17*(1), 1–16. https://doi.org/10.1007/BF03029445

McDonald, P. (2006). Low fertility and the state: The efficacy of policy. *Population and Development Review, 32*(3), 485–510. https://doi.org/10.1111/j.1728-4457.2006.00134.x

Miech, R., Pampel, F., Kim, J., & Rogers, R. G. (2011). The enduring association between education and mortality. *American Sociological Review, 76*(6), 913–934. https://doi.org/10.1177/0003122411411276

Mirowsky, J., & Ross, C. E. (2005). Education, cumulative advantage, and health. *Ageing International, 30*(1), 27–62. https://doi.org/10.1007/BF02681006

Molina-Mula, J., Gallo-Estrada, J., & Miquel-Novajra, A. (2019). Attitudes and beliefs of Spanish families regarding their family members aged 75 years and over who live alone: A qualitative study. *BMJ Open, 9*(4), Art. e025547. https://doi.org/10.1136/bmjopen-2018-025547

Mossakowska, M., Więcek, A., & Błędowski, P. (Eds.). (2012). *Aspekty medyczne, psychologiczne, socjologiczne i ekonomiczne starzenia się ludzi w Polsce.* Termedia Wydawnictwa Medyczne.

MRPiPS. (2016). *Informacja o sytuacji osób starszych w Polsce za rok 2015.*

Mularczyk-Tomczewska, P., Zarnowski, A., Gujski, M., Jankowski, M., Bojar, I., Wdowiak, A., & Krakowiak, J. (2022). Barriers to accessing health services during the COVID-19 pandemic in Poland: A nationwide cross-sectional survey among 109,928 adults in Poland. *Frontiers in Public Health, 10.* https://www.frontiersin.org/articles/10.3389/fpubh.2022.986996

Muresan, C., & Hărăguş, P.-T. (2015). Norms of filial obligation and actual support to parents in Central and Eastern Europe. *Romanian Journal for Population Studies, IX,* 49–81.

Murphy, M. (2017). Demographic determinants of population aging in Europe since 1850. *Population and Development Review, 43*(2), 257–283. https://doi.org/10.1111/padr.12073

Murphy, M., Glaser, K., & Grundy, E. (1997). Marital status and long-term illness in Great Britain. *Journal of Marriage and Family, 59*(1), 156–164.

Murphy, M., Martikainen, P., & Pennec, S. (2006). Demographic change and the supply of potential family supporters in Britain, Finland and France in the period 1911–2050 [Changements démographiques et disponibilité des soutiens familiaux en Grande-Bretagne, en Finlande et en France entre 1911 et 2050]. *European Journal of Population / Revue Européenne de Démographie, 22*(3), 219–240. https://doi.org/10.1007/s10680-006-9003-8

Murray, C. J., Salomon, J. A., & Mathers, C. (2000). A critical examination of summary measures of population health. *Bulletin of the World Health Organization, 78*(8), 981–994.

Muszyńska, M. M. (2011). The female-male gap in life expectancy in Poland. *Studia Demograficzne, 1(159)*, 23–36.

Mutchler, J. E., & Burr, J. A. (1991). A longitudinal analysis of household and nonhousehold living arrangements in later life. *Demography, 28*(3), 375–390. https://doi.org/10.2307/2061463

Mynarska, M., Baranowska-Rataj, A., & Matysiak, A. (2014). Free to stay, free to leave: Insights from Poland into the meaning of cohabitation. *Demographic Research, S17*(36), 1107–1136. https://doi.org/10.4054/DemRes.2014.31.36

Mynarska, M., & Matysiak, A. (2010). Diffusion of cohabitation in Poland. *Studia Demograficzne, 1–2*(157–158), 11–26.

Najwyższa Izba Kontroli. (2018). *Usługi opiekuńcze świadczone osobom starszym w miejscu zamieszkania.*

Nazio, T. (2019). Who cares? Securing support in old age. In *Population & policy compact.* Max Planck Society/Population Europe.

Newman, A. B., & Brach, J. S. (2001). Gender gap in longevity and disability in older persons. *Epidemiologic Reviews, 23*(2), 343–355. https://doi.org/10.1093/oxfordjournals.epirev.a000810

Nusselder, W. J. (2002). Compression of morbidity. In J.-M. Robine, C. Jagger, J. C. Mathers, E. M. Crimmins, & R. M. Suzman (Eds.), *Determining health expectancies* (pp. 35–58). https://doi.org/10.1002/0470858885.ch2

Nusselder, W. J. (2007). Recent trends in life expectancy and rectangularisation of the survival curve at advanced ages in the Netherlands. In J.-M. Robine, E. M. Crimmins, S. Horiuchi, & Z. Yi (Eds.), *Human longevity, individual life duration, and the growth of the oldest-old population* (pp. 131–146). Springer. https://doi.org/10.1007/978-1-4020-4848-7_6

Nusselder, W. J., Cambois, E. M., Wapperom, D., Meslé, F., Looman, C. W. N., Yokota, R. T. C., Van Oyen, H., Jagger, C., & Robine, J. M. (2019). Women's excess unhealthy life years: Disentangling the unhealthy life years gap. *European Journal of Public Health, 29*(5), 914–919. https://doi.org/10.1093/eurpub/ckz114

O'Donoghue, C. (2001). Dynamic microsimulation: A methodological survey. *Brazilian Electronic Journal of Economics, 4*(2), 77.

OECD. (2015). *Ageing and employment policies: Poland 2015.* OECD Publishing. https://doi.org/10.1787/9789264227279-en

OECD. (2017). *Preventing ageing unequally.* OECD Publishing. https://doi.org/10.1787/9789264279087-en

OECD. (2019a). *Health at a glance 2019: OECD indicators.* OECD Publishing. https://doi.org/10.1787/4dd50c09-en

OECD. (2019b). *International migration outlook 2019.* OECD Publishing. https://doi.org/10.1787/c3e35eec-en

OECD. (2019c). *Pensions at a glance 2019: OECD and G20 indicators.* OECD Publishing. https://doi.org/10.1787/b6d3dcfc-en

OECD. (2022). *Health at a glance: Europe 2022.* OECD. https://doi.org/10.1787/507433b0-en

Oeppen, J., & Vaupel, J. W. (2002). Broken limits to life expectancy. *Science, 296*(5570), 1029–1031. https://doi.org/10.1126/science.1069675

Ogg, J., & Renaut, S. (2006). The support of parents in old age by those born during 1945–1954: A European perspective. *Ageing and Society, 26*(5), 723–743. https://doi.org/10.1017/S0144686X06004922

Oksuzyan, A., Brønnum-Hansen, H., & Jeune, B. (2010). Gender gap in health expectancy. *European Journal of Ageing, 7*(4), 213–218. https://doi.org/10.1007/s10433-010-0170-4

Oksuzyan, A., Juel, K., Vaupel, J. W., & Christensen, K. (2008). Men: Good health and high mortality. Sex differences in health and aging. *Aging Clinical and Experimental Research, 20*(2), 91–102. https://doi.org/10.1007/BF03324754

Oláh, L. Sz., Kotowska, I. E., & Richter, R. (2018). The new roles of men and women and implications for families and societies. In G. Doblhammer & J. Gumà (Eds.), *A demographic perspective on gender, family and health in Europe* (pp. 41–64). Springer International Publishing. https://doi.org/10.1007/978-3-319-72356-3_4

Oliveira, M. R., Sudati, I. P., Konzen, V. D. M., de Campos, A. C., Wibelinger, L. M., Correa, C., Miguel, F. M., Silva, R. N., & Borghi-Silva, A. (2022). Covid-19 and the impact on the physical activity level of elderly people: A systematic review. *Experimental Gerontology, 159*, 111675. https://doi.org/10.1016/j.exger.2021.111675

Olshansky, S. J., Rudberg, M. A., Carnes, B. A., Cassel, C. K., & Brody, J. A. (1991). Trading off longer life for worsening health. *Journal of Aging and Health*, *3*(2), 194–216. https://doi.org/10.1177/089826439100300205

Omran, A. R. (1971). The epidemiologic transition. A theory of the epidemiology of population change. *The Milbank Memorial Fund Quarterly*, *49*(4), 509–538.

Omran, A. R. (1998). The epidemiologic transition theory revisited thirty years later. *World Health Statistics Quarterly*, *53*(2, 3, 4), 99–119.

Orcutt, G. H. (1957). A new type of socio-economic system. *Review of Economics and Statistics*, *39*(2), 116–123.

Österle, A. (2012). Long-term care financing in Central Eastern Europe. In J. Costa-Font & C. Courbage (Eds.), *Financing long-term care in Europe: Institutions, markets and models* (pp. 236–253). Palgrave Macmillan UK. https://doi.org/10.1057/9780230349193_13

Panek, T., Czapiński, J., & Kotowska, I. E. (2015). Metoda badania. Diagnoza Społeczna 2015, Warunki i Jakość Życia Polaków – Raport. *Contemporary Economics*, *9*(4), 25–35. https://ce.vizja.pl/en/download-pdf/volume/9/issue/4/id/407

Pascariu, M. D. (2018). *MortalityLaws: Parametric mortality models, life tables and HMD* (R package version 1.4.0).

Patterson, S. E., & Margolis, R. (2019). The demography of multigenerational caregiving: A critical aspect of the gendered life course. *Socius*, *5*, 1–19. https://doi.org/10.1177/2378023119862737

Perelli-Harris, B., Kreyenfeld, M., Sigle-Rushton, W., Keizer, R., Lappegård, T., Jasilioniene, A., Berghammer, C., & Di Giulio, P. (2012). Changes in union status during the transition to parenthood in eleven European countries, 1970s to early 2000s. *Population Studies*, *66*(2), 167–182. https://doi.org/10.1080/00324728.2012.673004

Pfau-Effinger, B. (2005). Welfare state policies and the development of care arrangements. *European Societies*, *7*(2), 321–347. https://doi.org/10.1080/14616690500083592

Pickard, L., Comas-Herrera, A., Costa-Font, J., Gori, C., di Maio, A., Patxot, C., Pozzi, A., Rothgang, H., & Wittenberg, R. (2007). Modelling an entitlement to long-term care services for older people in Europe: Projections for long-term care expenditure to 2050. *Journal of European Social Policy*, *17*(1), 33–48. https://doi.org/10.1177/0958928707071879

Pickard, L., Wittenberg, R., Comas-Herrera, A., Davies, B., & Darton, R. (2000). Relying on informal care in the new century? Informal care for elderly people in England to 2031. *Ageing and Society*, *20*(6), 745–772. https://doi.org/10.1017/S0144686X01007978

Pinquart, M., & Sörensen, S. (2003). Differences between caregivers and noncaregivers in psychological health and physical health: A meta-analysis. In *Psychology and aging* (Vol. 18, Issue 2, pp. 250–267). American Psychological Association. https://doi.org/10.1037/0882-7974.18.2.250

Potyra, M., Góral-Radziszewska, K., Waśkiewicz, K., & Gawińska-Drużba, E. (2023). *Population projection 2023–2060* (pp. 1–54). Główny Urząd Statystyczny. https://stat.gov.pl/obszary-tematyczne/ludnosc/prognoza-ludnosci/prognoza-ludnosci-na-lata-2023-2060,11,1.html

Preston, S. H., Heuveline, P., & Guillot, M. (2001). *Demography: Measuring and modeling population processes*. Blackwell Publishing.

Puur, A., Sakkeus, L., Põldma, A., & Herm, A. (2011). Intergenerational family constellations in contemporary Europe: Evidence from the Generations and Gender Survey. *Demographic Research, S11*(4), 135–172.

R Core Team. (2019). *R: A language and environment for statistical computing*. R Foundation for Statistical Computing.

Rau, R., Soroko, E., Jasilionis, D., & Vaupel, J. W. (2008). Continued reductions in mortality at advanced ages. *Population and Development Review, 34*(4), 747–768. https://doi.org/10.1111/j.1728-4457.2008.00249.x

Raymo, J. M., Pike, I., & Liang, J. (2019). A new look at the living arrangements of older Americans using multistate life tables. *The Journals of Gerontology: Series B, 74*(7), e84–e96. https://doi.org/10.1093/geronb/gby099

Rechel, B., Grundy, E., Robine, J.-M., Cylus, J., Mackenbach, J. P., Knai, C., & McKee, M. (2013). Ageing in the European Union. *The Lancet, 381*(9874), 1312–1322. https://doi.org/10.1016/S0140-6736(12)62087-X

Reher, D., & Requena, M. (2018). Living alone in later life: A global perspective. *Population and Development Review, 44*(3), 427–454. https://doi.org/10.1111/padr.12149

Reher, D. S. (1998). Family ties in Western Europe: Persistent contrasts. *Population and Development Review, 24*(2), 203–234. https://doi.org/10.2307/2807972

Reuser, M., Bonneux, L. G., & Willekens, F. J. (2009). Smoking kills, obesity disables: A multistate approach of the US Health and Retirement Survey. *Obesity, 17*(4), 783–789. https://doi.org/10.1038/oby.2008.640

Reuser, M., Willekens, F. J., & Bonneux, L. (2011). Higher education delays and shortens cognitive impairment. A multistate life table analysis of the US Health and Retirement Study. *European Journal of Epidemiology, 26*(5), 395–403. https://doi.org/10.1007/s10654-011-9553-x

Richards, T., White, M. J., & Tsui, A. O. (1987). Changing living arrangements: A hazard model of transitions among household types. *Demography, 24*(1), 77–98. https://doi.org/10.2307/2061509

Rickayzen, B. D., & Walsh, D. E. P. (2002). A multi-state model of disability for the United Kingdom: Implications for future need for long-term care for the elderly. *British Actuarial Journal, 8*(2), 341–393. https://doi.org/10.1017/S1357321700003755

Rise, J. E., Juel Ahrenfeldt, L., Lindahl-Jacobsen, R., & Andersen-Randberg, K. (2019). 33. The association between self-reported physical activity and physical performance: Does advancing age matter? In A. Börsch-Supan, J. Bristle, K. Andersen-Ranberg, A. Brugiavini, F. Jusot, H. Litwin, & G. Weber (Eds.), *Health and socio-economic status over the life course. First results from SHARE Waves 6 and 7* (pp. 319–326). De Gruyter Oldenbourg. https://doi.org/10.1515/9783110617245-033

Robine, J.-M., & Jagger, C. (2006). Lengthening of life and the population health status. In G. Caselli, J. Vallin, & G. Wunsch (Eds.), *Demography: Analysis and synthesis* (Vol. 3, pp. 285–303). Academic Press.

Robine, J.-M., & Michel, J.-P. (2004). Looking forward to a general theory on population aging. *The Journals of Gerontology: Series A, 59*(6), M590–M597. https://doi.org/10.1093/gerona/59.6.M590

Rogers, A. (1975). *Introduction to multiregional mathematical demography.* Wiley.

Rogers, A., Rogers, R. G., & Branch, L. G. (1989). A multistate analysis of active life expectancy. *Public Health Reports, 104*(3), 222–226.

Romaniuk, A. (2010). Population forecasting: Epistemological considerations. *Genus, 66*(1), 91–108.

Rosen, M., & Haglund, B. (2005). From healthy survivors to sick survivors — implications for the twenty-first century. *Scandinavian Journal of Public Health, 33*(2), 151-155. https://doi.org/10.1080/14034940510032121

Ross, C. E., Masters, R. K., & Hummer, R. A. (2012). Education and the gender gaps in health and mortality. *Demography, 49*(4), 1157–1183. https://doi.org/10.1007/s13524-012-0130-z

Rothman, K. J. (2012). *Epidemiology: An introduction.* Oxford University Press.

Rowe, J. W., & Kahn, R. L. (1987). Human aging: Usual and successful. *Science, 237*(4811), 143–149.

Rowland, D. T. (2009). Global population aging: History and prospects. In P. Uhlenberg (Ed.), *International handbook of population Aging* (pp. 37–65). Springer. https://doi.org/10.1007/978-1-4020-8356-3_3

Rubio-Valverde, J. R., Nusselder, W. J., & Mackenbach, J. P. (2019). Educational inequalities in Global Activity Limitation Indicator disability in 28 European countries: Does the choice of survey matter? *International Journal of Public Health, 64*(3), 461–474. https://doi.org/10.1007/s00038-018-1174-7

Ruggles, S. (2007). The decline of intergenerational coresidence in the United States, 1850 to 2000. *American Sociological Review, 72*(6), 964–989. https://doi.org/10.1177/000312240707200606

Rybińska, A. (2016). Life course development of young adults. Entry to adulthood. In I. E. Kotowska, A. Matysiak, & M. Mynarska (Eds.), *The life of Poles: From leaving the parental home to retirement. Insights from the Generations and Gender Survey (GGS-PL)* (pp. 10–11). Institute of Statistics and Demography, Warsaw School of Economics.

Ryder, N. B. (1975). Notes on stationary populations. *Population Index, 41*(1), 3–28. https://doi.org/10.2307/2734140

Salive, M. E. (2013). Multimorbidity in older adults. *Epidemiologic Review, 35,* 75–83. https://doi.org/10.1093/epirev/mxs009

Sanderson, W. C., & Scherbov, S. (2005). Average remaining lifetimes can increase as human populations age. *Nature, 435*(7043), 811–813. https://doi.org/10.1038/nature03593

Sanderson, W. C., & Scherbov, S. (2007). A new perspective on population aging. *Demographic Research, 16*(2), 27–58. https://doi.org/10.4054/DemRes.2007.16.2

Sanderson, W. C., & Scherbov, S. (2010). Remeasuring aging. *Science, 329*(5997), 1287–1288. https://doi.org/10.1126/science.1193647

Sanderson, W. C., & Scherbov, S. (2015). Faster increases in human life expectancy could lead to slower population aging. *PLOS ONE, 10*(4), Art. e0121922.

Sanderson, W. C., Scherbov, S., & Gerland, P. (2018). The end of population aging in high-income countries. *Vienna Yearbook of Population Research, 16,* 163–175. https://doi.org/10.1553/populationyearbook2018s163

Sandström, G., & Karlsson, L. (2019). The educational gradient of living alone: A comparison among the working-age population in Europe. *Demographic Research, 40*(55), 1645–1670.

Saraceno, C., & Keck, W. (2010). Can we identify intergenerational policy regimes in Europe? *European Societies, 12*(5), 675–696. https://doi.org/10.1080/14616696.2010.483006

Scherbov, S., & Sanderson, W. C. (2016). New approaches to the conceptualization and measurement of age and aging. *Journal of Aging and Health, 28*(7), 1159–1177. https://doi.org/10.1177/0898264316656517

Schoen, R. F. (1988). *Modeling multigroup populations.* Springer.

Schoeni, R. F., Freedman, V. A., & Wallace, R. B. (2001). Persistent, consistent, widespread, and robust? Another look at recent trends in old-age disability. *The Journals of Gerontology: Series B, 56*(4), S206–S218. https://doi.org/10.1093/geronb/56.4.S206

Schöley, J., Aburto, J. M., Kashnitsky, I., Kniffka, M. S., Zhang, L., Jaadla, H., Dowd, J. B., & Kashyap, R. (2022). Life expectancy changes since COVID-19. *Nature Human Behaviour.* https://doi.org/10.1038/s41562-022-01450-3

Schulz, E., Leidl, R., & König, H.-H. (2004). The impact of ageing on hospital care and long-term – the example of Germany. *Health Policy, 67*(1), 57–74. https://doi.org/10.1016/S0168-8510(03)00083-6

Siegel, J. S. (2012a). Measures of health status, functioning, and use of health services. In *The Demography and epidemiology of human health and aging* (pp. 217–267). Springer. https://doi.org/10.1007/978-94-007-1315-4_5

Siegel, J. S. (2012b). Models of aging, health, and mortality, and mortality/health projections. In *The demography and epidemiology of human health and aging* (pp. 731–773). Springer. https://doi.org/10.1007/978-94-007-1315-4_14

Silverstein, M., & Giarrusso, R. (2010). Aging and family life: A decade review. *Journal of Marriage and Family, 72*(5), 1039–1058. https://doi.org/10.1111/j.1741-3737.2010.00749.x

Singer, B., & Spilerman, S. (1976). The representation of social processes by Markov models. *American Journal of Sociology, 82*(1), 1–54.

Smits, A., Gaalen, R. I. Van, & Mulder, C. H. (2010). Parent–child coresidence : Who moves in with whom and for whose needs ? National Council on Family Relations Stable. *Journal of Marriage and Family, 72*(4), 1022–1033. http://www.jstor.org/stable/40864961

Sobiesiak-Penszko, P. (Ed.). (2015). *Niewidzialna siła robocza. Migranci w usługach opiekuńczych nad osobami starszymi.* Fundacja Instytut Spraw Publicznych.

Sowada, C., Sagan, A., Kowalska-Bobko, I., Badora-Musiał, K., Bochenek, T., Domagała, A., Dubas-Jakóbczyk, K., Kocot, E., Mrożek-Gąsiorowska, M., Sitko, S., Szetela, A., Szetela, P., Tambor, M., Więckowska, B., Zabdyr-Jamróz, M., & van Ginneken, E. (2019). Poland: Health system review. *Health Systems in Transition, 21*(1), 1–235.

Sowa-Kofta, A. (2018). *ESPN thematic report on challenges in long-term care.* European Commision, Directorate-General for Employment, Social Affairs and Inclusion.

Spasova, S., Baeten, R., Coster, S., Ghailani, D., Peña-Casas, R., & Vanhercke, B. (2018). *Challenges in long-term care in Europe. A study of national policies.* European Social Policy Network (ESPN). European Commision, Directorate-General for Employment, Social Affairs and Inclusion.

Spielauer, M. (2007). Dynamic microsimulation of health care demand, health care finance and the economic impact of health behaviours: Survey and review. *International Journal of Microsimulation*, *1*(1), 35–53.

Stanfors, M., Jacobs, J. C., & Neilson, J. (2019). Caregiving time costs and trade-offs: Gender differences in Sweden, the UK, and Canada. *SSM – Population Health*, *9*, Art. 100501. https://doi.org/10.1016/j.ssmph.2019.100501

Stolz, E., Mayerl, H., Rásky, É., & Freidl, W. (2019). Individual and country-level determinants of nursing home admission in the last year of life in Europe. *PLoS One*, *14*(3). https://doi.org/10.1371/journal.pone.0213787

Stonawski, M. (2014). *Kapitał ludzki w warunkach starzenia się ludności a wzrost gospodarczy* (Monografie). Uniwersytet Ekonomiczny w Krakowie.

Strzelecki, P. (2007). The multi-state projection of Poland's population by educational attainment for the years 2003–2030. *Studia Demograficzne*, *2/152*, 23–44.

Strzelecki, P. (2012). *Zastosowanie modelowania mikrosymulacyjnego w prognozowaniu ludności*. praca doktorska, Kolegium Analiz Ekonomicznych, Szkoła Główna Handlowa w Warszawie.

Strzelecki, P., Growiec, J., & Wyszyński, R. (2022). The contribution of immigration from Ukraine to economic growth in Poland. *Review of World Economics*, *158*(2), 365–399. https://doi.org/10.1007/s10290-021-00437-y

Styrc, M. (2016). *Interdependencies between marital instability and fertility*. SGH Publishing House.

Su, Y., Rao, W., Li, M., Caron, G., D'Arcy, C., & Meng, X. (2023). Prevalence of loneliness and social isolation among older adults during the COVID-19 pandemic: A systematic review and meta-analysis. *International Psychogeriatrics*, *35*(5), 229–241. https://doi.org/10.1017/S1041610222000199

Suanet, B., Broese van Groenou, M. I., & Van Tilburg, T. (2012). Informal and formal home-care use among older adults in Europe: Can cross-national differences be explained by societal context and composition? *Ageing and Society*, *32*(3), 491–515. https://doi.org/10.1017/S0144686X11000390

Sullivan, D. F. (1971). A single index of mortality and morbidity. *HSMHA Health Reports*, *86*(4), 347–354.

Szatur-Jaworska, B. (2011). Formy życia rodzinnego ludzi starych. *Polityka Społeczna*, *4*(8T), 12–17.

Szatur-Jaworska, B. (2012). Sytuacja rodzinna i potrzeby opiekuńcze ludzi starych w Polsce. In P. Błędowski, B. Szatur-Jaworska, Z. Szweda-Lewandowska, & P. Kubicki (Eds.), *Raport na temat sytuacji osób starszych w Polsce* (pp. 49–66). Instytut Pracy i Spraw Socjalnych.

Szinovacz, M. E., & Davey, A. (2013). Changes in adult children's participation in parent care. *Ageing and Society*, *33*(4), 667–697. https://doi.org/10.1017/S0144686X12000177

Szukalski, P. (2004). Projekcja liczby niepełnosprawnych seniorów do roku 2030. In J. T. Kowaleski & P. Szukalski (Eds.), *Nasze starzejące się społeczeństwo. Nadzieje i zagrożenia* (pp. 106–113). Wydawnictwo Uniwersytetu Łódzkiego.

Szukalski, P. (2008). Ewolucja umieralności i niepełnosprawności w świetle koncepcji rektangularyzacji krzywej przeżycia. In J. T. Kowaleski & P. Szukalski (Eds.), *Starzenie się ludności Polski – między demografią a gerontologią społeczną* (pp. 89–123). Wydawnictwo Uniwersytetu Łódzkiego.

Szweda-Lewandowska, Z. (2016). Niesamodzielni A.D. 2035 – w poszukiwaniu sposobów i źródeł wsparcia. *Folia Oeconomica*, *4*(315), 173–183. https://doi.org/10.18778/0208-6018.315.12

Szweda-Lewandowska, Z., & Kałuża-Kopias, D. (2019). Demand for the labor of foreign caregivers from the perspective of two generations: The elderly and their family caregivers. *Przedsiębiorczość i Zarządzanie*, *XX*(3), 79–93.

Tennstedt, S. L., Crawford, S. L., & McKinlay, J. B. (1993). Is family care on the decline? A longitudinal investigation of the substitution of formal long-term care services for informal care. *The Milbank Quarterly*, *71*(4), 601–624. https://doi.org/10.2307/3350421

Timoszuk, S. (2017). Wdowieństwo a sytuacja materialna kobiet w starszym wieku w Polsce. *Studia Demograficzne*, *2*(172), 121–138.

Titkow, A., & Duch, D. (2004). The Polish family: Always an institution? In M. Robila (Ed.), *Families in Eastern Europe* (Vol. 5, pp. 69–85). Emerald Group Publishing. https://doi.org/10.1016/S1530-3535(04)05005-8

Titman, A. C., & Sharples, L. D. (2009). Model diagnostics for multi-state models. *Statistical Methods in Medical Research*, *19*(6), 621–651. https://doi.org/10.1177/0962280209105541

Tomassini, C., Glaser, K., Wolf, D. A, Broese van Groenou, M. I., & Grundy, E. (2004). Living arrangements among older people: An overview of trends in Europe and the USA. *Population Trends*, *115*, 24–34.

Tomassini, C., Grundy, E., & Kalogirou, S. (2008). Potential family support for older people 2000–2030. In J. Gaymu, P. Festy, M. Poulain, & G. Beets (Eds.), *Future elderly living conditions in Europe* (pp. 71–98). INED.

Torres, C., García, J., Meslé, F., Barbieri, M., Bonnet, F., Camarda, C. G., Cambois, E., Caporali, A., Couppié, É., Poniakina, S., & Robine, J.-M. (2023). Identifying age- and sex-specific COVID-19 mortality trends over time in six countries. *International Journal of Infectious Diseases*, *128*, 32–40. https://doi.org/10.1016/j.ijid.2022.12.004

Triantafillou, J., Naiditch, M., Repkova, K., Stiehr, K., Carretero, S., Emilsson, T., Di Santo, P., Bednarik, R., Brichtova, L., Ceruzzi, F., Cordero, L., Mastroyiannakis, T., Ferrando, M., Mingot, K., Ritter, J., & Vlantoni, D. (2010). *Informal care in the long-term care system – European overview paper* (p. 67). CMT Prooptiki/European Centre for Social Welfare Policy and Research (INTERLINKS Report #3).

Tucker-Seeley, R. D., Li, Y., Sorensen, G., & Subramanian, S. V. (2011). Lifecourse socioeconomic circumstances and multimorbidity among older adults. *BMC Public Health, 11*(1), 313. https://doi.org/10.1186/1471-2458-11-313

Tuljapurkar, S., Lee, R. D., & Li, Q. (2004). Random scenario forecasts versus stochastic forecasts. *International Statistical Review, 72*(2), 185–199. https://doi.org/10.1111/j.1751-5823.2004.tb00232.x

Tymicki, K., Zeman, K., & Holzer-Żelażewska, D. (2018). Cohort fertility of Polish women, 1945–2015: The context of postponment and recuperation. *Studia Demograficzne, 2*(174), 5–23. https://doi.org/10.33119/SD.2018.2.1

Uhlenberg, P. (Ed.). (2009). *International handbook of population aging.* Springer Science+Business Media B.V.

United Nations. (2001). *Replacement migration: Is it a solution to declining and ageing populations?* Population Division, Department of Economic and Social Affairs, United Nations Secretariat (ST/ESA/SER.A/206).

United Nations. (2015). *Principles and recommendations for population and housing censuses. Revision 3. New York: United Nations (Statistical Papers, Series M. No. 67/Rev.3).*

United Nations, Department of Economic and Social Affairs, P. D. (2017). *Household size and composition around the world 2017 – Data booklet* (ST/ESA/SER.A/405).

United Nations, Department of Economic and Social Affairs, Population Division. (2019a). *Living arrangements of older persons around the world.* Population Facts No. 2019/2, April 2019.

United Nations, Department of Economic and Social Affairs, Population Division. (2019b). *Patterns and trends in household size and composition: Evidence from a United Nations Dataset* (ST/ESA/SER.A/433). https://www.un.org/en/development/desa/population/publications/pdf/ageing/household_size_and_composition_technical_report.pdf

United Nations, Department of Economic and Social Affairs, Population Division. (2019c). *World Population Ageing 2019: Highlights.* (ST/ESA/SER.A/430).

United Nations, Department of Economic and Social Affairs, Population Division. (2019d). *World Population Prospects 2019, Online edition. Rev. 1.* https://population.un.org/wpp/Download/Standard/Population/

United Nations, Department of Economic and Social Affairs, Population Division. (2020). *World Population Ageing 2019* (ST/ESA/SER.A/444). https://www.un.org/en/development/desa/population/publications/pdf/age ing/WorldPopulationAgeing2019-Report.pdf

United Nations Economic Commission for Europe – UNECE. (2015). *Conference of European Statisticians Recommendations for the 2020 Censuses of Population and Housing.*

United Nations Economic Commission for Europe – UNECE. (2017). *Recommendations on communicating population projections: Prepared by the Task Force on Population Projections* (p. 80). Document ECE/CES/2017/7.

United Nations Economic Commission for Europe – UNECE. (2019). *The challenging roles of informal carers.* Policy Brief on Ageing No. 22.

Vallin, J., & Meslé, F. (2004). Convergences and divergences in mortality: A new approach of health transition. *Demographic Research, S2*, 11–44. https://doi.org/10.4054/DemRes.2004.S2.2

van de Kaa, D. J. (1987). Europe's second demographic transition. *Population Bulletin, 42*(1), 1–59.

van de Kaa, D. J. (1994). The second demographic transition revisited: Theories and expectations. In G. Beets (Ed.), *Population and family in the Low Countries 1993: Late fertility and other current issues* (pp. 81–126). Sweets and Zeitlinger, Berwyn.

van de Kaa, D. J. (2002). *The idea of a second demographic transition in industrialized countries.* Paper presented at the Sixth Welfare Policy Seminar of the National Institute of Population and Social Security, 29 January 2002.

Van Den Berg Jeths, A., Hoogenveen, R., De Hollander, G., & Tabeau, E. (2001). A review of epidemiological approaches to forecasting mortality and morbidity. In E. Tabeau, A. van den Berg Jeths, & C. Heathcote (Eds.), *Forecasting mortality in developed countries: Insights from a statistical, demographic and epidemiological perspective* (pp. 33–56). Springer. https://doi.org/10.1007/0-306-47562-6_2

van den Broek, T., & Dykstra, P. A. (2017). Residential care and care to community-dwelling parents: Out-selection, in-selection and diffusion of responsibility. *Ageing and Society, 37*(8), 1609–1631. https://doi.org/10.1017/S0144686X16000519

van den Hout, A. (2017). *Multi-state survival models for interval-censored data.* Chapman and Hall/CRC.

van den Hout, A., Ogurtsova, E., Gampe, J., & Matthews, F. (2014). Investigating healthy life expectancy using a multi-state model in the presence of missing data and misclassification. *Demographic Research, 30*(42), 1219–1244. https://doi.org/10.4054/DemRes.2014.30.42

van der Gaag, N., Bijwaard, G., De Beer, J., & Bonneux, L. (2015). A multistate model to project elderly disability in case of limited data. *Demographic Research, 32,* 75–106. https://doi.org/10.4054/DemRes.2015.32.3

Van Imhoff, E., & Keilman, N. (1991). *LIPRO 2.0. An application of a dynamic demographic projection model to a household structure in Netherlands* (NIDI/ CBGS). Swets & Zeitlinger.

Van Imhoff, E., Kuijsten, A., & Van Wissen, L. J. G. (1995). Introduction. In E. Van Imhoff, A. Kuijsten, P. Hooimeijer, & L. J. G. Van Wissen (Eds.), *Household demography and household modeling* (pp. 1–15). Springer Science+ Business Media.

van Imhoff, E., & Post, W. (1998). Microsimulation methods for population projection. *Population: An English Selection, 10*(1), 97–138. http://www.jstor. org/stable/2998681

Van Oyen, H., Cox, B., Jagger, C., Cambois, E., Nusselder, W., Gilles, C., & Robine, J.-M. (2010). Gender gaps in life expectancy and expected years with activity limitations at age 50 in the European Union: Associations with macro-level structural indicators. *European Journal of Ageing, 7*(4), 229–237. https://doi. org/10.1007/s10433-010-0172-2

van Oyen, H., der Heyden, J., Perenboom, R., & Jagger, C. (2006). Monitoring population disability: Evaluation of a new Global Activity Limitation Indicator (GALI). *Sozial- Und Präventivmedizin, 51*(3), 153–161. https://doi. org/10.1007/s00038-006-0035-y

Van Oyen, H., Nusselder, W., Jagger, C., Kolip, P., Cambois, E., & Robine, J.-M. (2013). Gender differences in healthy life years within the EU: An exploration of the 'health–survival' paradox. *International Journal of Public Health, 58*(1), 143–155. https://doi.org/10.1007/s00038-012-0361-1

Vaupel, J. W. (2010). Biodemography of human ageing. *Nature, 464,* 536–542. https://doi.org/10.1038/nature08984

Verbakel, E., Tamlagsrønning, S., Winstone, L., Fjær, E. L., & Eikemo, T. A. (2017). Informal care in Europe: Findings from the European Social Survey (2014) special module on the social determinants of health. *European Journal of Public Health, 27*(Suppl_1), 90–95. https://doi.org/10.1093/eurpub/ckw229

Verbeek-Oudijk, D., Woittiez, I., Eggink, E., & Putman, L. (2015). Who cares in Europe? *Geron, 17*(1), 62–65. https://doi.org/10.1007/s40718-015-0119-y

Verbrugge, L. M. (1984). A health profile of older women with comparisons to older men. *Research on Aging, 6*(3), 291–322.

Verbrugge, L. M. (2016). Disability experience and measurement. *Journal of Aging and Health, 28*(7), 1124–1158. https://doi.org/10.1177/089826431 6656519

Vergauwen, J., Delaruelle, K., Dykstra, P. A., Bracke, P., & Mortelmans, D. (2022). The COVID-19 pandemic and changes in the level of contact between older parents and their non-coresident children: A European study. *Journal of Family Research, 34*(1), 512–537. https://doi.org/10.20377/jfr-695

Vergauwen, J., & Mortelmans, D. (2019). An integrative analysis of sibling influences on adult children's care-giving for parents. *Ageing and Society*, 1–25. https://doi.org/10.1017/S0144686X19001156

Verropoulou, G. (2012). Determinants of change in self-rated health among older adults in Europe: A longitudinal perspective based on SHARE data. *European Journal of Ageing, 9*(4), 305–318. https://doi.org/10.1007/s10433-012-0238-4

Vestergaard, S., Thinggaard, M., Jeune, B., Vaupel, J. W., Mcgue, M., & Christensen, K. (2015). Physical and mental decline and yet rather happy? A study of Danes aged 45 and older. *Ageing & Mental Health, 19:5*, 400–408. https://doi.org/10.1080/13607863.2014.944089

Wang, H., Paulson, K. R., Pease, S. A., Watson, S., Comfort, H., Zheng, P., Aravkin, A. Y., Bisignano, C., Barber, R. M., Alam, T., Fuller, J. E., May, E. A., Jones, D. P., Frisch, M. E., Abbafati, C., Adolph, C., Allorant, A., Amlag, J. O., Bang-Jensen, B., … Murray, C. J. L. (2022). Estimating excess mortality due to the COVID-19 pandemic: A systematic analysis of COVID-19-related mortality, 2020–21. *The Lancet, 399*(10334), 1513–1536. https://doi.org/10.1016/S0140-6736(21)02796-3

Warner, D. F., & Hayward, M. D. (2019). 32 The demography of population health. In D. L. Poston Jr. (Ed.), *Handbook of population* (pp. 839–857). Springer International Publishing. https://doi.org/10.1007/978-3-030-10910-3_33

Wattelar, C. (2006). Demographic projections: History of methods and current methodology. In G. Caselli, J. Vallin, & G. Wunsch (Eds.), *Demography: Analysis and synthesis* (Vol. 3, pp. 149–160). Academic Press.

White, A., Grabowska, I., Kaczmarczyk, P., & Slany, K. (2018). The impact of migration from and to Poland since EU accession. In A. White, I. Grabowska, P. Kaczmarczyk, & K. Slany (Eds.), *The impact of migration on Poland* (pp. 10–41). UCL Press.

Willekens, F. (1999). The life course: Models and analysis. In L. J. G. van Wissen & P. A. Dykstra (Eds.), *Population issues. An interdisciplinary focus* (pp. 23–51). Springer.

Willekens, F. (2007). *Multistate model for biographic analysis and projection* (2007/1; Working Papers). NIDI.

Willekens, F. (2014). *Multistate analysis of life histories with R.* Springer International Publishing. https://doi.org/10.1007/978-3-319-08383-4

Willekens, F., & Drewe, P. (1984). A multiregional model for regional demographic projections. In *Demographic research and spatial policy. The Dutch experience* (pp. 309–334). Academic Press.

Willekens, F. J. (1980). Multistate analysis: Tables of working life. *Environment and Planning A: Economy and Space, 12*(5), 563–588. https://doi.org/10.1068/a120563

Willekens, F. J., Shah, I., Shah, J. M., & Ramachandran, P. (1982). Multi-state analysis of marital status life tables: Theory and application. *Population Studies, 36*(1), 129–144. https://doi.org/10.1080/00324728.1982.10412568

Wilmoth, J. M. (1998). Living arrangement transitions among America's older adults. *The Gerontologist, 38*(4), 434–444. https://doi.org/10.1093/geront/38.4.434

Wingard, D. L., Jones, D. W., & Kaplan, R. M. (1987). Institutional care utilization by the elderly: A critical review. *The Gerontologist, 27*(2), 156–163.

Wizner, B., Skalska, A., Klich-Rączka, A., Piotrowicz, K., & Grodzicki, T. (2012). Ocena stanu funkcjonalnego u osób w starszym wieku. In M. Mossakowska, A. Więcek, & P. Błędowski (Eds.), *Aspekty medyczne, psychologiczne, socjologiczne i ekonomiczne starzenia się ludzi w Polsce* (pp. 81–94). Termedia Wydawnictwa Medyczne.

Wojtyniak, B., Stokwiszewski, J., Rabczenko, D., Goryński, P., Trochonowicz, A., Madej, T., & Zdrojewski, T. (2022). Life expectancy and mortality of the Polish population. In B. Wojtyniak & P. Goryński (Eds.), *Health status of Polish population and its determinants 2022*. National Institute of Public Health NIH – National Research Institute.

Wolf, D. A. (2001). The role of microsimulation in longitudinal data analysis. *Canadian Studies in Population, 28*(2), 313–339.

Wolf, D. A., & Gill, T. M. (2009). Modeling transition rates using panel current-status data: How serious is the bias? *Demography, 46*(2), 371–386.

Wolf, D. A., Mendes de Leon, C. F., & Glass, T. A. (2007). Trends in rates of onset of and recovery from disability at older ages: 1982–1994. *The Journals of Gerontology: Series B, 62*(1), S3–S10. https://doi.org/10.1093/geronb/62.1.S3

Wolff, J. L., & Kasper, J. D. (2006). Caregivers of frail elders: Updating a national profile. *The Gerontologist, 46*(3), 344–356. https://doi.org/10.1093/geront/46.3.344

Wong, M. K., Brooks, D. J., Ikejezie, J., Gacic-Dobo, M., Dumolard, L., Nedelec, Y., Steulet, C., Kassamali, Z., Acma, A., Ajond, B. N., Adele, S., Allan, M., Cohen, H. A., Awofisayo-Okuyelu, A., Campbell, F., Cristea, V., De Barros, S., Edward, N. V., Escobar Corado Waeber, A. R., ... Van Krekhove, M. D. (2023). COVID-19 mortality and progress toward vaccinating older adults – World

Health Organization, worldwide, 2020–2022. *MMWR Morbidity and Mortality Weekly Report, 72*, 113–118. https://doi.org/10.15585/mmwr.mm7205a1

World Health Organization. (1948). *Preamble to the constitution of the World Health Organization as adopted by the International Health Conference, New York, 19–22 June 1946.*

World Health Organization. (2002). *Active Ageing: A Policy Framework.*

World Health Organization. (2011). *World Report on Disability.*

Wróblewska, W. (2008). Summary measures of population health (Sumaryczne miary stanu zdrowia populacji). *Studia Demograficzne, 1–2*(153–154), 3–53.

Wróblewska, W. (2012). Wydłużanie trwania życia a zmiany w stanie zdrowia populacji. *Polityka Społeczna*, 14–20.

Wróblewska, W., Antczak, R., & Strzelecki, P. (2022). Zdrowie i opieka zdrowotna w okresie pandemii. In *Sytuacja osób w wieku 50+ w Polsce i w Europie w trakcie pierwszej fali pandemii COVID-19: raport z telefonicznego badania ankietowego SHARE Corona zrealizowanego w ramach 8. rundy badania 'SHARE: 50+ w Europie'* (pp. 35–55). Szkoła Główna Handlowa w Warszawie.

Young, H., & Grundy, E. (2009). Living arrangements, health and well-being. In D. Kneale, E. Coast, & J. Stillwell (Eds.), *Fertility, living arrangements, care and mobility: Understanding population trends and processes* (Vol. 1, pp. 127–150). Springer. https://doi.org/10.1007/978-1-4020-9682-2_7

Zeng, Y., Land, K. C., Gu, D., & Wang, Z. (2014). *Household and living arrangement projections. The extended cohort-component method and applications to the U.S. and China.* Springer. https://doi.org/10.1007/978-90-481-8906-9

Zeng, Y., Vaupel, J. W., & Zhenglian, W. (1997). A multi-dimensional model for projecting family households – with an illustrative numerical application. *Mathematical Population Studies, 6*(3), 187–216. https://doi.org/10.1080/08898489709525432

Zucchelli, E., Jones, A. M., & Rice, N. (2012). The evaluation of health policies through dynamic microsimulation methods. *International Journal of Microsimulation, 5*(1), 2–20.

Zueras, P., Rutigliano, R., & Trias-Llimós, S. (2020). Marital status, living arrangements, and mortality in middle and older age in Europe. *International Journal of Public Health.* https://doi.org/10.1007/s00038-020-01371-w

Polish Studies in Economics

Edited by Ryszard Kokoszczyński

www.peterlang.com

9 783631 894101